# ADVANCE PRAISE

"*That Hidden Road* is an illuminating travelogue not just on the
terra incognito of America, but of cancer survivorship. With bracing
honesty and generous humor, Rocco reveals the inscrutable routes,
by-ways, and pit stops of his courageous journey – and in doing so,
illustrates for a way forward for us all."

> — Adam Bessie, author of the graphic memoir series *Pink
> Ribbon Envy: Living with an Uncool Cancer*, and professor of
> English, Diablo Valley College.

"The further you read in Rocco Versaci's wonderful biking memoir,
the deeper you travel into the heart of America, and into his own
complex emotional world.  Cancer, divorce, religion, family, career:
this is a tale of one man's physical journey, but it's also a tale of love,
loss, resilience, and discovery.  An inspiring read."

> — David John Anthony, author of *Something for Nothing*

"In a confiding and supremely engaging voice, Rocco Versaci takes
his readers on an extraordinary journey, in the aftermath of extreme
personal difficulty, into his private heart and into the heart of
America. *That Hidden Road* is a fresh and imaginative memoir full of
humor, wit and many memorable adventures."

> — Christine Sneed, author of *Little Known Facts* and *The
> Virginity of Famous Men*

"A boldly original and absorbing memoir, candid and full of heart, *That Hidden Road* is a journey into the nature of what makes us human, a portrait on our histories and families and the secrets we keep from those we love most. Rocco Versaci's words, like the central trip of the book, lead us across the landscape of our emotions—we can feel the heat, the wind, the joy and the heartache bled into every single one of these lived-in words."

> — Robert James Russell, author of *New Plains, Mesilla,* and *Sea of Trees*

# THAT HIDDEN ROAD

*Rocco Versaci*

# THAT HIDDEN ROAD

*Rocco Versaci*

Apprentice House
Loyola University Maryland
Baltimore, Maryland

"Not in Kansas Anymore" appeared, in slightly different form, in the Spring 2014 issue of *Midwestern Gothic.* "Miss Fortune" appeared, in slightly different form, in the Spring 2015 issue of the *Georgetown Review.* A portion of "Operation Iguana" appeared under the title "Shallow End" in the Fall 2015 issue of *Midwestern Gothic.*

Excerpt from *The Phantom Tollbooth* by Norton Juster, text copyright © 1961, copyright renewed 1989 by Norton Juster. Used by permission of Random House Children's Books, a division of Penguin Random House LLC. All rights reserved.

First Edition

Printed in the United States of America

Paperback ISBN: 978-1-62720-133-9
E-book ISBN: 978-1-62720-134-6

Design: Nicole DeVincentis
Editorial Development: Alexandra Chouinard
Copy Editing: Alexandra Chouinard
Author photo by Shannon Lienhart
Cover photos by Rocco Versaci with assistance from Freddy Cleveland and Jim Odom

Apprentice House
Loyola University Maryland
4501 N. Charles Street
Baltimore, MD 21210
410.617.5265 • 410.617.2198 (fax)
www.ApprenticeHouse.com • info@ApprenticeHouse.com

Like all memoirs, *That Hidden Road* is a work of memory, research, and imagination. While I have made changes to certain details—including some individuals' names—I have taken pains to ensure that all of the facts and details are accurate and tell a truthful story.

*To anyone who ever wondered if they were on the right road;*
*and to Nick and Tony, who gave me permission to take this journey;*
*and to Shannon, who wasn't asked, and for not calling the authorities.*

"It is not down on any map; true places never are."
—Herman Melville

# Contents

# PART I

---

# Rough Terrain

"Wherever he was he wished he were somewhere else,
and when he got there he wondered why he'd bothered."
—Norton Juster, *The Phantom Tollbooth*

# 1

# Roll Me Away

"Linda thinks you're dead."

The words came to me slowly. It had been a rough morning, so just before lunch I decided to take a quick twenty-minute nap that stretched into an hour and a half, and now I was struggling to reenter the world. I tried to will my eyes to stay open, but they kept dropping shut as if I'd been drugged. My limbs felt like rubber and my face was gummy. I should have just let the call go to voicemail, but my hand somehow reached the phone and my fingers somehow opened it and my mouth somehow said "Hello?" and then my cousin Cathy told me that our other cousin Linda thought I was dead.

"She saw the card and started crying," Cathy said. I was having a little trouble following her thick Brooklyn accent. I wasn't sure if it was because everything was still a little out of focus, or because her voice was stretched through space between New York and California, or because I wasn't yet used to the acoustics of the cheap cell phone— my first, at age forty—that I bought out of necessity a few weeks earlier.

*The card*, echoed in my head. *Something about a card. What card?* I couldn't make sense of it, so I zeroed in on the other big noun. *Linda.*

"She called you?" I asked, mainly to buy some time so that I could catch up with the conversation.

"I just got off the phone with her," Cathy said. "She was *hysterical.*"

I heard my mother's voice in Cathy's. *Hysterical* was my mom's favorite way to describe any and all female friends, neighbors, and family members. In her estimation, the women she knew were always getting hysterical about something. Now Linda was getting hysterical. Because of a card. Oh yeah—*that* card. The Christmas card. I rubbed my eyes and pictured Linda, down in Miami, as she walked to her mailbox, opened an envelope, read the words on the card inside, read them again, and then ran inside to call Cathy.

"Didja see it?" Cathy asked.

I hesitated. "Um, no," I lied. The circumstances in which I saw that card were a little hard to admit, and in my sleep-addled mind I thought that if I confessed to seeing it, then all the rest would follow. As I got my bearings, I realized that there was something else that was a little hard to admit—the fact that when I *had* seen that card and the words on it, I didn't imagine how friends and family might react. At the time, those words were as direct and unambiguous as a club to the forehead.

We talked more about the card and the greatly exaggerated reports of my death, and then Cathy moved on to news about her son, her husband, and their passel of adopted cats, dogs, and birds. Listening to her voice—and again hearing my mother's—I rose from the bed and poked through the boxes that lined the walls of my room. In one of them was a battered copy of *The Phantom Tollbooth*, and sandwiched between its pages was the card.

The Christmas card, the one from my house, the one I stole. On the front was a picture I didn't take of my sons Nick and Tony standing on either side of my soon-to-be-ex-wife Elizabeth in front of a Christmas tree I didn't put up. Inside were the words that sent Linda running for the phone.

All the fuzziness was gone now, and I read the card's two curt sentences in the way I hadn't before—through Cathy and Linda's eyes, through the eyes of anyone familiar with my recent past. And then I felt myself smile, a habit I've had since childhood where I slip away from what's going on and see myself more as a character in a story than as the real me, in my life. Sometimes this has been a good thing, but I wasn't sure if this was one of those times. I saw that from a purely objective perspective, the card and its larger context was a little funny, but I also saw that nobody who got one would be objective. Still, I didn't begrudge Elizabeth whatever anger or confusion led her to mail them to everybody on my half of the Christmas card list. I was pretty confused myself and knew how that went. Plus, the implication of those words wasn't completely wrong. *Something* had died, but at the time I couldn't have said what.

•

That card is on my mind again, but I'm not sure why.

The southbound traffic is surprisingly light for a Wednesday morning, and I start to say this out loud when I realize that I already did, five minutes ago. Instead, I stare at the ocean off to my right as Shannon drives.

Neither of us wants to talk because the only thing to talk about, really, is where we're going and what I'm going to do once we get there, so I reach over and let NPR fill the silence between us. The news is the same. A little over a month earlier, in April, some machinery at a British Petroleum drilling operation in the Gulf of Mexico exploded, and since then oil has been pouring freely from a broken pipe wedged into the sea floor. On the radio, one correspondent intones that the soiled wildlife and dim prospects of staunching the flow anytime soon will likely make this the worst ecological disaster in U.S. history.

I switch it off, and we're drowning in silence again.

"I'll be okay," I finally say.

"Will you?" Shannon says. She shakes her head as if to dislodge the words that have been piling up there. "If you're out of touch for more than three hours any day, I'm calling the authorities."

"The authorities," I repeat. Before I can ask, "Who are the authorities?" she laughs at how ridiculous she knows she sounds.

"Seriously, though…" She lets the sentence trail off into more silence.

We exit I-5 and Shannon steers us through shrinking streets until we're at the parking lot for the beach.

"Are you really going through with this?" she asks for probably the eightieth time this week, and I know that even now, as we look for a spot, part of her hopes I'll change my mind so that we can drive back to the house where we've been living together for the last two years.

"The die is cast," I say, showing her my palms. "Out of my hands."

"Oh, bullshit."

•

Like any big plan, this one had stages.

First was the Daydream Stage, and it involved a lot of *what if*?s. What if I got on my bike and started riding? What if I just kept going? What if I went all the way across the country?

Next was the Internet Stage, which led to the simultaneously reassuring and annoying discovery that my *what if*?s were nothing new. Lots of people rode across the country. In fact, lots of people did much more. One guy had been on the road for over fifteen years. Just as I resigned myself to the fact that it's impossible to have any truly original ideas anymore, a line from one site caught my eye. It said that every tour—hitting the open road on your bike was called *touring*, I learned—was different. Okay. That suited me. Mine would be different. How, I wasn't sure.

The rest of this stage was spent researching what to pack, where to pack it, which way to go, where to stay, and most importantly, what to ride.

Which quickly led to the Money Stage, the stage that signaled true commitment. My first purchases were a couple of books on touring and some official maps from the Adventure Cycling Association, a Montana-based group that had mapped routes up, down, and around the country. The rest of the stuff I bought consisted mainly of toiletries, tools, camping gear, medical gear, and biking gear, which far and away contained the priciest items. Before I could get racks and bags— and just like that, *panniers* was added to my growing bike vocabulary—I had to settle on a bike.

I soon found out it's easy to spend a lot of cash on a good touring bike. I also found out these bikes can be hard to find. The sea of spandexed bikers that floods the roads every weekend are seated atop aluminum, carbon, or titanium, none of which is suitable for someone who's planning to pile a ton of gear on his or her frame. For that you need steel. Steel is durable, but it's heavy and inefficient for those bikers who count pedal cranks and compare average mile times— which is to say, most bikers. And because the average bike shop caters to most bikers, not many of them stock touring bikes. I wasn't crazy about buying one over the Internet; I wanted to be able to climb aboard, so I got on the phone. After spending half of a morning on calls, I found a shop that carried one of the three models in my price range. I abandoned my Cheerios mid-bowl and took off in my car.

The shop was a Trek Superstore, and the bike was the Trek 520. It popped up on a lot of my Internet searches and had good reviews. Back in the early 1980s, it was one of several steel bikes manufactured by Trek, but now it was the only one.

I stepped into the shop and was confronted by a giant cardboard Lance Armstrong. He shuffled back and forth in front of me, and I was about to say something when a dark-haired head wearing black horn-rimmed glasses poked out from behind and smiled.

"Welcome to Trek," he said. "Can I help you find something?"

When the rest of him emerged from behind the cardboard, I could see his nametag, which read, "Ask Me—I'm WILL." I told Will why I was there and what I was looking for. He set Lance down on the counter behind him, shouted to a co-worker by the shoe area that he couldn't get him to stand up right, and then walked me upstairs and to the back corner, where a two-tiered rack stood filled with bikes. He reached up, grunted a few times, pulled a bike free, and set it in front of me.

I reached to touch it. Long, sleek frame. Gleaming silver chain. Bold, metallic finish of "Root Beer Brown," according to the tag.

"Can I take it for a ride?"

A smart shopper and someone with even an inkling of what he was getting into would have taken the bike on a serious ride and been prepared with a list of questions. But I was neither of those things. I rode the bike around the parking lot a couple of times and pretended to weigh its pros and cons, but I had already decided that this was it, this was the bike that was going to take me across the country. In fact, I had already named it "Rusty," as in, *Rusty, you and I are going to kick some serious ass together.*

The final step was the Planning Stage, during which I figured out how to get from here to there. To do this, I relied on the ACA maps I bought. Problem was, there was no clear-cut route from San Diego to Greenville, North Carolina—the place I picked to finish partly because of its proximity to the Atlantic Ocean but mainly because my cousin Tom lived there—so I cobbled a route together out of four existing ones. That still brought me only as far as Virginia. I would have to figure out some way to get down to Tom's house from there, but I assumed that I could work that out when the time came.

More worrisome was the matter-of-face tone of doom that pervaded the touring books and maps. The books advised starting out with one- or two-night trips to get a feel for the many problems that arise on long-distance tours, and the maps warned—at least three times per map—that the routes I planned to take could be "very dangerous" and were for riders with "several years of experience."

If I've had years of experience doing anything, it was enjoying summers off from my teaching job at the local college. Losing myself in a stack of novels, goofing off with my two sons, watching TV—these were the things I knew cold. But biking? When we moved to California from Indiana, we had an eighteen-month-old baby named Nick, an orange tabby cat named Bogart, and a red Dodge Neon named Leon. We had another car, too—a gold Omni whose parts I was constantly replacing—but we sold it before we left. It wouldn't have made the trip, and it was too expensive to ship. The plan was that Elizabeth would drive Nick to doctors' appointments, parks, and play dates, and that I would bike to school. This commute turned out to be about thirteen miles round trip, a total that would have impressed these mapmakers not at all. But there was no way I was going on an overnight practice run. I knew that if I did, I might realize that pedaling my forty-two year old ass for thousands of miles and who knew how many weeks—or *months?*—was one of my crazier ideas. Maybe the craziest.

Shannon had her own reactions to each stage.

During the Daydream Stage, she said, "Okay, you can do this."

During the Internet Stage, she said, "You're really doing this?"

During the Money Stage, which started when I unloaded Rusty from the back of my car and continued as packages arrived from strange-sounding companies like Tubus and Ortleib, she said, "You're not seriously going to do this, are you? *Are you?*"

And during the Planning Stage, when I was careful not to repeat the words "very dangerous" or "several years of experience," Shannon's main comment was, "Whatever."

At some point she decided that I was going and there was nothing she could do, so she planned and threw a big send-off the weekend before I left. It was meant to be festive, but whenever one of our friends mentioned how "impressed" they were with what I was doing, my stomach clenched. At that point, I hadn't done anything except spend money and pretend. I loaded up Rusty and put him on display, and person after person would grip the top tube and rear rack, grunt as they tried to lift him, and look at me with wide eyes that said, *You're going to ride this?* It was my weekend to have Nick and Tony, and I spotted the two of them, at different times, both trying and failing to raise Rusty's wheels off the ground.

Somewhere between Daydream and Internet, I told them what I was thinking of doing and asked if it was all right with them—a question, Shannon reminded me later, that I did *not* ask her. I said to myself that if they seemed at all apprehensive, I would bail on the idea. But they were okay with it. Enthusiastic, even.

At first.

The night before I left, we took the two of them out for dinner. I told them I would call every day and aimed for a light mood, but the prospect of spending two or more months apart hung between us like a thick cloud of smoke. At fourteen and eleven, Nick and Tony are more comfortable talking about sports and television shows than their feelings, which is something Shannon understands much better than I do. After a too-short phone conversation, I'll say to her, "They don't have much to say to me," and she'll tell me, with much more patience than I deserve, "They're *boys*." During dinner, I kept fishing for what they thought about my trip, but all I got were shrugs. Until we were almost done.

Nick's fork hovered over a piece of pie that was oozing hot apple onto the plate. His brow was wrinkled—something that happens when he's thinking, which is most of the time. He looked up at me. "Just be careful, okay?"

Tony was patting Oreo crumbs into a leaning tower of soft serve with the back of his spoon. A tuft of brown hair hung in front of his eyes, and he flicked his head sideways to get it back in place. He stared at his bowl so intently that until he spoke, I thought he was focused on something in his ice cream.

"I couldn't even lift it," he said.

•

The five or so minutes I had allotted between dipping Rusty's tire in the ocean and actually rolling away is a bit off. Once I slosh my way out of the water, I have to carry Rusty back to the parking lot, dry off, put on my socks and biking shoes, and load up the six bags, each one heavier than the one before.

A half hour later I'm pointed east down the neatly asphalted river trail that will lead to road after road into who knows where. Shannon stands next to me with her camera, and the same silence from the car returns.

"I feel like I should say something profound," I finally offer.

Shannon hugs me and backs up. To cover her tears, she lifts her camera and snaps a few shots of me as I pedal away.

Fact is, I'm not prepared for any of this, and it takes all of four minutes to figure that out. As I weave around the runners and dog walkers who fill the trail this morning, I'm sweaty and panting, my muscles are straining, and even Rusty resists as I fight to keep the two of us balanced under an impossibly heavy load, made just a little bit heavier by the voice in my head that keeps repeating, *This is a big mistake, you moron.*

When people heard my plan and inevitably asked *Why?*, I was ready with *An adventure! A new writing project! To see the country!* and these all sounded more or less convincing. More convincing to my friends and less convincing to my dad, who has had to work this new development in his younger son's life with some older developments that he *still* hasn't processed completely. I had another set of answers that I kept to myself, along the lines of *I want to find myself* (a phrase that made me wince), *I'm restless, I need to feel strong again*, but these didn't seem quite right either. What occurs to me now, as I negotiate a ninety-degree turn onto the bridge over the San Diego River floodway and almost topple over, is that what I'm doing, plain and simple, is running away from some of the disasters that I had encountered and—if I'm being completely honest here—*created* these last few years.

# 2

# Mistah Secrets

Here's a job that doesn't exist but should—Disasterologist.

I picture someone with a clipboard and a box of pens sitting next to a bright red phone. When it rings, it means disaster. Tornado, wildfires, maybe even an oil spill. The call doesn't come *during* the disaster; there's too much going on then. But once the air is calm, the fields are done smoldering, and the last petroleum-soaked heron is cleaned, this person begins to trace the complicated, even counterintuitive chain of events back to some kind of ground zero. Maybe a technician set the power load incorrectly on a transformer or maybe a contractor bought discount bolts that didn't pass inspection—who knows? The disasterologist will trace event back through event until there are enough details to tell a convincing origin story.

I'm sure that people already do this kind of work or some version of it, but the disasterologist that I have in mind would examine personal disasters. That way, if a guy was interested in knowing how he arrived at a particular place—in front of Sea World, say, wobbling along on an overloaded bicycle—he could simply call someone to figure things out.

But that job doesn't exist, so I'm on my own.

A leading candidate for my ground zero is the bathroom just off the upstairs hallway in my parents' townhouse. My brother Vince and

I shared this bathroom for several years, but when I was twelve, he left for college and it became my territory alone. That bathroom saw its share of the usual, like a shameful amount of self-pleasure, but I used it for other things, too. When I was in high school and discovered old James Dean movies, I would sometimes go in that bathroom while my parents watched television downstairs and sneak a cigarette. I would stand on the toilet and blow the smoke directly into the bathroom fan. Or I would swipe a can of Miller Lite from the fridge downstairs and practice my shotgunning technique. Gouging the hole at the base of the can with a metal nail file was easy; swallowing everything when I popped the top was not.

But what I remember most about that bathroom as a kid was the mirror that covered the entire wall above the counter. I would stare at myself for a long time until I felt some part of me slide away. In the mirror, I saw hands rise up to rub a face and pinch arms. *This is me*, I would think. *This is all real. My life.* As I repeated these thoughts in my head, sound would grow thick around me as if I was underwater. My skin felt like wax, and when I pinched my arms, it felt like it was happening to somebody else—to this kid in the mirror.

"Whaddaya doin' in there?" my mom would eventually shout from the bottom of the stairs.

"Nothing!"

Then I slowly came back to myself, trotted downstairs, and took my place on the gold shag carpeting to watch *Dallas* or *The Love Boat* or *The Jeffersons.*

"What's goin' on up there?" my mom asked, obviously annoyed.

Shrug. "It's a secret."

"Mistah Secrets!" she said.

As a kid, Mistah Secrets was pretty good at entertaining himself. One way was puzzles. I had some favorites—Batman fighting the Joker, Superman being squeezed by the tail of a giant dinosaur, the Loch Ness monster towering over a small rowboat of frightened men.

I spent hours in the basement making, breaking, and remaking those puzzles. I loved to dump the pieces into a big pile on the folding table and turn them into a picture. Vince told me all the time that there was a right way to make a puzzle—find the straight edges, build the frame, and then work toward the middle—but I wouldn't do it like that. I worked on clusters and connected them up when I saw patterns emerge. It took longer, but so what? It was more fun because each time was different. The real problem was that I didn't take care of my puzzles. There were too many shelves in our basement toy closet, so the spaces between them were pretty tight. To make the boxes fit, I smashed them on top of each other until their corners collapses and pieces leaked out. When I would haul them out again a couple of weeks later, I found puzzles with gaping holes, extra pieces, or both.

I liked to read, too. My parents didn't. At night when my mom watched television from the La-Z-Boy that she bought for my dad as a birthday present but always sat in herself, she would sometimes flip through magazines like *People* and *Star Weekly*. My dad would read the *Chicago Tribune* at his place at the kitchen table, and when he was done with the articles, he would do the Jumble.

I read whatever I could get my hands on, but mostly—at first— comic books. There was something about the pictures and how they told a kind of truth that words alone couldn't. When I reread my issues of *Super Villain Team-Up* or *The Incredible Hulk* or *Man-Thing*, I barely even looked at the words; instead, I pored over images that I still recall all these years later—a close up of Dr. Doom's eyes behind his titanium faceplate, the Hulk breaking out of the Toad King's armored restraints, the Man-Thing lumbering into the swamp with a dead clown cradled in his mossy arms.

After my mom threw out my comics—*I thought they were trash!*—I moved on to "real" books. The first of these were spy and horror novels, and Robert Ludlum and Stephen King were my new heroes. Others followed. There was a bookstore within easy walking distance from my house, a used bookstore a little bit further than that, and a whole city of books—or at least that's how I imagined it—available from the Bantam catalog that I sent away for after seeing an ad in the back of my paperback copy of *The Illustrated Man*. My bookshelf began to sag under the weight of all the books.

My reading seemed to bother my parents, especially my mom. Every Christmas, I gave her a list of the titles I wanted, and she always made a face and said, "You're gonna look like a book!" She once forbade me to buy any more, but I couldn't help myself. I walked down to the Printer's Ink one day after school and came home with *The Postman Always Rings Twice* and the latest issue of *Hockey Digest*.

When I walked through the door, my mom reached for the bag and asked, "What's in there?"

I opened it so that she could see. "Just a hockey magazine. Geez." Mistah Secrets was too sly for her. Because the book was so thin, I stuffed it under my shirt.

Another time I was upstairs reading *Watership Down*. It was a Saturday night, and my parents and brother were downstairs waiting for *Fantasy Island* to come on. I heard the familiar *ka-chonnng* of my mom releasing the La-Z-Boy. I looked up from my book and waited for one of three things to happen. She would either walk into the kitchen, her slippers smacking distinctively against the linoleum; or she would come upstairs, her weight—like anyone's—making the third and seventh stair *pop*; or she would just shout at me from the bottom of the stairs.

"Whaddaya doin' up there?" Number three.

"Reading!"

I couldn't see her face but I could imagine her expression as she shouted back, "Put that book down and come watch TV with the rest of the family!"

As my mom would say, "it wasn't all fun and games" for Mistah Secrets. There were, after all, Sundays. Even the best Saturday nights—drinking Cokes and playing Dungeons and Dragons at my buddy Paul's house—existed under a cloud of doom. The weekend was pretty much over, the next day was Sunday, and Sunday meant church.

Church was pretty serious stuff to everyone in our house except me. We had church bulletins on the fridge, crucifixes and pictures of the Pope and St. Francis on our walls, and other holy objects all over the place, like a thin wooden cross on a stand that mysteriously appeared on my dresser one day. My brother and I didn't go to Catholic school, but we were marched through the sacraments of baptism, confession, communion, and confirmation. This last sacrament demands that you make a serious and sacred covenant between yourself and the Church, and my church asked me to do that when I was eleven years old. We had to take a saint's name to become part of our own, and we needed a "sponsor" to guide us along. For my sponsor I picked Vince, who was seventeen at the time, and in this role, he made me write an essay about the saint whose name I chose and why I chose him. I knew that the real reason wouldn't fly; I picked St. James because my favorite fictional character at that time was James Bond.

On Sunday mornings I had to wear these awful brown suede shoes that my mom bought from Kinney's and a silky shirt with buttons at the neck that she got from Kmart. When winter came, I had to wear black galoshes over the shoes, only I had never heard the word "galoshes"; my mom and dad called them "rubbers." Once I used this word—its other meaning a complete mystery to me—the more streetsmart kids let me have it. I can still see Jimmy Vitek's crooked leer as he asked every Sunday in winter for five years, "Hey, are those your rubbers? Did your mom give you those rubbers?"

CCD—Catholic Sunday school—delivered religious instruction. Our teachers were moms in the congregation who did a lot of volunteer work for the church, and every once in a while a nun or priest would come in. It wasn't all bad. One Sunday we learned that, in an emergency, anybody could baptize somebody else. All you needed was some liquid, a guy about to die, and no priest in sight. For the next few weeks I fantasized about finding an accident scene where I could save somebody's soul by licking my thumb and making the sign of the cross on his forehead.

But most of the time it was a drag. One year our teacher assigned each of us a week when we would have to lead the class in prayer, combining the two things I hated most—public speaking and praying. I knew better than to say anything to my family, or else I would be forced to practice in front of them. All during the week leading up to class, I muttered the prayer I came up with over and over, editing it down so that when my week arrived and I trudged to the front of the room, it was a single sentence that I exhaled in a rushed whisper: "OhLordpleasehelpustoimproveourselvesasweawaitthedayofyourarrivalamen."

Church every Sunday, no exceptions, and the services were likewise unbending. Marching up and down the aisles. Atonal responsive readings. Unified shuffling sounds as everyone performed the Catholic calisthenics of sit-stand-kneel. No meaningful discussions ever took place after church unless the priest gave some kind of directive that my dad or Vince wanted to make sure I had heard. Questions and debate were not encouraged.

In church and at home, rules were a very big deal. No meat on Fridays, no food or water an hour before communion, confession every eight weeks. We did what we were told. When we moved from our apartment in Darien to our townhouse in neighboring Downers Grove, we were technically out of the St. Mary's parish—the one my parents had attended since moving to Chicago—and within the boundaries of a new one. I remember my dad had to fill out forms and made an official request to remain a member at our original church. When I asked him why we couldn't just go wherever we wanted, he said, "Whaddaya want? Those are the rules."

And following rules meant that breaking those rules brought punishment, the fear of which loomed large in my young mind. *God sees everything*, I was told more than once. Even guardian angels—an idea intended, I suppose, to give comfort—seemed creepy. An invisible person *who's always there right next to me?*

I'm tempted to reimagine my younger self as a little cynic who saw that all the rules and fear were part of the church's real purpose— control—but the truth was I was just a scared kid. Later, I started to resent the fear, and then I wanted to see what I could get away with. Mistah Secrets made things interesting and showed me that I could get away with a lot, especially after I started driving. We always went to the 9:15 mass, but somehow I convinced my parents to let me attend the 10:30 service alone.

So of course I broke holy the Sabbath day. I never went to the 10:30 mass, or any other one. Sometimes I went to the Suburbanite Bowl--open early on Sundays—and played pool for an hour or so. I never seemed to get much better despite my visions of becoming a high school Paul Newman, hustling suckers for money.

Other times, if the weather was nice, I drove to a park with a smuggled book—real sinful stuff like *Rosemary's Baby* or *'Salem's Lot.* If it was cold or rainy, I read at Wag's, a twenty-four hour restaurant that reeked of coffee and smoke.

Walking back into the house and knowing that I had broken at least two of God's commandments and would again next Sunday, I got a little rush. The whole deception seemed transparent, and every time I came home at noon after cruising by the church to make sure the service had let out, I expected to get caught. Or at the very least, catch a suspicious look. But all I got were half-hearted questions.

"Who did the service?" my mom would ask.

"The old guy."

"With the lip?"

"The one who groans."

"Oh, that one." She shook her head. "I can't stand that one."

One Saturday night during my senior year in high school, I went to a party with some friends and drank a beer. Then I drank another. Then I drank several more until I needed the wall's help to stand up.

After the police arrived and everybody ran—or in my case, was carried—my friends drove around and hoped I would sober up. I didn't, so they had no choice but to deliver me to my shocked parents. I'm tempted to invent a scene here, but I really don't remember much of that night beyond the party.

The next morning I was in no condition to make it to church, but neither was I in any condition to fight them about going. Twice during the service I had to go to the bathroom in the vestibule to throw up. The second time was dry-heaves, and if anyone had walked in on me as my body twisted in mute agony, they might have called an exorcist.

My mom spent most of the week looking at me, shaking her head, and repeating, "I just can't get ovah this…" My dad didn't say a thing. No comments, no lecture, no questions about where I was, why I got drunk, or if this had happened before. He didn't speak to me until the following Saturday, when he told me that we were going to confession. After I was right with God and those dark stains on my soul were scrubbed clean, we were back to normal.

At least for a while.

# 3

# Astronomy 101

Most of San Diego County is built over and around an interlaced pattern of canyons formed by runoff from mountains to the east that are, at present, kicking the holy hell out of my ass. I make the mistake of checking my map's elevation chart, which tells me I'm in the midst of a four thousand foot climb that's not ending anytime soon, especially at the rate I'm moving. My legs hurt, but the worst pain resides in my butt, the lower cheeks of which feel clamped in a red-hot vise. I'm beginning to understand that those training rides I took with Rusty were not the same animal—not even the same Goddamn *species*—as spending several hours climbing a mountain on the back end of the first day of some half-baked cross-country journey.

Shortly after Highway 79 turns into a narrow mountain road punctuated by little houses and the occasional bait shop, I see another rider approaching from the other direction. His bike looks light, and the only thing he seems to be carrying is a lone water bottle. He's wearing an electric green and yellow jersey that burns bright against the wooded backdrop.

I flag him down.

"Hey," I say, as he slows to a stop in front of me. "You know what's up ahead?"

"Not too much," he says. Then he gestures at Rusty. "Out for a while, huh?"

"Going cross country," I say and immediately feel lame. The other side of the country feels so far removed from my present reality, it might as well be Oz.

"Nice," he says. He looks over my load more closely, craning his neck to take in all the bags. I imagine he's counting them, judging their weight, guessing their contents.

"I probably took too much," I offer, trying to read his gaze.

He looks back to me. "You can always send things home along the way."

Having spent the better part of the day alone and inside my own head, I feel unguarded, so I ask, "I'm wondering what I got myself into."

He starts to say something and stops. Then he nods and tries again. "It's only your first day," he says. "You'll find your rhythm."

By the time I finally stop about an hour later in the little mountain town of Pine Valley, I'm shivery and achy and ready for this first day to be over.

And I wonder how I'm going to do this again tomorrow, and the next day, and all the days after that.

And I think, *Rhythm, my ass.*

The next afternoon, with the mountains behind me, I look forward to some easy biking back down to sea level.

Turns out I have no idea what I'm in for.

In most states, it's illegal to take a bicycle onto an interstate highway; you're allowed to only if there's no other way to get from Point A to Point B. From my current Point A at the eastern end of Old Highway 80, there's only one way to get to my intended Point B of Ocotillo, and that's Interstate 8.

The drop begins almost as soon as I roll onto the shoulder from the entrance ramp, and in a few seconds I'm hurtling down at thirty, then thirty-five, then forty miles an hour. I'm braking, but I can't do that the whole way down. I read that constant braking on a steep downhill creates friction that can heat the wheel rims to the point where the tube ruptures.

I'm not alone on this road. Semi-trucks roar past me every ten seconds or so. The shoulder is wide, but its left third is an unbikeable rumble strip designed to wake up dozing drivers, and its right third is piled with fallen rock shards from the mountainside. Not all of these rocks are kind enough stay to the side, so I focus on my little strip of speeding ground to make sure I don't hit an errant chunk, fly off Rusty, and slide onto the highway.

Then there are the crosswinds.

Roaring out of the Yuha Desert below and amplified by channels in the mountains, these winds rip across the traffic with frightening power. At several points, the winds are strong enough to shove me eight to ten inches to the right. The first time this happens, it's so sudden that I cry out and nearly topple over; by the fourth time, my fear is only pee-inducing.

It's the longest eight miles of my life.

When I finally reach the bottom, I pull over beneath an underpass, dismount, kneel in the weeds, and throw up. If I'm being generous with myself, I might say it has something to do with dehydration or the stack of pancakes I ate an hour earlier in Jacumba, but the truth is that it's a fear puke, plain and simple.

I straighten up, rinse and spit with water from one of my bottles, and look forward to the twenty-five mile ride to El Centro, my destination for the night. The grade ahead is flat, and it feels like there's a tailwind, too.

But then I start riding.

If there's a worse state-maintained road in America than the Evan Hewes Highway, I don't want to see it. Going way beyond "washboard," this road is falling apart, and I'm moving in a crazy zigzag pattern to avoid the divots and cracks that will easily swallow my front tire if I don't pay attention. I wouldn't be surprised to find out the local National Guard outfit takes regular mortar practice on this road. Mercifully, the vehicles are few and far between; all the drivers have no doubt fled to I-8, which runs parallel to the Evan Hewes. I'm tempted to head over and risk getting a ticket there instead of being rattled apart here.

Further down, after the road changes from outrageously shitty to just kind of crappy, I pass an abandoned shack on my left. When I'm about fifty feet past it, I decide to circle back and snap a picture.

I haven't yet attempted to make a U-turn on Rusty when he's fully loaded, so I take it too tight and turn the front wheel almost perpendicular to the frame. I need momentum to finish what I started, but the hot wind that was pushing me from behind now smacks me full in the face. As I'm suddenly stopped, I start to tip over, and the only thing I can do is set my feet down, but they're held fast by my pedal cleats.

Falling from a bike is nothing new to me, but each time is a lesson in helplessness learned as if for the first time. Even when I've fallen at a pretty good clip, the moments between loss of balance and impact stretch out to a cruel degree. There's the initial slip where your tire catches the lip of a driveway or you hit a patch of leaves or you lose momentum and start to tip over, and you see everything coming. Sidewalk. Gravel. Weeds that may or may not be hiding broken glass. Instinctively, you tense up. If you're quick, you might get a hand out to cushion the fall, but this could backfire in a broken wrist or fingers.

I land on my left side, my knee and shoulder taking the most of the impact. When I hit, I feel a solid jab where my elbow is tucked against my ribcage, and all the air goes out of me.

I disengage my feet from the pedals and crawl out from underneath Rusty. I stand and slowly move my shoulder and flex my knee. Not too bad. Scrapes up and down my leg and arm, but both are functioning. That said, I know from experience the real pain won't start until tomorrow morning. As I bend to pick up Rusty, I immediately rethink that theory.

I freeze, and then I slowly straighten up. What I need is a deep breath, but when I try to fill my lungs, I feel a stabbing pain in my left side.

*Okay, just relax.*

I bend over, more slowly this time, and make sure Rusty's okay, focusing on him instead of imagining a splinter of rib puncturing my liver or lung. I wheel over to the side of the road by the abandoned house. Actually, "house" is being generous; it's barely four walls and a roof. The front part of that roof is in mid-collapse, and it's only a matter of time or a few rainstorms before it topples and knocks the rest of the structure backward, like a set of rotting-wood dominoes. It's hard to believe that someone once lived here.

•

One Saturday night, we took Nick and Tony to Qualcomm Stadium with friends and their two kids for a monster truck and tractor rally. It wasn't really our thing, but we were trying to be social with the only other young couple at the Unitarian Fellowship that Elizabeth had us join, and their kids loved monster trucks. The evening was a rarity for us: a bona fide Saturday night two-family outing complete with Cokes, Crackerjack, and cotton candy. As trucks with gigantic wheels spun and skidded over dirt hills and the night air thickened with exhaust fumes and dust, Nick—remembering a baseball game that the two of us had gone to the month before, a game where Padre centerfielder Mark Kotsay threw us a ball in between innings—asked what happened to all the grass.

"It's underneath," I said. "They put the hills on top."

"How?"

"With trucks," I said. "Big ones. Way bigger than these." I gestured to a big black behemoth with horns affixed to its roof that at that moment had just landed on top of another, smaller truck, crushing its cab.

He studied the chaos in front of us, less interested in the trucks he saw than in the immaculately manicured lawn he remembered.

"It's gonna die," he said.

•

The next morning, my pain theory proves correct; everything is sore and it hurts to breathe. I have a lot of time to think about it because I'm on the road to Glamis, which a guy at a fruit stand in Brawley told me was "a whole lotta nothing."

He wasn't kidding. There's little vegetation out here other than spots of brown scrub that freckle the smooth white dunes on both sides of me. Even the wildlife is minimal—mainly tiny white lizards that scurry from the shoulder and disappear into fine-grained sands. I look beyond a few brown and green bottles wedged into the sandy hillside and stare at the bleached horizon. The things that live here have to work hard at it. Water comes in drops, in the mornings, on the tips of spiky leaves. Food is small and fast, and it may be a long time before a meal happens by. True, we've built houses and schools and roads on this terrain, and we've figured out how to move electricity, gas, and water through it, but the fact is, the desert is an inhospitable place with a perilously thin margin for error. And I'm trying to cross it on a bicycle.

The entirety of civilized Glamis is two structures—a massive RV storage lot and the "Glamis Store," a wood face building designed to look like an old trading post. A couple of pickup trucks are parked in front of this store, and one of them has a bumper sticker that reads, OFF ROADERS EAT MORE BUSH.

Inside, I take off my sunglasses. Behind the counter, a TV broadcasts more news from the Gulf. The cleanup crew has now enlisted the help of shrimp boats with boom nets meant to corral the oil. A helicopter provides an image that looks like a Jackson Pollack painting come to life—specks of white circling orange smears across the mottled green water background.

"Help you?" a woman asks as she walk over and shuts off the TV.

I smile and introduce myself as "a teacher from San Diego," believing that my profession is so well-loved that anyone would fall over themselves to help me out.

She just stares at me.

"And, uh, anyway, I was wondering if there was somewhere around here I might set up a tent or something…"

"Talk to him," she says, pointing with her chin at a guy in a base-ball hat stacking beer in a wall cooler.

I re-deliver my spiel to the same unimpressed stare, and when I'm done, he gestures to the RV lot across the street. "You can set up a tent behind the fence over there if ya want."

"Is it okay if I fill up my pack here with some water?"

"We got bottles for sale."

"Is there a sink or something?"

"We got bottles for sale," he says again and points to the end of the coolers without looking at me.

There are rows of twelve ounce bottles of water for sale at four dollars each. Sixteen ounce bottles go for six bucks apiece. I pass.

Outside, a big guy in cutoffs and sandals is checking out Rusty while his wife and two kids sit at one of the picnic tables in front of the store.

"You crazy?" he asks me, laughing.

He fires questions at me and I try to answer them. Meanwhile, his wife watches their kids with one eye and us with the other. When he asks me where I'm staying tonight, I point to the RV lot.

"You can camp with us if you want."

His wife looks like she's about to say something but stops.

The invite is tempting because I'm sure that it includes dinner, which will no doubt be a lot better than the two Clif Bars I had on the menu tonight. Probably some kind of roasted meat. I can imagine the campsite, too. A big RV. Chairs. One of those folding picnic tables. A gigantic grill. Probably a generator to power lights, and maybe even a television. Hot water and comfy beds. All the pleasures of home.

"Where's your site?" I ask.

"In the flats about seven miles back." He points in the direction I came from. "'Bout half a mile off the road."

Their ATV is parked just to the left, and it doesn't take long for me to figure out that there's no room for either me or Rusty on that thing. I do a quick calculation. It's fourteen more miles than I planned to bike. Plus another mile of wheeling Rusty, fully loaded, through the sand and then camping in that same sand. Goodbye, some kind of roasted meat.

"I appreciate it," I tell them, "but I think I'll take my chances here."

"Okay," he says. "But take these." He hands me three bottles of water from their cooler. His wife looks a little relieved. Could be the last thing she wants is some crazy biker filling her husband's head with ideas about roaming the land, alone.

The store closes down at two o'clock, but I hang out in the patio area until the sun dips low enough for me to pitch my tent in shade. I find a decent spot against the fence about a hundred yards off the road. There's a huge storage container at my back, and I figure this will block the night wind. There's no level ground close to the fence, so I have to set up on a slight incline.

Camping in a one-person tent is not for the claustrophobic. My tent is barely big enough for me, let alone the gear I bring in—an inflatable pad and pillow, sleeping bag, flashlight, journal, and my entire handlebar bag. Through a series of contortions, I unroll and inflate my sleep pad and pillow and set up my sleeping bag. This takes way longer than it should because every time I twist or do anything with my left arm or breathe, my ribs protest. It hurt like hell when I woke up this morning and didn't get much better throughout the day.

The desert sky is pinkish as the sun sets somewhere behind me, and I can see the pregnant moon as it starts to announce itself in the sky. It's Friday night, and if I were back home I would be picking up the boys for the weekend. Then Pizza Night, followed by games or a movie or tossing a football around outside. They're still young, so these things are fun to them, but before long they'll step more fully into their own lives—friends, work, college, and beyond.

When I spoke with the two of them earlier, they were their typical quiet selves on the phone, their updates ending almost as soon as they began. *Yeah. Good. Okay. Love you.*

In front of me are train tracks. A couple of long freighters have come and gone since I arrived, and in the distance I can hear the faint whistle of another one approaching. All around, the night comes alive as the clicks and croaks of desert animals begin to fill the air. The clear desert sky is now a deep blue that makes the fluttering stars seem that much brighter.

What I don't know about astronomy could pretty much fill the space above me, but I do know that stars are humbling illusions. What we see in the sky aren't the stars themselves; it's their light, which left those stars years and years ago—some long before I was even born. They're so far away they might have died ages ago, and all that's left are their final light particles, still crossing the black space between there and here.

Astronomers estimate there are over one hundred billion stars in our galaxy, and any one of those stars might, like our sun, provide just the right combination of heat and light for life to thrive on some planet in its orbit. It's supreme arrogance to believe that we're alone, that in the unimaginable vastness of space, the only intelligent life exists in our infinitesimal corner of it. But then again, we might as well be alone. Those other planets, like the suns they depend on, are lifetimes away. If there is some other world out there, and if there are people on that world, and if one of those people happens to be a father, sitting alone and feeling sorry for himself in the middle of a desert, watching the night sky and thinking about his sons, I'll never know, never meet him, never be able to ask him what the fuck he's doing there.

# VOICES FROM THE ROAD

# 4

# Dennis Hopper Is Dead

On my fourth day out, I'm standing in the heat and the wind at a gas station called "Wheelie's 76" in Palo Verde, California, having just inhaled a S'mores-flavored energy bar, a Milky Way, a banana nut muffin half the size of my head, a pint of chocolate milk, and a one-liter bottle of fruit punch Gatorade. Even though I've been on the road for less than a week, I've already learned that I'll be hungry again before long, but right now I'm sated and a little woozy. As I walk Rusty to the bathroom behind the building, I hear liquid slosh around in my stomach, and I can picture little chunks of muffin floating in a sea of brownish-red fluid or whatever color chocolate milk and fruit punch Gatorade make when mixed. I pull open the heavy door to the bathroom, and this soup lurches in my stomach as the stench hits me.

The best I can say about the space in front of me is that it's big. All the better to accommodate the pile of sanitary pads and dirty diapers on the floor by the garbage can, the half-eaten burrito by the sink, and the used clumps of toilet paper that someone dropped on the floor to the right of the toilet. I breathe through my mouth, do my business, and get out of there as fast as I can. Just as I'm about to roll back onto the road, my phone chirps. It's a text from my buddy Jerry in Chicago. He's getting married in a little over a month, and I'm supposed to be his best man. Understandably, he's worried that I won't make it, so he's been checking my progress through calls and texts. This one is different, though. It's only five words long.

*Dude, Dennis Hopper is dead.*

•

I first saw *Easy Rider* in the sixth grade. Spread out on the gold shag of our living room and ignoring my mom's complaints from the kitchen that I was too close to the TV, I ate a bowl of Fritos and watched. And even though it was edited for television—*ridiculously* edited, I found out years later—I was immediately sucked into the story of Captain America and Billy the Kid.

It was beyond me then to pick up on the movie's cautionary messages; I completely missed Peter Fonda's line "We blew it" and didn't dwell too long on the closing image of both men dead alongside their burning motorcycles. I may have liked to read, but at that age I didn't read very critically, so I absorbed road stories through a filter that blocked everything except the thrill of escape, which was everything my unthrilling home life was not. Church was bad enough, but there was more. Spelling tests and phonics workbooks. Report cards and parent-teacher conferences. Chores, schedules, routines. Dad to work at seven, back home at five, dinner at six. *Hey, what's your dad do, anyway? I dunno. Goes to an office.* Two weeks' summer vacation spent on another driving trip to New York to see the same relatives and friends. Rinse and repeat.

So I began to do a little easy riding myself. Of course, it wasn't on a motorcycle; it was on my bike. Well, Vince's bike, really, even though he never used it. He doesn't remember how he picked this particular bike, but it's possible that he saw an ad from the early 1970s that I found on the Internet. It was for the new "Roadmaster" series of bikes by AMF, and beneath the words EASY RIDERS, two boys—brothers, I like to imagine—are atop separate bikes. In the foreground, the older one sits on a blue "Flying Wedge," which had a five speed stick shifter on the top tube, and in the background, the younger one sits on an orange "Renegade." That was our bike, the one I aimed at the open road. And by "road" I mean sidewalk, and by "open" I mean carefully bordered by trim lawns and little fences made of white plastic posts connected by white plastic chains. I would have liked a helmet with the stars and stripes on it like in *Easy Rider*—it seemed wrong even though I couldn't say why—but they weren't for sale in good old Downers Grove. The best I could do was my plastic Chicago Bears helmet. Back then kids didn't wear helmets at all, so after a few cracks from some older kids, I tossed it back in the basement. But none of that dampened the strains of "Born to Be Wild" echoing in my head.

Not long after I saw the movie, I found an ad for posters in one of my comic books. Hidden in the three-column list beneath photos of Bruce Lee in his bare chest, John Travolta in his white suit, and Farrah Fawcett in that orange swimsuit were the words *Easy Rider*. I talked my mom into writing a check for me, and six-to-eight weeks later I stood on my bed with a fistful of thumbtacks in one hand and a full-color image of Fonda and Hopper tooling down the road in the other. If my parents had known a little more about movies, or about 1960s drug culture, or about how bored Mistah Secrets was getting at home, they would have been upset about much more than the holes in my unblemished tan wall, which is what my dad yelled about when he got home from work.

•

Back in the Wheelie's 76 parking lot, the dry gusts that have pum-meled me all day blow hot across my face. I read Jerry's message again and try to come up with a response, but I'm blank. I can feel the sugar I ingested start to congeal in my gut, and I take a long drink of water to wash the stickiness from my mouth. I put my phone away. Palo Verde doesn't look like much, but its geometric fields are green and lush and a welcome change from the desert that I just pedaled through. I have over two hours of biking left in the day. Closer to three, really, given the wind. My destination is Blythe, a town on this side of the Colorado River.

I have to get back on the road, but I can't move.

*Dennis Hopper is dead.*


It's late afternoon by the time I make it to Blythe. All day the winds have been a blow dryer aimed straight at my face, and by the time I pedal through town, cross a railroad, cross a canal, and then pull up to a bait and tackle shop, I can barely make my legs move. A big wooden sign out front is decorated with white ornaments. As I get closer, I see they're catfish skeletons. One is just a huge skull with its mouth agape, hanging from the bottom of the sign on a strand of blue twine.

The owner of the bait shop—a guy named Wayne—is a member of a group called "Warmshowers," an online network of hosts for riders on tour. It's an awful name, immediately calling to mind images of kinky and unclean sex acts, but I'm relying on it to help get me across the country.

The bait shop is one part of a compound. Next to it is a small house, and out in back I can see three or four trailers arranged around a little pond. I wheel Rusty over to a bench, where a guy with one arm loads ice and water into a pickup truck. He looks in my direction and nods.

"Hey," I say. "I'm looking for a guy named Wayne."

He raises his chin and his eyes appear under the brim of his baseball cap.

"Place ain't Wayne's no more," he tells me. "You gotta talk to Melissa."

Before I can answer, a short, round woman with long hair comes out of the shop.

"You our biker?"

"That's me."

She smiles and moves in to deliver a spine-cracking hug. Then she steps back, puts her hands on her hips, and gives me the rundown.

"Well, we don't have much but you're welcome to what we got, so set your tent up in back and feel free to use the shower in the house if you want, and when you're all settled in come visit with us folks out front." She takes a breath and looks me up and down. I can only imagine what she sees.

"If you're hot, you might want to jump in the canal," she tells me, pointing back over my shoulder. "We had a fella here from France who just dove right in, clothes and all."

I turn and take a look. The black water looks like it would swallow me whole.

"Maybe just a shower," I say.

"Suit yerself," she says. "Come visit later."

After a shower that's hot—not warm—and doesn't do much against seven hours of wind-packed grit, I head to the front lawn.

About six or seven people sit on and around folding chairs, and one of them directs me to a galvanized metal tub full of ice and Bud Light. It's a Saturday night, and clearly this is the place to be. Some of them live in the trailers out back, and the rest are from town. Unfortunately, my brain is too addled from the day's ride to retain their names. Except for one guy—Rod. He's probably about my age, maybe a little older. He's got a big beer gut and a dragon tattoo crawling up his calf.

The questions start rolling in. *Where you from? Where you going? What do you do for a living? You a married man?*

"'Course he ain't married," Rod answers for me. "You know of any wife that'd let her husband take off on a bicycle?"

"I know a few wouldn't mind if they did," one of the women says.

Rod's quite the character. When I tell him where I'm headed over the next few days, he lets me know that he's driven his truck all over Arizona and that one particular stretch is a big climb. In his words, "a lot like my ex-wife…a real bitch." He holds a meaty forearm almost vertical to illustrate the grade. "This hill, your bike…good luck." He's got all kinds of suggestions for what I ought to do instead, including—to his own great amusement—"buy a motorcycle," and he emphasizes the finer points of these suggestions by poking the air with his beer bottle. I tune most of this out and instead wish Dennis Hopper was here to deal with this turd.

Later that night, Melissa joins me out at the picnic table next to my tent and sets a big plate of chicken, potatoes, and beans in front of me. While I'm eating, she tells me about running the shop, some of the other bikers she's hosted, and the future of America.

"I tell ya, I'm scared for where we're heading."

"What do you mean?"

"World's coming apart. Earthquakes, tornados, all that oil down south. It's just not safe anymore." She shakes her head, and continues. "And you know, the Chinese're buying up all kinds of land and businesses and such. We're heading for something pretty bad."

"War?"

"Worse," she says. "My brother's in the military, and he told me they've been given all kinds of equipment to protect from germs and viruses and whatnot. He told me, 'Missy, you better start stockpiling,' and that's exactly what we been doing."

I take a look at the property in the glow of the lights from inside the houses and trailers. With its ample living space, water supply, and proximity to the railroad, this place wouldn't be a bad spot to hole up and wait things out. So long as ol' Rod was somewhere else, of course. I could just see him in the post-Apocalypse; he would sit around, drink all the beer, and complain. *That ain't no way to make a Goddamn fire; what you oughta do is….* Yeah, fuck that guy. Feed him to the zombies.

The more Melissa talks, the less crazy it all seems. We definitely have disaster on the brain today, with all these books and movies and TV shows set in some future wasteland. Maybe it's a collective fantasy to see if we have what it takes to survive.

The next morning, against my better judgment, I stop for breakfast on my way out of Blythe at McDonald's. Adults and kids on their way either to or from church fill the tables and form four packed lines in front of the counter. I find a corner booth and sit down with my food—two greasy sausage biscuits and a yogurt cup full of still-frozen strawberries. The fluorescent light overhead flickers in some indiscernible rhythm, and a steady, ambient chatter bounces off the walls around me. All of this makes me feel like I'm slipping into a trance, so I choke everything down and hit the road again.

After I cross the Colorado River, I make my way across the Ranegras Plain, a stark stretch of eastern Arizona that's occasionally interrupted by little desert towns in the process of fading away. One of these consists entirely of a long-abandoned gas station that still has its final price posted—$1.27 per gallon unleaded. Another one is Hope, and there's a sign on its far side that might have something to say to me if I could only ignore the mistake.

YOUR NOW BEYOND HOPE.

# VOICES FROM THE ROAD

# 5

# Unnatural Disasters

Pain radiates from my ribs and my ass. The ribs aren't too bad while I'm riding, but as soon as I dismount, or bend over, or twist, there's a sharp stab that makes me seize up. Perversely, my saddle sores are on the opposite schedule. When I'm off the bike, they're fine; when I'm on the bike, the burning builds steadily and to the point where I have to rise from the seat to get some relief. When I do, my shorts stick to the sores before releasing and the pain is sharp enough to bring tears to my eyes.

I decide to stop in Salome, where I have a choice of three buildings: a bar/restaurant, a convenience store, and a place called Sheffler's Motel. I head to Sheffler's.

Like a lot of motels I've seen on these dusty desert highways, Sheffler's is a simple, one-story building with parking spaces in front of the doors. Chairs sit beside each door so that people can visit at night. Right now there aren't any takers. No cars, no people. Just a few cats napping in the shade of some dying bushes.

I call my boys, then Shannon, then my dad. Tonight, he's happy to hear from me as usual, but he can't hide his feelings about my trip. When I share some details about Glamis, I'm not sure if I do it to keep him informed or to provoke a reaction.

"All alone? Whaddaya mean?"

"It was the desert," I say. "No one was there."

"What if something happened?"

"Like what?"

"I dunno. Animals. Wolves."

The conversation moves through the typical script; I tell him I'm eating, I tell him I feel good—I know enough to keep quiet about my saddle sores and ribs—and he mutters, once again, that this whole thing "isn't normal."

Then he adds, "What about the boys? Are you calling?"

There's an accusatory tone in his voice that rankles.

"I just talked to them."

"Say hello to Mom."

I know what's coming, and there's nothing I can do about it. She's going to ask me a question, the only one she ever asks me anymore.

"How's Elizabeth?"

•

In late October of 2007, I was living out of a couple of suitcases in the spare room of my buddy Daniel's apartment. Daniel kept several cockatiels and didn't believe in cages, so the entire space was a giant aviary, complete with stray feathers and piles of white shit everywhere. One of his birds liked to perch on my shoulder and bite my neck just below the ear. In the two weeks I had been there, I made a habit of leaving before they woke up so that I could eat breakfast in peace and without pain, so it didn't seem strange to me that it was still dark out when I got ready to bike in for my morning class. The cell phone I had owned for less than a week rang, and when I looked at the screen I saw Elizabeth's number. Our last few conversations had degenerated quickly into shouts, so I hit "silence" and tossed it into one of my rear bags.

The sky looked like muddy water. There was a smell, too, but I couldn't quite place it.

The traffic was light as I approached school, and my phone rang again. *I'll call her back when I get to my office,* I told myself, not really believing it.

When I pulled up to the college entrance, two police officers stood in front of blockades. I wheeled up between them.

"What's going on?"

"Campus is closed."

"Why?"

They looked at each other, and then back at me. One of them raised his eyebrows and said, "The fires."

My phone rang again, and this time I answered it.

In our brief conversation, Elizabeth mentioned that all the area schools were closed. She was watching the news and when she talked about what might happen, she kept using the pronouns "we" and "us," as in "Where should we go?"

Daniel didn't have cable, so I biked over to a Best Buy near school. It was empty except for a few people who were clustered together in front of a wall of televisions.

Wildfires, whipped into raging infernos by desert winds, had engulfed San Diego County. With estimated speeds of over eighty miles per hour, these winds—known throughout southern California as the Santa Anas—spread the fires at a rate that was nearly impossible to combat or contain. There were nine fires in all, but two large fronts had come together to the east and the south, and this wall of flames was moving steadily westward. Several towns were under evacuation orders, and footage showed clogged highways, overcrowded school gymnasiums, and brown-gray smoke blocking out the sun. The bottoms of the TV screens in front of me were a steady ticker of lists—the status of the fires, the school closings, the locations of the temporary shelters. News helicopters hovered over Qualcomm Stadium and provided the scope of the evacuation, capturing images of the lot overstuffed with tents, cots, National Guardsmen, and crowds of people.

Cameras on the ground recorded the dazed look of people who had fled their homes and no doubt wondered if anything would be left when they returned. One shot showed a man stroking the nose of a horse, trying to calm him in a corner of the parking lot.

I watched until I couldn't look at one more patch of fire on a hilltop, one more resident being interviewed in front of a blazing home, one more helicopter dumping barely visible loads of red chemicals on a forest inferno.

Outside, everything was quiet. This section of town normally teemed with traffic and activity, but now it was still and empty. The smell of charred wood filled the yellow air as ash drifted around me. I could feel the winds now, hot and angry, and I could picture the flames they pulled behind them. And as I stood there, fire raging toward me from the east while the family I wrecked lay a few miles to the west, I had no trouble believing, if only for a few seconds, that it was the end of the world.

•

In the morning, before I leave Salome, I find the one channel that's even remotely watchable. The TV is from another time, complete with rabbit ears, bad horizontal hold, and some serious color issues. Through the fuzz and flutter, a talking head expresses dismay in low tones.

The oil spill, again. Despite the poor reception, I can make out a satellite picture of the Gulf smeared with a dark stain that the voice says is now almost the size of Missouri. This cuts to a reporter at some gas station on one of the highways out of the area. She reminds us these were the same roads clogged with people during Hurricane Katrina, and there's a similar exodus now. One woman tells the camera she could taste oil in her mouth, and after a sleepless night when she thought about her kids inhaling the stuff—the tarry brown mess seeping into their little pink lungs—she decided to pack up and head north.

I'm close to the screen now, squinting into green light at the images. Empty harbors and beaches, dismayed locals, underwater footage of sludge billowing forth from the broken pipe beneath the surface.

This last shot of the brown cloud lingers. In purely visual terms, absent any context, the contours of the oil spreading into the water might be beautiful, like slow-motion footage of a dark rose that expands endlessly into bloom.

I make it to Wickenburg that night and stay with the family of a woman I work with. They're loud and friendly and keep asking me about the "race" I'm in, and they seem a little disappointed when I keep telling them there's no race, only me. Their oldest daughter is away at college taking summer school classes, so they set me up in her bedroom. Despite the comfortable bed, I can't sleep. I think about Nick and Tony and the things they might be doing at home, like playing football in the street, helping with yard work, or going to the beach. At some point I must drift off because suddenly I'm standing on sand with the two of them, and we're looking out at the ocean. There's a shadow undulating on the water, moving toward shore.

"What is it, Dad?" Nick asks.

"I don't know."

But I do know. I know when the blackness hits the sand and starts to seep into the grains. We should move, but we're all stuck as we watch the stained sand spread toward us. It's not black, though. It's brown. And as it gets closer, chunks of dark sand fall away into a churning brown soup. I feel the shift beneath my feet, and I know it's too late.

The three of us tumble into the mess. I hold their hands tight and try to raise them up, but I just push myself further down. *Kick*, I think, and I try to get my legs going but they're slow, smothered by thick, oily muck. I squeeze hard but it's too slick and their hands slip away. I'm flailing now and I reach out to grab hold of them but there's nothing, then something soft, then I'm holding the top of the blanket in my hands while my legs are tangled up in sheets. I lie there panting and sweating and I swear to God I can taste oil in my mouth.

# 6

# Learning to Ride

Arizona Highway 89 slides out of the south in Flores and snakes its way up and into the mountains for about three thousand feet. The lion's share of this climb—about two thousand feet of it—takes place between Congress and Yarnell over maybe nine miles of road. It's tough to say for sure because of all the twists and turns. From Yarnell, the road rolls gently through a series of sleepy little ranches until it decides to climb again for another thousand feet in looping switchbacks that eventually crest at over six thousand feet before dropping down into Prescott.

From where I'm standing in this dirt lot adjacent to Moe's Grab 'n' Go, a gigantic fiberglass chicken to my right, all I can see of the route is its first part: a slice of road in the rock that angles up before disappearing into a curve of mountain.

I lean against the chicken. I'm not sure what it's advertising or why it's even here. At this particular moment, its main purpose seems to provide commentary on my state of mind. I've been warned about my chances on this climb from Rod in Blythe, and I'm pissed when I think he may be right.

As I stand there, I become aware of a blue sedan to my left and the gray-haired guy in the passenger seat who's checking out me and Rusty. I smile and nod at him.

"How ya doin'?"

"You're going up there?" he asks me, then points to Rusty. "On that?"

"That's the plan," I answer. "Heading to Prescott." I pause. "Is it as steep as it looks?"

"Son," he says, "it don't look steep. It *is* steep."

His wife comes out of Moe's with a plastic sack in her hand.

"This gentleman here is riding that there two-wheeler to Prescott," he tells her.

"Oh dear," she says, then gestures at the road that I've been studying for the past twenty minutes. "Getting up to Yarnell is bad enough, but those switchbacks south of Prescott..." her voice trails off.

"And construction," her husband adds, as if he's suddenly remembered. "Down to one lane for a stretch. Hope you're ready to wait."

Okay, enough of The Good News Couple. I say goodbye and climb aboard Rusty. Time to see what I can do.


The climb to Yarnell is slow going. In addition to the usual ribs and ass pains that I'm getting used to, my heart feels like it's going to pound its way through my breastbone, sweat blinds me, and my hands—pulling back on Rusty's bars to get some leverage as I pedal up the slope—start to tingle. Every so often a vehicle passes on my left, giving me a wide berth. Way off to the right are dark purple mountains poking the horizon like a jagged underbite, but I can't stare too long in that direction because I need to watch the road. And I can't look too far ahead on that road because it's scary steep and there's not much to see anyway before it curves into more climb. I need a distraction.

•


Somewhere in one of my parents' old photo albums is a picture of nine-year-old me sitting on my bike in front of our house. All of its important details are on display. Thick, knobby tires. Long, snakelike handlebars. Metallic orange frame and a silver banana seat, also metallic. Back then, the whole world was metallic.

At the bottom of the picture are my training wheels. I had them on my bike for a long time. An embarrassingly long time, actually. My other neighbors all rode without them. Even kids a grade or two behind me. One summer, my Aunt Angie, one of my mom's sisters, came to visit from Miami. She arrived with a box of grapefruit for my parents and a box of seashells for me and Vince. A few days into the visit, Aunt Angie found it odd that a ten-year old still needed training wheels. I became her project.

We worked at it for the better part of the week, but I couldn't go more than a few feet before I would wobble, panic, and plant my feet. The kind of balance needed was completely beyond me. One afternoon, I didn't get my feet down in time, and I tumbled onto the sidewalk, landing on my elbow. It was skinned raw and bleeding, and I said that I was done. Aunt Angie just nodded and said that was fine.

After my mom patched up my elbow, I retreated to the basement with some comic books. At dinner, Aunt Angie casually mentioned that she saw Noelle, my eight-year-old neighbor, doing a wheelie.

The next morning, I rolled my bike off the patio before anyone else was up. I set my right foot on the pedal and my eyes on the end of the sidewalk about a hundred feet ahead. I took a deep breath and went for it. My arms shook, but I clenched the grips at the ends of the handlebars and tensed my legs to keep them from doing what they very much wanted to do, which was to hit the firm, stable ground. I pedaled and grew steadier. The faster I pedaled, the steadier I became. I still remember that powerful feeling of new movement. It must be like learning to crawl and walk, but while those memories are lost to us, riding a bike for the first time is something we can remember and hold onto. I rode right to the end of the sidewalk and then hopped off before gravity could knock me down. I ran back to tell Aunt Angie, who came outside in her nightgown and made me do it for her all over again.

After that, I was on that bike every day it wasn't raining or snowing. My mom and dad didn't worry so much about what might happen to me out there. Of course there were dangers, and I'm sure we lived near a few weirdoes, but parents back then didn't hover; they just assumed the world was safe and its people kind. Plus, they thought I would stick close to home.

I didn't. I went much further than my parents knew, certainly more than they would have allowed. The suburban streets branched and split like capillaries, and I would ride for what seemed like a hundred miles without encountering any major traffic. I pedaled furiously into different neighborhoods where kids I didn't know went to schools I never heard of, winding my way deeper and deeper into this strange new world to see how lost I could get. Then I would try to find my way out. The blood pulsed in my temples as I turned down street after street and hoped I wasn't just guessing. My mind repeated one question until it was almost a prayer. *Can I find my way home?*

I always did. And after I rolled my bike onto the patio, I would grab a Push-up from the freezer, climb upstairs to the scratchy couch where I did most of my reading, and settle into the indentation that matched the curve of my back.

Before long, though, I started to think about getting on my bike again, riding far beyond my home, out where there was always another corner to turn or another hill to climb.

When you're young, life moves fast even though it doesn't seem that way at the time. Looking back, I see a rapid series of *thens*—*then* I inherited Vince's ten-speed, *then* I was taking driver's education, *then* I was using our 1977 brown Impala to get around.

They kept coming. *Then* college, *then* marriage, *then* a career, *then* kids, *then* a series of homes in neighborhoods like the ones where I used to bike and imagine living in one day. When I rode as a kid, I believed the road to the promised land was hidden out there somewhere, and if I just looked long enough, I would find it. I must have held tight to that belief, because the trajectory of my life took me right into what I thought I was looking for, and before long I was in for the biggest *then* of all—then finding out what it *really* means to be lost.

•

I pull into Yarnell sweaty and thrashed, but with a little gas left in my tank. I look back the way I came, and I can barely make out the road where I stood by that chicken about an hour ago.

I throw up my arms and extend two fingers—the middle ones.

"FUCK YOU, ROD!" I yell at the horizon.

For the next couple of hours, I roll through the ranchland north of Yarnell. It's just me and cows, their dark, triangular heads turning in slow arcs as I pass. Eventually, I see a signpost that says "Wilhoit," the last town before Prescott. I don't see any of the 664 people who supposedly live here, but it's possible that there are at least two or three of them in a tiny store off to the side of the road.

Fifty feet beyond this sign is another that reads

CURVES<br>
MOUNTAIN GRADES<br>
NEXT 15 MILES

Great.

# VOICES FROM THE ROAD

# 7

# Coexist

With Prescott a few hours behind me, I pull into a Chevron station in I'm-Not-Sure-Where, Arizona, and am about to park my bike in front of a guy when I notice his shit-kicker boots, black leather pants, torn jeans jacket, tattooed neck, and dark tangled hair—all details screaming he's someone to stay far the hell away from, and that's exactly what I do. Rolling past the spot where he squats with a cell phone to his ear by a cage full of propane tanks, I park near a bench by the front door and head inside to pee. When I come back out, I notice what I hadn't before: the bench sits in front of a big white Harley, and now this big white Harley's owner—even scarier looking up close—stands, thumbs in pockets, next to Rusty.

"Mind if I get a shot of your rig?" he asks, brandishing his phone.

"Be my guest," I tell him.

"My old lady'll get a kick outta this. Name's John, by the way."

We shake hands, and he takes a few shots with his phone before stuffing it into a pocket on his jacket. Then he pulls off his shades and asks one of the two questions that I've been asked several times already since I left over a week ago.

The two questions are "Where are you going?" and "Where are you from?" My unscientific research—which is based, admittedly, on an extremely limited sample size—has led me to conclude that the question asked reveals something about the person asking. The "Where are you from?" people have lived in the same place for many years and can tell you something important, or at least interesting, about most of their neighbors. They've worked at the same job and shopped at the same stores and eaten at the same restaurants for years.

The "Where are you going?" people ride motorcycles or drive campers. They read maps not because they're planning a trip necessarily, but because they like to look at the dense tangle of roads across the land. They find themselves saying the names of the places on these roads out loud and wondering what they're like and who lives there.

I'm not sure which question I would ask if I met someone like me. John, on the other hand, doesn't have that problem.

"Today, Grand Canyon," I answer. "Eventually, North Carolina."

He tilts his head back and whistles. Then he extends his hand again and I shake it again. "You are one hardcore motherfucker," he tells me.

John and I obviously have different concepts of "hardcore." I'm staring at a guy who's probably been in bar brawls and had knives or guns pulled on him. I don't have any stories like that; the worst I can claim is puking on a guy's car in college and then running away when he shouted at me from his apartment window.

John pulls out his phone and checks to see if the picture's been sent. Then he confesses that things haven't been going so well with his old lady. In fact, she kind of tossed him out. He had done a little work for her brother, a plumber, and there was an incident involving some tools. Words were said.

"Naturally, she took his side," John tells me. "She's a good woman, but she can be a bitch. 'Specially when it comes to that brother a hers."

John decided to hit the road for a while before things got worse. He's been sending her messages for the last week, none of which have been answered. He finally tried to call, but all he got was their machine.

"She better be feeding Dexter."

"Dog?" I picture a pit bull, thick chain around its muscled neck.

"Cat," John says. "Friendly little guy."

He steps over to his Harley and rummages around in one of the rear compartments. On the front of his bike is one of those stickers where symbols from the world's major religions spell out the word COEXIST.

"Which way you goin'?" he asks, brandishing a map.

We sit down on the bench and I trace my path. My finger runs around the Grand Canyon, rises up to the North Rim, moves northeast into Utah, then heads back west into some barren territory before turning east again on winding, desolate roads. I feel like my hand's going to drop right into the map, swallowed up by the sand, solitude, and a hundred other disasters waiting for me.

"Whoa," John says. "That run's a fuckin' bear. Why you goin' that way?"

I don't really have a good answer for this. "It's the way people go, I guess. Guys on bikes."

"Fuck guys on bikes," he says, smiling. "What are *you* gonna do?"

For the next forty-five minutes we pore over the map. He shows me some other roads I can take and gives me a rundown on the towns along the way. In one of them, he tells me, there's an abandoned gas station, but the water spigot in back still works.

"Lotsa little secrets the map don't show," he says. Staring into his mirrored sunglasses, I imagine him winking.

As I roll up Highway 64—the highway that leads to the south entrance of Grand Canyon National Park—it's clear that I'm entering a major destination spot. Cruising past me at speeds and proximities that make me clutch my handlebars a little tighter are cars, cars with trailers, campers, RVs, RVs towing cars, and—my favorite—RVs towing SUVs with three or more bikes affixed to the back. The billboards along the highway acknowledge the grandeur to come, but they frame it through the lens of crafty marketing that scares sightseers into thinking they'll miss out on all that grandeur if they don't see it via river rafting, or helicopter, or from the new glass sky deck. The full-color pictures are enough to make even preliterate children ask from the back seat, "Can we do that?"

This is my third visit to the Grand Canyon. In 1994, Elizabeth and I had been married five years and took a three-week trip during the summer while we were in graduate school. About ten years later we returned with the kids. And now here I am again.

After I set up my tent and lock my bike at a six-bucks-a-night "hiker/biker" site inside the park, I set out on foot. My saddle sores are happy that I'm up and walking, but my ribs are now protesting a little, and I'm not looking forward to twisting around in my tent tonight. The path I'm on winds through trees that soon clear away as I hook up with the rim trail. At first, all I can see is sky, but as I get closer to the edge, the land spreads down and out across the northern reaches of Arizona. I take a few pictures, but the images on my camera's screen are a ridiculous contrast to what I see in front of me.

A family drifts into view. Father, mother, son, daughter. Dad wears a blue Polo shirt tucked into plaid shorts, and his wrist is strangled by an expensive-looking watch. Mom is fit and trim, her long hair held in check by a pink visor, and the two kids—high school age and maybe twins—have their own cell phones that they're now working in different ways. I imagine that Sis texts a friend back home while Brother checks out eating options, which is the topic under discussion among them. Dad suggests the steak house at the Lodge, but Mom wrinkles her nose, no doubt at the thought of all that red meat.

Then Sis, who's wearing a cowboy hat, moves near the edge. Dad whips out his camera and calls to her, "Smile, Cowgirl!"

•

Elizabeth had a hard deadline to get our Christmas cards out right after Thanksgiving. She settled on a formula she liked, and when October turned to November, she worked on it with rigid efficiency. Wanting to avoid the standard model—long-winded letters that arrived by the armload every year—she used a checklist. More of a spreadsheet, really. Accomplishments on the left, names across the top, a scattershot of big black Xs in the middle to show who had done what. She then folded this up with a picture and stuck it inside of a card which might contain a quick note, depending on the recipient.

I was always the weak link in the chain of production. My two jobs were simple ones, but I dragged my ass getting them done.

First was to take the picture that accompanied the card. Every year I set up our camera on a tripod and posed us in front of a huge magenta bougainvillea bush in our yard. Between the camera's tricky self-timer and the fact that I was trying to capture presentable and simultaneous smiles on two young boys, the picture-taking process ate up most of a morning. The last one I shot was eleven months before I left that house, left that marriage, and it was a beauty. Tony was just long and light enough for the three of us to hold him up horizontally in front of us. Everyone was smiling.

My second job was to send the cards to the people on my half of the list—my friends, my family—along with a quick note. The year I left, Elizabeth took over both jobs.

•

I head in the opposite direction of the family and follow the "Trail of Time." It's a series of spaced pedestals that feature a hunk of some kind of rock along with a corresponding geological date. The further I move west along the trail, the further I move back in time. It's still a work in progress; some rocks, like Hermit Shale, are present on the pedestals only by name. I watch a couple ahead of me stroll along the trail, a toddler in tow. He's the only one paying any attention to these markers, rubbing his hand over the rocks when they're there and searching all around the stand when they're not.

The dates are mind-boggling. Near the point where I join the trail, the rocks are five hundred million years old. By the time I get to the heart of Grand Canyon Village, the number has climbed to just over two billion.

I look out into the Canyon. Two billion years old. I once read that it would take over thirty years to just count to *one* billion. What's the proper response to something this old? Awe, sure, but something else, too.

When you get right down to it, the supreme majesty of the Grand Canyon is all about loss. These magnificent red and green mesas and hoodoos exist because time has removed, a fraction of a pebble at a time, trillions of cubic feet. Time works the same way on people but with less impressive results. Take a man and a woman who are at one point as close to each other as two people can be, and look at them years later after the things that held them together have been subtracted and eroded. If you saw them at a restaurant—and you probably have—silently forking through their rice pilaf as if looking for something to say to each other, you would never think you were looking at one of the natural wonders of the world.

# 8

# Crossroads

The next morning I'm at the intersection of Highways 89 and 160. This is where the route John showed me begins. When we talked, I was completely sold on the idea. Now I'm not so sure.

If I head north on 89, I've got detailed turn-by-turn directions, a complete listing of services that each town along the way offers, and the phone numbers of the people providing those services. I've got elevation charts. I've got narrative histories of the area and various precautions to take. I've got the accumulated comments, observations, and experiences of perhaps thousands of bicyclists who have traveled the route at various times of the year.

If I head east on 160, I've got a disintegrating map that gives the names of places and little else. I've got these words from a guy with a snake tattoo on his neck riding a Harley with a COEXIST sticker on its side—*Fuck guys on bikes. What are* you *gonna do?*

Cars and campers fly by in batches of threes and fours. Weekend travelers on their way home. I catch only glimpses and pebbles as they speed by.

My ribs and saddle sores are as bad as ever, and now there's something new—a painful twinge in my right knee. The road doesn't help with any of this. It looks like builders took large concrete squares and laid them down one after the other. To fix the spaced joints, some crew splattered them with tar in the hopes that they would even out. They didn't. Every fifteen feet or so, I'm jolted by another joint. The rhythm is such that it feels like I'm biking down an elongated staircase. With each *cha-thunk*, I imagine my vertebrae pounding together and spraying bone dust over surrounding tissue. I try to stand at each jolt, but there are too many of them and my calves begin to ache.

After two miles of this, I want to drop into the soft sand beyond the shoulder and go to sleep.

After four miles of this, I imagine Rusty's bolts coming loose until he falls apart and I'm left sitting on a pile of parts holding the handlebars.

After six miles of this, I start shouting with every jolt.

After eight miles of this, I want to strangle John.

After ten miles of this, I want to find the person who designed the road, the people who built it, and the workers who tried to fix so that I can whip them all with a tire tube.

I pull to the side of the shoulder. The sun is directly overhead, and it must be in the high-90s. Straddling Rusty, I stretch my hands far above my head and then twist from side to side. The road ahead quivers apart into heat waves.

Why didn't I just stick to the original plan?

I shake off the question. This is the road I'm on, and there's really only one thing to do. Keep pedaling.


Near the heart of the Navajo Reservation, I find one thing—a tired-looking motel in Tsegi—and lose another—contact. I walk all around the gravel lot, along the row of trailers behind the main building, even across the highway, holding my phone overhead and waving it gently to coax some errant signal my way, but the message is the same. NO SERVICE.

I return to my room. It's still light out, but the dark-paneled walls and heavy curtains make it seem like midnight. So I pass out for about an hour, wake up, and turn on the television to sort through the two or three channels where the images are all ghosted.

One is broadcasting from—where else?—the Gulf of Mexico, and today's focus is the unspoken consensus that recovery will be slow, if it happens at all. To reinforce this grim prediction, they show clips of sea turtles and pelicans covered in brown goo while volunteers dab at them with paper towels.

I turn it off and almost immediately the room phone rings. I stare at it through two more rings before answering.

"Hello?"

"Are you kidding me?"

"Hey Babe," I say. "I haven't had service all day."

Shannon gives me a synopsis of her last few hours, most of which were spent worrying. Her imagination had me swallowed by the sand, falling into a canyon, and/or kidnapped by drug dealers.

"Sorry," I say, but it's a pretty lame apology.

"You're not alone in this, you know."

"I know, I know," I say. "How'd you find me, anyway?"

She looked at Google Maps and figured out where we last spoke. There were few roads I could take, so she started calling the even fewer motels that popped up.

"Good thing I didn't camp," I say.

Silence. Then, "Next time I'm calling the authorities."

I head outside, and when I open the door, I'm struck by three things at once: the rush of hot air, the brightness, and the two dogs that rise from the dust and trot towards me.

I move down the sidewalk, and these two dogs are joined by three more. I look behind me, and back by the edge of the building there's another one asleep in the dirt. The ones at my feet nose my legs to see if I have anything for them. A couple of doors down, someone cut the bottoms off of two plastic milk gallons and set them out. One holds a shallow puddle of filmy water, and the other has a few bits of kibble.

I dump out the water and head back to my room.

I clean and refill the makeshift dish in my sink, and when I set it back down outside, the dogs cluster and start lapping at the water for all they're worth. From out of the bushes, a long-haired black and white dog ambles out and wedges his head in between two smaller dogs. A little black puppy, not much bigger than my foot, circles around the drinking dogs, unable to get in. On his third trip around the pack, I scoop him up.

Back in my room, I fill the ice bucket with water, but it's too high for him. I try to hold him over the water, but he's fidgety and won't drink while he's suspended in midair. Then I get another idea. I plug the sink and open the cold water tap. As the basin is filling, I hold the puppy on my chest. He's probably got fleas that are jumping onto my clothes and hair, but his black fuzz feels good as he nuzzles under my chin.

When the sink is full, I set him on the side, and he drinks.

After he's had his fill, he looks up at me and whines, his nose twitching. I pick him up and head back to the bed, stopping at my bike to fish out a package of brown sugar and cinnamon Pop-tarts. His head tilts when the silver wrapper crinkles, and he immediately tries to wriggle his way to my hand.

I feed him a piece at a time, and for a little guy he's got a huge appetite. When he's done, it's back to the sink for some water and then outside again.

Most of the dogs have wandered back to their shady spots, and I set the puppy down by a couple of the others, who immediately start to sniff and lick his snout. I spot a few more dogs hanging out around the trailers in back. Orphans, all of them. I think back to the wildfires that ripped through San Diego right after my marriage ended. One of the stories that emerged in the wake of that disaster was about the animals left behind as their owners fled. Dogs, cats, hamsters, fish. The small ones always get hit the hardest.

~

The next morning I'm in Monument Valley, which takes up a good portion of Arizona's northeast corner. The landscape in front of me is a big bowl of shade studded with monoliths that are just beginning to catch the morning light. From a distance, they look like the heads, hands, and backs of huge beings rising up out of the earth, and the names of some of these formations—the Thumb, Three Sisters, the Mittens—reinforce this vision. Far to the east, the mountains are hard to make out. They're gray and blurred and look as if they've been smeared against the sky with a piece of kids' sidewalk chalk, the kind that comes in a bucket and is as thick as a baby's forearm. When they were younger, my boys and I used chalk like this on the driveway to draw monsters, planes, and scenes like the one I'm staring at. The sun, mighty and bright, is climbing up the other side of those mountains, but right now it's just a tiny finger of orange running along their tops.

Like the Grand Canyon, Monument Valley is Time's canvas. In prehistory, this entire area was a basin collecting layers and layers of sediment that eventually hardened into shale and sandstone. Over time, the earth below shifted in slow and mighty turmoil, lifting all of the land as far as I can see into a plateau. Then rain and wind took over, carefully carving away the vast majority of that plateau until all that remained were these sandstone giants, some standing over one thousand feet tall. I imagine somewhere down the road there's a visitor center where they show a movie compressing these millions upon millions of years of slow change into a few minutes, creating the illusion that we can wrap our minds around what's at work here.

To the land around me, the time I've spent on this earth doesn't add up to much. These rocks looked the same when my grandparents first stepped off the boat from Italy in the early 1900s, and they'll look the same to my grandchildren's grandchildren hundreds of years from now, assuming any of us are still around.

Up ahead to my right, a lone fin of purple rock commands the horizon. It looks imposing enough on its own, but in relation to the ranch near its base, which looks like a model from a child's train set, it's enormous. Bordering the left side of this scene is a two-lane highway that tapers off into the distance and is spotted with vehicles. Despite the magnificent rock on the right and the cars on the road on the left, my eye is drawn to the houses in the middle, and I wonder about the people who live in that space.

•

I got a little lost in college. I had enrolled as an education major because I wanted to be a high school English teacher. Actually, my plan was to become *the* high school English teacher. A guy so cool, so funny, so full of insight about books and movies and all kinds of shit that his students couldn't help but be inspired. They would actually look forward to Mr. V's class. I even planned to ride a motorcycle to school, right after I learned how.

But I hated the education courses. Too much theory and too many case studies. What I really liked was reading and writing stories, so I switched majors from English Education to just plain English and started filling my schedule with classes about Joseph Conrad, metafiction, and the art and craft of the short story. For a minor, I doubled down and chose comparative literature. Now I was reading Tolstoy along with Twain, the *Bhagavad Gita* along with *Bleak House*. As graduation loomed, I had amassed over one hundred units in literature and creative writing. The next May, I would earn a bachelor's degree but not a teaching credential or anything else that might translate into some kind of a salary.

Once a week during the fall of my senior year, I would head to the placement office and get depressed about my options. The only things I could reasonably apply for were jobs in sales or as a management trainee. I couldn't see myself sitting behind a desk, or going to meetings all day, or wearing a suit and a tie and maybe a hat, just like my dad did when I watched him trudge off to an office five mornings a week. The thought of it made my stomach hurt.

One day there was a new name among the interviewers. The Peace Corps. I knew a little bit about it and even more after I went to the library. I signed up for an interview the next day. The whole thing seemed perfect—living in a village in some faraway land and helping people a lot less fortunate than I was. It might even be something to write about; I couldn't seem to find a lot of material in the suburbs where I spent most of my life. It would be an adventure. And one that *mattered*, was how I saw it.

My parents saw it differently. I told them in early November. They were visiting for the weekend, and after I explained the two-year commitment, the places I might get sent, the interview I already had and the others to come, there was silence from my dad. The silence remained three weeks later when I was home for Thanksgiving, and it was still there a month after that when I returned for winter break.

One night he blew.

We were midway through dinner when my mom asked me questions about the whole thing—*Where would I go? What would I do? How long would it be for?* and, of course, *What would I eat?* As I answered, I watched my dad from the corner of my eye. He worked his jaw with more and more force, and I could tell that everything he had been turning over in his head and gut was about to come out. He took a deep breath and then slammed his knife and fork down on either side of his plate.

"You keep asking questions, he'll think this is okay!"

My dad's outburst did not end the silence; it reinforced it. Nothing was settled that night, or the next night, or over the entire break. Vince got into the act, too. He wanted to set up a little challenge for me while I was home to see if I could live with the kind of austerity the Peace Corps demanded, the assumption being, of course, that I couldn't. No phone, no television, no going out with friends, no hot water. He typed up four single-spaced pages of rules and even included a contract at the end that I was supposed to sign. My dad nodded as Vince went through each point. I didn't sign; instead, I kept quiet and returned to school a few days early. I understood my parents giving me a hard time, but my *brother*?

And theirs wasn't the only pushback. I had thought of the Peace Corps as a solo adventure where I might find something out about myself and hopefully do a little good along the way. But Elizabeth and I had been dating for a while, so my idea had the effect of accelerating our relationship. *I'm going to join the Peace Corps* soon became *Let's get married and join the Peace Corps*. If possible, her parents were even less thrilled about their child going to Africa than mine were, and at some point amid the thick envelopes from her parents where a little too much was said and the brief phone calls with my parents where not nearly enough was said, it was clear that straying from convention was creating too many problems, so we backed down and revised the statement yet again, this time to *Let's get married*.

Our wedding wasn't huge—mostly her parents' church friends— but it was festive, and everyone was happy, including me. I was twenty-one, just a few months out of college, and stupid in the way that most twenty-one-year-olds are. I had no real capacity to imagine what might be waiting ten or fifteen years down the road. I had spent most of my time in school reading books, and I had only a superficial sense of who I was or what mattered to me. I liked the idea of getting married because it made me feel that my life was heading somewhere, that this was what I was supposed to do. The Peace Corps may have not worked out, but we had a new plan—work for a couple of years to earn some money and then head to graduate school. It seemed like a winner.

Yet before we got married, a part of me resisted. Elizabeth was a year ahead of me at college, so she worked as a teacher in the Chicago suburbs while I finished my senior year in Champaign. Whenever we talked about engagement, I felt like I was watching myself have these conversations instead of really having them.

I hesitated, in part, because I was still in school and broke, but then Elizabeth and her mom picked out a ring. Her parents bought it, Elizabeth sent me a check to pay them back, and then they mailed it to me so that I could give it to her. It was an embarrassing series of transactions, and if Nick or Tony told me a similar story, I would try to slow things down and ask them if they really wanted to get married. But Mistah Secrets wasn't about to share these details with anyone. *Wait and see*, he thought. *Things work out.*

Needless to say, we didn't have a good engagement story. I drove up from school one weekend and we went to dinner at a Bennigan's, where—because she worked—Elizabeth picked up the check. At some point during the meal I passed the ring over to her and asked if she would marry me.

A year and a half later, we had dinner with a couple she worked with, and we heard all about how he proposed to her. Something about taking her up in a plane and hiding the ring in a map that he asked her to grab while they sailed through the clouds. They kept going back and forth, taking over the storytelling from each other, their eyes glistening with a kind of love reserved for couples in a Disney cartoon. I felt my neck getting hot and I kept waiting for them to ask us about our story, but they were so wrapped up in the fairy tale their lives would inevitably become that they never did.

The ride home was quiet. And even though we didn't know it at the time, we reached a kind of agreement in the car that night that we would translate any awkwardness or discontent or disagreement with each other into silence.

But maybe I'm being too harsh. More than once, Elizabeth told me that I had a "negative memory"—I only remembered the bad things. Maybe she was right and this is why it all came to an end eighteen years later.

•

Deeper in the valley, I stop and turn around. Nothing looks the same as before. The towers glow in the mid-morning sun, and longer shadows stretch through their ridges so that they appear to be leaking something dark. I see the massive purple wedge that I passed a while earlier, when it was dark and cold. Now it glows red and tan. As the sun continues its steady march across the sky and I roll down the highway, these towers of rock—the very bones of the earth—continue to shift and change into new versions of themselves.

It's easy to see the desert as a wasteland, especially when you're on a bike fighting heat and headwinds, but there's beauty in the sandy ripples on the dunes and in the subtle differences between the ones formed by wind and those formed by the skittish animals that survive here. There's beauty in the morning sun that peeks over rock at such a low angle that even the tiniest pebbles cast shadows of thick black fingers. There's beauty in the wind and its near-infinite variations of sound—the crackling of brittle vegetation, the whispers through sand, the whistle through a biking helmet.

And there's beauty in the desert's lesson of endurance. Its animals, plants, and rock formations have all weathered heat, storms, winds, and the subtractive power of Time.

I think back to that family at the Grand Canyon, and how that could have been some future version of me, Elizabeth, Nick and Tony. No bird-filled apartment, no alternate weekends with my kids, no Christmas cards that send distant relatives into a panic. Every road has detours, of course, but some are harder to find your way back from than others.

# VOICES FROM THE ROAD

# 9

# Durango

My first glimpse of Durango is through the cracked windshield of Chuck Carpin's Ford F150. As we roll down from the hills and approach the city limits, the sun glints off of the Animas River, which crosses our path up ahead. Centuries ago, when Spanish explorers wandered the land that is now Colorado, they came upon this winding ribbon of water and watched it disappear into the dark, forbidding canyons of the San Juan Mountains. As the waters flowed into the unknown, these men no doubt envisioned disasters like churning rapids with the force to separate riders from their rafts, rocky jaws with the power to grind those rafts to splinters and mash those riders to pulp, and massive eddies that would swallow the debris into cold blackness. Those explorers knew the value of a river, but they also knew its dangers, and they named this one accordingly—*El Rio de la Animas Perdidas*, "The River of Lost Souls." This moniker seems at odds with the brightness of the day and the obvious joy the town's citizens take in the Animas. From where I'm sitting, I can see joggers and bikers on the trail beside the river as well as a team of rafters on the river itself. Chuck turns left before we cross the bridge, and I know I should be more attuned to the blinding greenness around me, but as he tells me about the "no-good shit" his daughter married, I stare at that delicate spiderweb crack in the windshield and wait for the bump in the road that will force it to give way and rain shards of glass in my lap.

After I abandoned Highway 89 for Highway 160, I had been navigating on the fly with four separate maps—one from a gas station, one given to me by a couple of Canadian motorcyclists, one I found on a bench outside of a diner, and the one on my phone when I had coverage, which wasn't often. Appearing in large block letters on all of these maps, **DURANGO** dominated its little corner of southwest Colorado, where it lay nestled at the foothills of the Rockies. In my mind, the Continental Divide stood as a major crossing—the highest point of the whole journey and the place beyond which I would be in this thing for good, no turning back—and Durango looked like the perfect spot to marshal my forces for what was going to be a long, hard climb.

Since I crossed into Utah, the ache in my ribs had dulled, but saddle sores continued to be my constant, burning companion. Both, however, paled in comparison to my right knee, which had grown steadily worse since I felt the first twinge four days ago in Tuba City.

At some point on a shortcut through some canyon road, I crossed the unmarked border between Utah and Colorado, and three new problems emerged.

First, the bugs. Every time I stopped to rest, or to eat a Clif Bar, or to make sure my phone *still* wasn't getting service, I was assaulted by squadrons of whistling gnats that flew into my ears and up my nose.

Second, the rollers. With each climb, no matter how modest, I felt the strain on my knee, and the pain sharpened. The downhills were worse; my knee would tighten up as I coasted, and when I had to start pedaling again, I could barely move my leg.

Third, I had no idea where I was. This road was supposed to lead to Cortez, but because no one was around and my maps and phone were useless, I didn't know if Cortez was over the next hill—it wasn't—or the twentieth—still no.

After about an hour and a half of this, I started to hear traffic in the distance and caught a glimpse of a highway far off to the right. But seeing your salvation and getting there are sometimes two different things. The pain in my knee forced a crazy economy of effort. I pedaled as much as the knifing sensation would allow—typically three full cranks—and then coasted as far as possible. Then another three cranks, another stretch of coasting, and on and on all the way into Cortez.

At a bike shop in Cortez, one of the mechanics, a young guy named Jake, offered to put me up, and after a night's fitful sleep on his couch, I continued on with every intention of biking the fifty or so miles to Durango. But first I hit the Wal-Mart outside of town, got a knee brace and some Ibuprofen, and waited for the miracle of modern over-the-counter pain relief to work its magic.

There was no magic. Even with a brace hugging my knee and a handful of little white tablets, the knifing pain just under my kneecap started up again fifty feet out of the parking lot and wouldn't stop. Each downstroke on the right made me suck air through my teeth and even cry out a couple of times. The hell of it was that this stretch was not tough biking. Cortez and Durango were roughly the same elevation, and the road's shoulder was smooth and wide—a rarity on the trip so far.

After a few miles, I unclipped my shoes from the pedals and slowed to a stop, putting all weight on my left leg. Even kicking my right leg over the rear rack made me wince. I moved to the far side of the shoulder, laid Rusty on the grass, and limped a few steps to test my knee. The road ahead rose and fell before it bent out of sight between the forested mountains. I envisioned myself repeating this same process of dismounting, hemming and hawing, and remounting every two miles all the way to Durango. Sighing, I turned to face the oncoming traffic, and stuck out my thumb.

I knew from experience that when your body turns against you, there's not much you can do.

•

A little more than four and a half years before I walked out of my marriage, my son Tony and I were wrestling in our playroom. He was five at the time but still tough to corral, so I had to resort to cheap maneuvers like tickling his ribs. He squealed and arched his back, and when he did, he knocked his head against my chest. It hurt way more than it should have. My yelp must have sounded serious because Tony turned to me, his little eyes and mouth open in concern, but I started tickling him again to let him know I was all right.

Later, though, I ran my thumb over my right nipple. There was a lump about the size of a pencil eraser beneath the skin, and it hurt every time I touched it. I figured it was some kind of bruise, and I put it out of my mind for the next couple of weeks. But like a tongue prodding a sore tooth, I kept feeling to see if it was still there and if it still hurt. Yes and yes. I finally went to see my doctor, who ordered a series of tests.

The first was a mammogram. Male breast cancer—rare, but it does exist—was the concern, and this test would rule it out. Or confirm it. I had to go to the women's center of a nearby hospital. The center had its own parking lot, a fact brought to my attention by the lot's security guard.

"If you're picking up, you need to go by the entrance," he said, one hand firmly attached to his belt and the other pointing to the building.

"Uh...I'm not. Is this the lot where I park?"

"This is the lot for the women's center. Are you picking someone up?"

"No. Do I park in there?" I nodded toward the lot.

"Sir, it's the lot for the women's center. Pick ups go there," he said, leaning toward my open window. With one hand still on his belt, he set his other on the roof of my car and motioned toward the entrance with his head. I turned and saw a lady in a wheelchair waiting for a ride in a coordinated system of pick ups and drop offs that I was clearly complicating.

"I'm here for me, okay?" I said. "I am having a procedure done at the women's center."

I couldn't read his eyes through his dark sunglasses, but he straightened up and took his hand off the car. His other hand finally left his belt.

"Oh, I'm sorry. Yeah, yeah…park right in here."

I started to drive off.

"Sorry about that. It's just that…uh…"

"I get it. No problem."

Once inside, I sifted through copies of *More*, *Ladies Home Journal*, and *Town & Country* and tried to ignore the fact that I was the only man in sight.

After about ten minutes, a nurse called my name. She led me to a room, told me to take off my shirt, and stood me next to a large machine with two dinner plate-sized metal squares that looked like a big mechanical mouth. Then she left.

My ears began to register the ambient noise. Footsteps clacking outside, faint at first and then louder and then fading; muted chatter among nurses, doctors, and patients; the ring of a dropped instrument echoing down the hall. I didn't know it at the time, but these noises were part of the soundtrack to my anxiety, and it played constantly over the following months.

A soft knock on the door was followed by a technician with short black hair, a pair of glasses perched low on her nose, and a pink ribbon on her lab coat. She ran through a list of questions about my medical history, and I heard myself repeat "no" without really processing what she asked. Those must have been the right answers because she never looked up from her sheet. Her glasses looked like they were going to slide right off of her face, and I fought the urge to reach over and push them back. And then—as if I said something out loud—she readjusted them herself.

Her hands moved me closer to the machine and pushed me against the cold edges of the plates to compress as much flesh in there as possible.

"Hold still," she said, running her hand over a switch. The machine whirred as the plates squeezed together, a little part of my chest in between them.

When it was over, I said, "That wasn't bad."

She waved her pen at my chest. "Women who are larger up there have a worse time of it."

A consult with the doctor followed about twenty minutes later. She hung my scan on a light box and studied it. Then she pointed to a spot, moved her head closer, and squinted.

"Have you ever used steroids?"

I looked down at my body and thought about making a joke, but I just said no.

"Well," she said, "it's not a malignancy. It's something called gynecomastia."

She sat down and began writing on her clipboard.

"What do we do about it?" I asked.

As she wrote, she told me that if it got more painful or if I became self-conscious about it, she could refer me to a surgeon, who could remove it. The process was fairly simple. Strictly outpatient.

"The only concern," she added, still scribbling, "is why it's there."

"Should I be worried?"

Her pen stopped and she looked at me for the first time. "Not yet."

•

One of my books on bike touring said that if you have to hitch-hike, make sure your bike is visible and your helmet is on. People were much more likely to give a ride to someone who looked helpless and harmless because most psychos wouldn't bother with a ruse involving such elaborate props.

Five minutes after I stuck my thumb out, a gray pickup pulled onto the grassy patch behind me, a man in a baseball hat at the wheel.

"Break down?" he asked, hopping out of the cab.

"Sort of," I said. "My knee's a little messed up."

He told me his name was Chuck Carpin and must have been in his sixties, but when we shook hands, he nearly pulled me off my feet. I could see the cables flexing beneath the skin of his forearms as he took first my bags and then Rusty from me and set everything gently among his power saws and toolboxes.

In the truck we got to talking. Chuck was a Vietnam vet whose daughter had also served in the military. Air Force, the both of them. She was currently living in Albuquerque with her feckless husband. I heard all about him as well as Chuck's neighbor, a "real shit-for-brains" with a few pit bulls that developed a taste for Chuck's chickens. That ended after he shot at the dogs, killing one and wounding another. Unfortunately for Chuck, he couldn't solve his son-in-law problems with the same directness.

Like a lot of people in Colorado, Chuck was from somewhere else. Columbus, Ohio, as it turned out. "Buckeye all the way," he told me.

When he did, I looked down at the jersey I picked to wear that day. It was bright orange and blue with a gigantic "I" for the University of Illinois.

"I appreciate you picking me up then," I said, indicating the jersey. "Seeing how I'm wearing this and all."

He looked over and smiled. "Well, I like to lend a hand to someone in need. I'd a picked you up even if you had a Michigan shirt on."

He paused, then winked at me. "Probly."

Twenty-five minutes after he picks me up, Chuck drops me off at Hassle Free Sports, a bike shop in Durango. As I step out of the truck and my right foot hits the cracked asphalt of the parking lot, I have to grab the door edge for support. Sitting in air-conditioned comfort has caused my knee to stiffen, and it feels even worse than it did this morning.

"You all right?" Chuck asks.

"I think I just need to stretch it," I say, and almost believe it.

We unload my gear, but Chuck looks reluctant to leave. He fishes around in his pocket and hands me a card.

"My cell's on there," he tells me. "If you need anything, give me a call."

I suddenly remember something a biker I met told me about his own cross-country adventure as a twenty-one-year-old. He said that whenever he got into trouble, he just sat down and waited for someone to come save his ass.

"Thanks for saving my ass," I say as we shake hands.

As Chuck climbs back into his truck, I ease myself down against the wall of the bike shop. He backs out, rolls down his window, and pauses in front of where I'm slumped. "Be safe now."

*As if.*

•

After the mammogram my doctor sent me to the lab, where a nurse drew seven vials of blood and gave me a big brown plastic container to collect my pee for a 24-hour period. The sample had to stay cold, so I put the container front and center on the top shelf of our fridge. But whenever I retrieved it, I had to dig it out from behind the milk and juice.

About a week later the results came in. My blood showed the presence of something called Beta hCG, or Human Corionic Gonadtrophin.

"Which is what?" I asked my doctor.

He was a small, quiet man who spoke with an even tone that didn't give much away. "It's a hormone that could be responsible for the gynecomastia."

"But why is it there? How high is it?"

"Let's take it one step at a time. We'll run some additional tests and go from there."

When I got home from the doctor, the house was empty. Elizabeth had taken the boys to the beach. At that time, neither of us had cell phones, so the delivery of this news and whatever it meant would have to wait.

In the meantime, there was the Internet.

It didn't take long to get an answer. I found out that hCG is known as the "pregnancy hormone." Very high in expectant mothers, at low levels in other women, and virtually absent in men. One sentence in the long explanation stood out—"Very high levels of hCG in men often indicate the presence of a tumor."

I tried to make sense of that word. I ran my eyes down and up the "u" like a slide, bounced them over the "m," and then circled the "o" a few times.

But what were "very high levels" for a man?

Rereading the words on my screen, I got an idea for a test of my own. I went upstairs and rifled through the bathroom cabinet under Elizabeth's side of the sink. Like my side, it was a maelstrom of toiletries and cleaning supplies. I sifted through the debris until I found what I was looking for, tucked away in the back corner. The date on the end flap of the box didn't inspire confidence. It was more than two years old, but it was all I had. I followed the directions as best I could, and waited.

Five minutes later I was staring at a blue "X" on a white plastic stick.

*Congratulations,* I thought. *It's a tumor.*

I knew I should stay off the Internet in the days that followed, but I couldn't.

Hunched over the keyboard nightly, I translated medical jargon into images of my body wasting away in a hospital bed, my skin grow-ing thin and sallow, my two boys staring at an empty seat at the table. Elizabeth wasn't interested in visions of doom, or even anxiety; I heard "You'll be fine" enough times to figure out that if I thought the oppo-site, I should keep it to myself. Mistah Secrets was ready and willing to help.

The tests rolled in. A chest X-ray. More blood draws. An uncom-fortable testicular exam by my doctor. An even more uncomfortable testicular ultrasound by a female nurse.

In the blur of procedures, this one stands out. I can't remember the nurse's name, but I do remember that she was young and attrac-tive and that I did not represent myself well during the exam, which involved cold jelly and a large plastic wand.

Like most men, I'm incredibly squeamish and—I'll say it—a big baby when it comes to my balls. As the nurse pressed the wand against and around each one, I held her wrist in a death-grip. I kept flinching, and my penis shriveled up like a mushroom in the sun. It was shrink-age of a kind I had never seen before, way beyond dips-in-icy-pools shrinkage, way beyond all-day-outside-on-a-cold-Chicago-winter-day shrinkage. I had visions of this woman telling stories later that after-noon to all of her nurse friends, and I'm ashamed to admit that this imaginary scene completely eclipsed in my mind the possibility that a tumor might be lurking in one of my balls.

But nothing turned up. My doctor ordered another round of blood tests, and aside from the elevated hCG, these all came back negative for anything out of the ordinary. The last step was a CT scan.

I can't speak for all CT scans, but those involving the abdomen are unpleasant. You start by drinking two barium shakes, each the size of a Starbucks *venti* coffee. The ones the nurse handed me were supposedly orange flavored, but it was hard to tell. There might have been something "orangy" about the drinks, but I was too focused on choking down the chalky, lukewarm sludge to notice. She told me there was no rush, but every few minutes she poked her head around the corner of the waiting room and asked, "How we doing there?"

It doesn't take much to put me back in that moment, climbing onto the table as Kim, the technician, explains the procedure. She puts a hand on my shoulder, arranges me on the table, wiggles my right foot and smiles.

"Just relax."

She swabs the inside of my arm and then deftly inserts a needle for an IV drip of iodine, which will act as a dye when they scan my pelvis.

Kim retreats to the booth, and the table slides me feet-first into the white tunnel. A prerecorded male voice instructs me over the machine's steady hum.

"Remain still.

"Breathe in. Hold it.

"Release."

The voice is annoyingly calm. I picture a guy named Geoff-with-a-G, who wears a turtleneck sweater and types on his MacBook.

My head is scanned first, and for that I'm completely inside the tunnel. I've heard stories of people freaking out during such tests, but I just close my eyes and listen to Geoff, that well-toned, healthy asshole.

As the scans move lower, I extend further out of the tube and into the open. I stare at the ceiling when I feel those two tumblers of barium hit.

"We're going to start the iodine," Kim tells me via intercom. "You'll feel a little warm."

Within a few seconds, a puddle of heat spreads at the back of my throat and then slowly leaks down the length of my spine and pools just behind my balls. As if this wasn't enough, the barium now joins the fun by pressing urgently against my sphincter.

"We're almost done," Kim says, as if sensing my discomfort.

The CT machine slowly spits me all the way out and Kim returns to remove the needle. I need to get to a bathroom, fast, but I can't resist asking Kim how everything looked.

"The radiologist will read them and call your doctor."

I pause. "But did you see anything?"

We're the only ones in the room. Placing her hand on my arm, she looks me in the eyes and speaks quietly. "I'm no expert, but everything looks normal."

It wasn't. My doctor called three days later to tell me that I had a mass near the base of my kidneys. The official diagnosis was a retroperitoneal germ cell tumor. The next step was a biopsy to see whether it was benign or malignant.

After another ill-advised trip to the Internet, I was the owner of two new facts. The first was that my condition had a story. When we're embryos developing in the wombs, germ cells travel from our growing brains to our sex organs. Sometimes these cells get stranded along the way, and most of the time, that's it for them; they spend the rest of our lives hidden in some quiet corner of the body. But sometimes, to combat the monotony of being stuck, they embrace chaos. They divide and multiply and divide and multiply again and again into tumors that spread up into the abdomen, through the lungs, and back home to the brain, at which point, or shortly after, the journey—along with everything else—ends. Since it was there before I was born, my stranded germ cell was, technically, older than I was. It was with me when I fell into a pool at five or six, when I learned to ride a bike at ten, when I began skipping church at sixteen, when I got married at twenty-one, when I became a father for the first time at twenty-eight, and when I became a father for the second time at thirty. And while I went about my business, that cell waited to reveal itself, which it finally did when I felt that tiny lump on my chest at thirty-five.

The second fact brought me back to the gold shag carpeting of our living room, where—at twelve—I sat in front of the TV and cried at the end of *Brian's Song*. What I learned was that a germ cell tumor multiplied and divided its way into Brian Piccolo's lungs and brain and killed him. I remembered the scene that made me cry. Billy Dee Williams and James Caan run together in slow motion while the title music plays. And then, because I was in front of my computer and because we live in an age where nearly all media history exists, literally, at our fingertips, I found the clip on Youtube and watched it over and over until Elizabeth and the boys got home.

I had a biopsy in early July. I was back in the CT tube, this time lying on my stomach while an IV dripped not iodine but a drug that was supposed to dull the pain and make me forget the discomfort. It didn't do either very well. As I lay there, the radiologist inserted a huge needle—I made the mistake of looking at the instrument tray—into my back, checked the monitors in the other room to see its position in relation to my tumor, came back to readjust the needle, left to check again, and on and on. Every time he moved that needle, I could feel it probe and poke inside of me.

When he was finally happy with the position, I heard a series of short snaps as he pulled the trigger on some device attached to the needle. The tech assisting him was Kim from my first CT. She smiled weakly at me, and I saw in that smile that she remembered telling me everything looked normal. I smiled back and didn't let on that I remembered too.

That Fourth of July was that weekend, and we went camping. The biopsy results weren't in yet, so it was tough for me to think about much else. I tried to bring it up a couple of times, but the conversations went nowhere, so I tried my best to be Camping Dad. As I sat cross-legged in a creek, the cold water flowing over the lower half of my body, I watched Nick and Tony build a stone enclosure for a crayfish they caught. He kept trying to scrabble up the sides, but my boys were determined to keep him trapped. Nick was the engineer and Tony the labor in this little operation, so as Nick pointed out spots that needed to be shored up, Tony hunted for a perfectly-sized rock to place. I marveled at how well they could work together, given the blood feud that developed in the back of our minivan the day before.

I kept picturing our answering machine, a small black box that hung on the wall between the end of the counter and the kitchen table. Was it blinking? Was the information waiting there for me, or was it still being gathered, debated, double-checked? The box wasn't much larger than a paperback book, and sometimes answering the phone dislodged it from the screws on the wall behind it. It seemed too slight a contraption to bear the weight of this news.

When we got home I forced myself to unload all the gear from the car and turn the water back on before going inside. Then I went to the bathroom. No rush. As the boys ran upstairs and Elizabeth started sorting laundry, I slowly dried my hands. Then I moved down the hall into the kitchen.

The light was blinking. It could be anybody. I took a deep breath and pushed the button.

It was my doctor. He said to call him.

The tumor was malignant. Choriocarcinoma. This kind of cancer usually presented in the genitals, but mine had skipped that, heading for a spot right behind my abdomen, so I was considered Stage II. The treatment was the same as for Testicular Cancer—three cycles of chemotherapy that would stretch over nine weeks. I found all of this out a few days later when I met with an oncologist. He was a tall, white-bearded man who explained the specifics with a nasal twang and a deadpan delivery. I came to understand that his job was not to set me at ease; it was to explain what would happen. My particular chemotherapy was to be a cocktail of three drugs, and for each cycle I would spend about four hours every morning of the first week with an IV drip of these drugs. For the second two weeks, I would come in on Mondays for just one of them. I would also be given other drugs to help mitigate the worst of the side effects. Of course, as I found out, these other drugs aren't always so successful, and they come with side effects of their own. As he told me all of this, Elizabeth wrote notes in the margins of the handouts he gave us.

"Any questions?" he asked.

"It doesn't sound too bad," I responded lamely.

He looked at me. "It's actually quite intense."

I nodded as if I understood. Of course, I didn't.

# 10

# *El Rio de las Animas Perdidas*

My plan is to rest for a day before I attack the Divide. Based on my map, Highway 160 will climb steadily and then dramatically to just under 11,000 feet at the summit, Wolf Creek Pass. I've been telling myself that after that point I'll be home free; I should enjoy a nice drop into the Colorado plains before Kansas, where I plan to be swept along by tailwinds. But whenever I try to envision a gentle cruise through Middle America, all I can see is a mountain road pointing straight up.

My hosts for the night, a young couple on the eastern edge of town, won't be home until late afternoon. This gives me most of the day to putter around Durango. With my knee in its current state, I'm able to maneuver Rusty only in the most delicate manner possible, coasting more than pedaling. Fortunately, I'm on a river trail that allows for such casual drifting.

It's a popular place. There's a young woman in a floppy hat and sunglasses who's walking seven dogs, the smallest of which is about the size of my foot and the largest of which comes up to my waist. She seems remarkably in control as we pass each other and say hello. There are two young mothers powering a couple of thick-tired jogging strollers. One of the women wears a shirt with a giant peace symbol beneath the words "Peace, Love, and Burritos." A little later a team of rollerbladers wearing shirts that say "The Wheel World" cruises by, and right after them is a unicyclist who nods and tosses me a "Hey bro."

To my left is the Animas River. I dismount and sit on a wooden bench in the shade, and from it I watch the water flow in currents dotted with white, foamy ridges. Some of the branches spiraling help-lessly downstream are snagged by a dark, spongy tree limb that sticks up from the surface, its other end held fast by the silt below. It bounces with the current, and if I blur my vision it looks like a bony finger that either wags in judgment or beckons me to follow. I can't decide.

At the post office, I completely unpack Rusty and lay everything out in front of me. Clothes, maps, tools, spare bike parts, camping gear, and the crazy assortment of things from my handlebar bag like Chapstick, gum, tiny bungee cords, spare batteries for my bike clock, and directions to Jerry's wedding in Chicago, which is in three weeks.

For the next hour I sort through this mess and try to decide what I need and what I don't. By the time I'm done, two flat-rate fee boxes sit on the counter, their bulging sides held in check by layers of pack-ing tape. I've freed myself of maybe fifteen pounds, but it feels like it should be more.

•

I waited to call my family and tell them about my cancer. It was an awful secret, all coiled and waiting and ready to do damage if let loose. I've seen my parents fret over blown circuits and strange car noises, and I couldn't imagine how they'd react to something like this.

I ruined Vince's day first. The second after I said "I've got cancer," there was silence, and a second after that, he shouted, "Jeannie! Pick up the phone!"

His wife is a nurse, and after she picked up the phone and I repeated my heavy news, she went into medical mode. What tests did

I have? What did they find? What drugs would they give me? I spelled most of the words for her, and she said she would call an oncologist friend at the hospital where she worked. As for my parents, Vince said it would be best to call when they were over for dinner that Sunday.

Sunday came, and I called. Vince and Jean had prepared them. After I spoke, they got quiet, asked me a few questions, and no doubt asked more of Jean after we hung up. Every few days they called. My dad would ask if I was eating—always the number one concern in my Italian family—and then he would hand the phone to my mom.

"We're praying for you," she said in a tone that was meant to reassure.

A few weeks later I heard from my cousin Cathy, who heard from our Aunt Angie, who heard from my mother that I "was sick but getting some medicine and should be better soon." Cathy asked me what I told my parents.

"Everything," I said.

"Your mom made it sound like you've got the flu."

•

Durango, it turns out, is a model of how to change without falling victim to the unchecked growth that plagues many tourist towns. The city was settled in the 1880s, and it is one of many "Home Rule Municipalities" in the state of Colorado, meaning that it creates its own charter and governs itself. This autonomy has allowed Durango to control which businesses enter its boundaries.

I'm learning all of this from a guy named Bruce as I sit in Durango Coffee with my knee sheathed in an ice-filled baggie. He's a retired firefighter who comes to this coffeehouse every morning and has been telling me a story about the uproar created when Barnes and Noble attempted to move in downtown. Recognizing the threat to Maria's Bookstore, a local favorite, people sprang into action. Like antibodies attacking a virus, they organized a letter-writing campaign to the Barnes and Noble corporate division, warning them that if they implanted themselves in the heart of Durango, there would be boycotts. They also pledged their support to Maria and started a petition they took to the planning commission. The threat of such resistance must have spooked the Powers That Be; even though Durango has Fort Lewis College, Southwest Colorado Community College, an educated populace, several used book stores, and even more coffees houses, there isn't a Barnes and Noble within one hundred miles of town.

This protective attitude pervades the town. Earlier, when I asked a woman how to get to a Starbucks, she grudgingly told me that there was one a few blocks away but quickly added that there were some great local places nearby, like Durango Coffee, to which she provided turn-by-turn directions. After we parted, I looked back and saw her watching me to see which way I would go.

•

I'm falling in and out of sleep in a hospital room that smells of disinfectant and stale body sweat. A steady drone emanates from a wall-mounted TV. I'm in a hospital gown, blankets up to mid-chest, a pillow propped under my head. A plastic cup of juice with a bendy straw stands alone on a small wheeled table right next to an IV stand that I'm connected to by a long, thin tube.

For the days leading up to my first morning of chemotherapy, this was what I imagined it would be like.

In reality, my treatments didn't take place in a hospital; the chemo center was in the same building as my oncologist's office. But it had a separate entrance, no doubt to keep the Afflicted from scaring the About-To-Be-Diagnosed or the Shakily-Negotiating-Remission.

A pink-gowned woman named Maria took my pulse, blood pressure, and temperature, and then handed me off to other nurses.

At one end of the room was a counter stacked with boxes and

bottles. The rest of the space housed ten large recliners with IV stands next to them.

"Sit anywhere, sweetie," said one of the nurses, a short dark-haired woman named Dorothy, who I later found out was a breast cancer survivor.

Six recliners were already filled. As the days progressed and the faces in those chairs changed, I realized I had been walking around with the arrogance of the healthy in a carefree land. Somewhere between wrestling with Tony and stepping into this room, I had left that land and crossed the border into a strange new country, one with far too many citizens.

Citizens like Ricardo, a man in his sixties who had been fighting leukemia for the last two years.

And Monica, a mother of three with ovarian cancer.

And Dan, a man in his fifties whose weight dropped over seventy pounds in two months and was still falling, much to the consternation of his doctors and their tests, none of which had turned up—in his words—"Jack shit."

And Carlton, a man in his seventies who was likewise not doing well; a few minutes after I got there, a nurse named Cheryl—a tall, willowy woman with short gelled hair—told him that his cell count was too low for him to get his regular treatment.

And people like the two in the corner of the room on that first day—a woman who was asleep and a white-haired man named Russ.

Russ was always there when I arrived in the morning and would still have a bag of meds on his IV stand when I left at noon. After he asked about my cancer and I told him, he shook his head.

"So young," he said. "Disease has no conscience."

You could say the same about the treatment. People refer to chemotherapy as "medicine," but that's not exactly accurate; the chemicals that drip out of bags, down tubes, through needles, and into a patient's blood are actually poisons designed to kill rapidly growing cancer cells. But to do this, the treatment kills the patient a little bit, too. The fact that my own cancer was so treatable was good news that concealed a terrible truth: because it's a cancer that afflicts young men, the chemicals can be more damaging and caustic. I stopped reading the literature on the long-term consequences of my treatment after seeing words like "kidney and lung damage."

During this time, Elizabeth kept the boys occupied and out of the house, but I craved time with them. My favorite was late afternoon, when I would doze on the floor of the playroom as they stacked big cardboard bricks over and around my body. Then I would gather my strength and rise like the Krakken, lumbering after them while they shrieked in delight. Other times I would read the cards that seemed to arrive every day in the mail, let people take me to lunch, or enjoy the company of dinner guests who arrived at our door with arms full of food that I had a hard time eating. A few years later, one friend told me about the lecture he and his wife received from Elizabeth about topics of conversation that were off limits. No unpleasant world events, no school or departmental politics, and absolutely no cancer.

The side effects came on gradually and then dramatically. Fatigue put me on the couch for hours. Jitters kept me awake at night. Numbness crept into fingers and feet. Pain gripped my wrists.

I was in the shower one morning when I looked down to see a black clump of something sitting atop the drain like a big spider. I pinched the side of my head and came away with a thick tuft of hair between my fingers. Rather than wait it out and watch my head become a patchwork of bald spots, I decided to shave it off. It took longer than I expected. I cut first with scissors, then buzzed with electric clippers, and then shaved with a razor. When I dragged the blade across my scalp, it sounded like scraping sandpaper with a butter knife.

I stared at myself in the mirror, a kid again, and wondered, *Is that me?* My fingers explored the rough terrain of my skull, new and not new. It was a part of me I had never seen before even though it was there my whole life, hiding.

Then there was Chemo Brain.

I first heard this term from Sara, the woman asleep in the corner on my first day. It refers to the spacey feeling that accompanies treatment. For me, it was as if a thin plastic film separated me from the rest of the world. I was tired, but my slowed interactions with everything around me were more than just fatigue. Sounds were dulled and came to me very slowly, like I was moving at a different speed than everything and everyone else. Food tasted funny, as if everything I ate was an artificial substitution for the real thing. Even water became thick and metallic in my mouth. Sara went through the same thing. She had a garden where she grew plump, fire engine red tomatoes. Unfortunately, they tasted wrong to her now, and it broke her heart. She brought some bags in for the nurses, who tried to conceal their delight. Sara, a vegetarian, was horrified when I told her that the only thing that tasted good to me was red meat. Specifically, the double cheeseburgers at Burger King. While other food nauseated me because nothing tasted how it should, those double cheeseburgers never disappointed; I could down two or three without a problem. On my last BK run, that juicy meat tasted so good I felt tears in my eyes.

"Oh my God," Sara said. "That's awful."

Sara didn't have kids and wasn't married, but she had two good friends who helped her out as she battled breast cancer. Hers was a vicious cycle. Doctors would start her on something that would push her into remission, but it wouldn't last. Then a new drug cocktail, then remission again, then recurrence. She had been going through this process for nearly three years, and it showed. Even though I didn't know her pre-cancer, I recognized her pale skin, thin hair, and bloated face and arms—she had to wear compression sleeves to force out the fluid that collected there—as by-products of long-term chemo. Her current treatment had her in every Monday, so I saw her each week, and despite her condition, the room was always livelier when she was around. When I came in bald for the first time, wearing sunglasses and a bandana, her face exploded into a smile. "Bad-ASS!" she yelled.

Like me, she worked on crossword puzzles during treatment, but she was much better at them than I was.

"Yo," I might say. "A three-horse sled. Six letters."

She would pause to think, but barely. "Troika."

Sara had gone through every test out there. Later, when my doctor ordered a PET scan, I called her. She laid out the details and told me to bring a blanket because the room got really cold. She could recite every drug she had been given since starting treatment, which went on much longer than anyone thought.

"When I was thirty-nine, my doctors said I wouldn't see forty," she told me once. "Now I'm forty-two."

Chemo Brain kept me from following the plot of a simple sitcom or more than two or three pages of a book, but I had no trouble imagining scenarios of disaster that all coalesced around a question that I could never voice aloud: *What if it doesn't work?*

I had already fallen into the slim minority of so many things. It was rare for a germ cell to get stranded during gestation, more rare for that stranded cell to develop into a tumor, and even rarer still for that tumor to be malignant, much less fall into the class of choriocarcinomas, the most serious kind and the category that represented less than one percent of them. Why shouldn't I also fall into the minority who didn't respond to the treatment?

As I became drained by this and other thoughts, I could feel my emotions rise to just beneath the surface. It didn't take much.

Listening to messages from friends at work.

Watching my sons' argument about which Matchbox car was the coolest devolve into a wrestling match that I lacked the strength to break up.

Looking at all the unread books on my shelf.

~

During my fourth week of treatment, one of the nurses, Paula, had trouble getting the needle into me. The pain was intense and got worse every time she tried and failed to find a vein in my hand. I clenched my body until it finally went in and the medicine began to drip. She apologized and asked me if I needed anything, but I just smiled and shook my head. After she left, I could feel my throat tighten.

"How are you doing?" Sara asked from the seat next to mine.

I told her I was all right.

"We have a group that meets every Thursday," she said. "Right next door."

"You're in that?"

"I kind of started it."

The group had about a dozen people, all led by a moderator, Michelle. Sara and I were the youngest, and the condition of people ran the gamut from not sick at all—Kathy, whose husband had died of esophageal cancer, still came to the group—to people in the final stages of their particular cancer.

Ron, a New Jersey transplant in his fifties, had acute lymphoma. Rising up between his collarbone and jaw was a lump the size of an apple that I had a hard time looking away from. I quickly gathered that he and his wife Eileen had been the focus of recent meetings. That night, Ron announced that he was done with treatment. They had taken one more shot but had known there was only about a ten percent chance of success.

"I wish I could've gone to Atlantic City one more time," Ron said, his gray skin pulled tight into a smile. "I miss the boardwalk." He paused, took a deep breath, and nodded. "I'm okay with it."

His wife clutched his hand. She started to shake her head, and her eyes were red. "I'm not. I'm not ready for him to go."

People shifted in their seats. On the Internet, I read about "not letting go." There was one story of a man, life slipping away on his deathbed, whose wife stood over him and hissed, *Don't you dare leave me.*

"But if it's time, and Ron's ready," Michelle asked, "is that fair?"

I was a little dazed by how suddenly intense the meeting had become. I thought that the whole support group thing would be a gradual process. I wasn't quite ready to meet a man who, it turned out, would be gone within two weeks.

Eileen admitted that it wasn't fair, but that was how she felt. Wasn't it important to be honest?

So we talked about honesty for a while. Or rather, they talked while I listened. At the break, Ron and Eileen left amid a flurry of hugs. He was pretty worn out and she wanted him to rest.

Michelle found me at the food table, picking through the cookies. "Too heavy?" she asked.

Yeah, it was. But listening to Ron and Eileen, I felt like that plastic film over me had been pulled back, at least a little. I told her I was fine.

And later I told the group that even though my illness had made me the center of attention and I had visitors a few nights a week and I got calls almost every day, I still felt alone. I saw a few heads nod. I told them that coming to the group and hearing from others made me feel less alone.

"What do you want to talk about here that you can't talk about at home?" Michelle asked.

I thought about this and then finally said, "My shit."

At home, if I couldn't share my anxieties about Nick and Tony growing up fatherless, then I certainly couldn't share the unpleasant physical details, like how I felt my lower bowels slowly congeal over the course of any given morning so that when I finally went to the bathroom, I would grunt, sweat, and in the end deposit a sad little pile of black pebbles.

Too much information? Not for the people in that group, who knew that shaping your illness into some kind of story—complete with uncomfortable details—was a way to get some control over it.

Not much, but some.

I kept coming to the group, even after my hCG levels dropped, and even after I was done with my treatment altogether. In fact, I was still a member of that group almost a year later, when Sara died.

•

It's late afternoon. I phone my boys and Nick answers.

"Well, I had a hell of a day," I tell him. I've gotten more casual with how I throw around my "hells" and "shits," and I can tell by their snickers that they like to hear the old man curse.

I tell Nick about hitchhiking with Chuck.

"You got a ride?"

"My knee's been killing me. I didn't think I could make it."

"So you're not really biking across the country." It's a statement, not a question, delivered in that withering tone that only a fourteen-year-old can muster. I have no response.

"Well, I mean…are you okay?" he asks.

I tell him I am and he tells me about going to the beach, what book he's reading, and how he's seriously considering switching team allegiances from the Cubs to anyone else. I work my way through this conversation, and then another one with Tony, but I'm distracted by Nick's frank assessment.

I ride to the other end of town on the river trail and pedal as little as possible. As I dip into a shady grove, I see other bikes. A few cruisers and some mountain bikes, all with ratty seats and handlebar grips patched with duct tape. Then piles of garbage bags. Then the men. Most are bearded and wear tattered jeans, flannels, and—in a couple of cases—an army jacket. No helmets, no bike gear. There are maybe a half dozen guys either stretched out in a patch of dirt or sitting at a picnic table, and it occurs to me that here in Durango, where participating in some kind of outdoor activity seems to be a requirement, even the homeless ride bikes.

One of the men notices me and raises a hand in greeting, but I hurry away, telling myself it's because I'm expected by my hosts.

A half hour later I'm in front of a big two-story house. The residents, Jason and Dee, are a couple in their late twenties. Along with their four-year-old daughter Jody and their fifteen-year-old dog, they occupy the top floor and usher me into the bottom floor, where I'll be staying. It has its own bathroom, laundry room, and kitchen with a fully-stocked fridge.

During dinner, I entertain them as best I can with stories from the road. Later, stretched out on the soft mattress downstairs, I think of those men down by the river.

The next day I'm back in downtown Durango, killing time until later. I was supposed to stay with Jason and Dee again tonight, but I told them that I was heading to Pagosa a day early. This lie was easier than trying to explain what was going through my head, especially since I don't quite understand it myself. Every time I try to put it into words, all I come up with is *stranded*. Like those branches on the Animas, tossed from rock to shore and back again. Like a lost germ cell with nothing better to do than grow into a tumor.

Late in the afternoon I get down to the clearing I saw yesterday, which is empty except for a guy hunched over a can of beans at a picnic table. His bike leans against a tree behind him, and even from twenty or so feet away, I can see the mismatched pedals and cable housings.

As I approach, he looks up. A spoonful of beans hangs in the air between the can and his mouth.

"Hello, young man."

"Hey," I answer. "How are you?"

He sets the spoon back in the can.

"Oh, been better, been better."

"I have some stuff here I hope you'll accept."

I pull a white plastic bag from the back of my bike, and his eyebrows go up as I empty it in front of him. Bananas and apples, little bags of trail mix, a few pouches of tuna. He moves his beans aside and pokes through the pile, settling on the trail mix. He squints at the package as if trying to read in dim light.

"Well now," he says. Then he nods toward the other side of the table. I sit down.

"Name's Chester," he says.

I tell him mine and try to form my next words. There's so much I want to know right now. I want to ask him what happened, how he got here—was it one incident that changed everything, or was it a lot of little things?—but before I can say anything, he points at my bike.

"Not from around here."

I look at Rusty, loaded with bags and lying on his side like a beached whale.

"California."

"Long way from home."

I want to answer that somehow, but I can't speak. After a minute, Chester raps his knuckles twice on the table, and the hard knocks echo off the trees around us. Then he tells me a story of his own. How he used to be uptight. How it got so bad that he would wake up with an ache in his chest that stayed with him all day. How he finally had to leave behind the things that made him feel that way. I wasn't sure what those things were and Chester didn't offer specifics.

"Now I got that," he says and points a callused thumb at his bike. Then he nods at the river behind me. "And I got that."

I turn to the water and listen to it rush over rocks.

When he speaks again, it's as if his voice comes from far away.

"There're worse ways to spend a day."

~

I set up my tent by the river. I don't know if it's legal or not, but

I make a little space for me and Rusty at the edge of the clearing. The men began to appear as the sun started to fade, and now—in the dusk—they fashion shelters near their bikes. I know I'm out of place here; all told, Rusty, racks, bags, and gear probably cost more than these men see in a year, maybe longer.

I walk over to a table where some of the men have gathered, and Chester introduces me to them.

Like Chester, they all have their stories, though some are less coherent than others. Common themes are lost jobs and homes. One guy's wife took his daughter and left; another is heading south to stay with his sister in Louisiana. Like a migratory flock, most will spend the summer by this river and head to New Mexico when the weather turns cold.

In the dim corners of the clearing, there are others without bikes. One man gathers twigs for no apparent reason. Another sits by a bush, mumbling.

I have something in my shorts pocket, and I head over to the guy collecting sticks. He stops suddenly when I come near him.

What can you say about a man getting ready to sleep in the dirt next to a river? In the failing light, I see beneath a tangle of hair that his eyes are red and unfocused. There are holes in his jeans and flannel shirt, and his hands and face are caked with dirt.

"It's not much, but here."

He looks at my hand, then sets down the sticks. He reaches out and holds what's in it, not quite pulling it away. We stand like that for a few seconds, our hands wrapped together around a Clif Bar I picked up at some gas station a few days ago.

He nods and then looks at me like he's about to say something else but doesn't. The bar disappears into his pocket and he goes back to collecting sticks.

Then it gets late and I'm tired, mostly from trying to ignore the dull ache behind my kneecap. The men at the table have drifted off to their spaces, and I approach Chester. I'm planning an early start in the morning and doubt I'll see him.

"Safe travels, brother," he tells me.

Back in my tent, I listen to the flow of the Animas, amplified by the dark. I remember my last conversation with Sara. Michelle told the group one night that Sara was on hospice care. A few of us nodded and exchanged looks. We all knew what this meant. I called Sara the next day, but she didn't have much energy to talk. I told her how much she helped me through my treatment and how sorry I was and how I wished there was something I could do.

She just sighed, "It is what it is."

When I leave Durango the next morning, some dark clouds are gathering behind me. My plan is to ride to Pagosa, the last town before the road starts to rise. Tomorrow morning I'll attempt to cross the Continental Divide at Wolf Creek Pass.

My knee feels better than it did, but it's far from okay. When I think about the climb tomorrow, I see myself sitting on the side of the road waiting for another ride. But if I can't make it on my own, then what's the point?

I keep checking those clouds behind me. They gain on me until their eastern swell is just overhead. The temperature dips, and a few errant drops hit me before they taper off. As I continue to move toward Pagosa, the crosswinds kick up. Normally this would annoy me, but as I check over my shoulder, I see the wind is blowing the storm north. The clouds darken as they extend behind me, and thick blue streaks color the horizon—heavy rain in the distance. After a few miles, it's clear the wind will continue its northward push.

I've dodged this storm for the time being.

# VOICES FROM THE ROAD

# 11

# Eight Miles High

The next morning, I roll onto Highway 160. Last night, ten minutes after I got a room at an Econolodge outside of Pagosa, the rain came in thunderous sheets, and now the bright morning sun's reflection in the wet asphalt is blinding.

In town, I'm reunited with the San Juan River. It flows south from here, fed by several tributaries, including the Animas, and heads into the Navajo Reservoir in New Mexico. Then it cuts west across that state and turns up into Utah, where I first met it back in Mexican Hat.

At Treasure Falls, I stop to stretch. My knee is holding up okay, but the ride has been gentle so far. That's about to change. The falls—an icy knife of water tumbling off a cliff's edge in the distance—is the last point of interest before the real climb begins. I watch a few tourists take pictures, and I know I'm prolonging the inevitable. Each stop makes it a little bit harder to get back on Rusty.

As I remount, I see the sign: WOLF CREEK PASS SUMMIT 8 MILES.

Eight miles doesn't sound like much, but when those are mountain miles, it's another story. I'm looking at two, maybe two-and-a-half hours of steady grinding up a steep ascent.

I see the road ahead rise, bend, and disappear into the heights. I'm guessing that I can see only about a quarter mile of it, but I'm no judge of distances, even at this point in my trip. I start to wonder what the road looks like beyond where it vanishes from my sight.

But I can't think about what's ahead; if I'm going to do this, I need to focus on the right here and the right now.

I begin my climb in the cold and the dark. Sheer rock walls reach up and block the sun, and at seven thousand feet—roughly the elevation at the base—it's a little chilly. Ponderosa Pines rise above me and will continue to shield me from the sun as I climb. It's slow going, and my only companions down here are fallen trees and shards of stone dislodged from above. I downshift, but not all the way; I want to make sure I still have gears to drop into when my legs are ready to give out, which might not be too far off. My hands fidget on Rusty's bars, and I move them around, trying to find a comfortable grip. Now I'm focused too much on my hands, and I can't settle into a rhythm. I curl my fingers around the brake hoods and park them there. I'm sweating, but the cold mountain air chills me. My right knee aches, but it's manageable. So far.

I'm not even at the first bend yet. The road ahead seems impossibly long, but I can't think about what's up there. I need to focus on where I'm at.

Each time my right leg bears down, I think *This one*. I fall into a rhythm. *This one…this one…this one…*

Two blue and white jerseys on superlight bikes whip by. A couple of guys on a Sunday morning ride. The same kind of people who are no doubt riding up and down the coast back home, packs of riders trying to wring out every last drop of energy from themselves before gathering at some coffeehouse with a view of the ocean.

That's where I should be, enjoying a nice coastal ride. Not by myself in the middle of the country. Not climbing the Goddamn Rockies.

*No. This is where I am.*

Cars labor past me, their engines wheezing against the grade. The air is still, for now. Up at the top it's probably crazy cold. I can picture travelers bundled up, snapping pictures of pine-studded mountains. If I make it that far, what next?

*No. Stay in the moment. This one...this one...this one...*

I pedal into partial sunlight now, and I see that I'm at eye level with some of the trees and above others. As I approach the first switchback, I'm suddenly engulfed by more bikers. They flow by me like a river around a rock. I stare at their unencumbered bikes and immediately feel every ounce of gear that I'm carrying.

I decide to stop until they're all out of sight. I look down at the ribbon of road below me. The last biker—and older guy, bringing up the rear—wants to talk as he slips by.

"Where you from?" he asks.

"San Diego."

"Right on!"

He disappears around the bend and I start to pedal again. My knee is killing me and I tell myself I have to stay on Rusty, I have to keep going. Before I can stop them, my eyes slip down to my odometer. I haven't covered even two miles of this climb.

It's hopeless.

*No. This one...this one...*

These words slip out of my mind and into my mouth. "This one...this one..." They're an echo of something I've heard before, but I can't remember what.

I'm in full sunlight now, and I look down on a vast carpet of pines. Water falls over the rocks to my left, and I can see the powerful stream below. This is Wolf Creek, headwaters of the San Juan River. Here, the water is diamond-clear, fresh from the melt above. But back in Mexican Hat—where these same waters carry the dislodged soil of Colorado, New Mexico and Utah—the river churned brown and thick.

•

My levels of hCG were closely monitored throughout my treatments, and when I went in for what was to be my last cycle of chemo, Maria showed me the latest results.

Level of hCG, zero.

I hadn't allowed myself to get too hopeful, but there it was, that wonderful nothing.

As she was taking my blood pressure, my vision blurred and I felt my breath catch.

Maria stopped fumbling with her stethoscope and put a hand on my shoulder.

"You're happy, right?"

I was, but after the treatments were over, I didn't get the immediate relief I expected. Some of the side effects, like the numbness in my hands and feet, actually got worse. And I was still tired. I couldn't make it all the way up the stairs in our house without having to stop and catch my breath. I took to counting the stairs when I went up. When I hit seventeen, I was at the top. One day I was stuck on fourteen. I could see just into our bedroom and spy the top corner of something blue propped on my night table. It was a card that Nick and Tony had made out of construction paper. On the front, Tony had drawn picture of a shark, and inside, Nick had written, "Dad you are stronger than a great white shark." Resting on the stairs. Sleeping ten to twelve hours a day. I didn't feel so strong.

And I felt alone again. That chemo room with its recliners and soft pastels and gentle hum of activity had become a kind of home where I sat in my chair and fell right into the rhythm of conversation about Russ's new drug protocol or Sara's strange rash or my own obsession with blood test results. Once you get used to the fear, chemotherapy becomes a constant reminder that people are working to keep you safe. Each day you're wrapped in a blanket of medicines ending with –cin and –sone and –con, reassured with sheaves of paper bearing numbers in solid columns, and tended to by a family of medical professionals carrying charts and pushing carts. It's beside the point that the safety provided is an illusion—the illusion has power. I imagined the hCG in my system as a pack of black liquid creatures that were slowly crawling out of hidden corners of my body now that they were no longer held in check by the drugs.

At my house, the unspoken directive was to get back to normal—pay bills, maintain cars, fix broken sprinklers.

Three months later, it was time for my first post-treatment blood tests and CT scan.

During the days leading up to the procedures, most of my thoughts were crowded out by the details of what was to come—pretending to read a magazine while I waited for my name to be called, climbing into the chair where the nurse would draw my blood, squeezing the red ball while the nurse wrapped a rubber tube around my bicep, looking away as she felt for a vein, and tensing my legs as she slipped the needle into me. These images played in an endless loop in my mind, and as bad as this was, it was nothing compared to the waiting that came after. Those few days before the results came back were a prison where the best I could hope for was a stay of execution, but all I could imagine were footsteps growing louder in a corridor until they stopped outside my cell and were replaced by a voice that grimly intoned, "Son, it's time."

I was haunted by time—especially the time I had left. Before all of this started, I hadn't worried too much about my future, but now the thought of all those years stretched out ahead of me was as oppressive as a conversation where I had something important to say but wasn't allowed to speak. Sometimes I went to a movie and sat through two showings, not paying attention either time. Sometimes I parked my car on the coast in the morning and faced west, staring at the ocean for what seemed like hours. And sometimes—like a kid on my bike back in the Chicago suburbs—I drove around to nowhere specific, turning down one strange street after another until I didn't know where I was. I felt spent. Used up. Done.

•

And then, somehow, I'm passing cars and trucks parked next to a clearing where a giant sign reads THE GREAT DIVIDE. I slow Rusty and ease to a stop in front of it. I take a deep breath of cold air, dismount, and take off my sunglasses. A guy in a Mets hat offers to take my picture in front of the sign, and I let him. Big smile and a peace sign, but it feels like a pose.

The road ahead levels and then drops out of view into a place I can't see. I'll find out soon enough what lies ahead, but right now I'm standing on the spine of the country, where rock parts water. Behind me, *El Rio de las Animas Perdidas*—the River of Lost Souls—will flow into the San Juan and then join the Colorado as it continues to cut the Grand Canyon, provide power, and water crops before emptying into the Pacific. In front of me, on the eastern side of the Divide, all water heads down into the Great Plains and gives life to its people and the tributaries that feed the Mississippi, which carries the trade of a nation as it flows first to the Gulf of Mexico and then to the Atlantic. I know that everything comes together at some point, that all of the water around me will one day evaporate, rise into clouds, and fall as rain somewhere else. There's a metaphor here, but I can't see it. I'm distracted by the feeling that I just came close to something—a memory?—but missed it, and either I'll find it or it'll find me somewhere down the line.

# 12

# Guy Limps into a Doctor's Office…

I'm staring at Paul Newman. He's young and lean and angled across a pool table, his left hand arched over the felt as his right hand squeezes the end of a cue. A cigarette points from the corner of his mouth. Behind him, men wearing hats and smoking cigars watch him get ready to shoot, and there's no doubt in any of their faces that the ball he's aiming at will end up in the pocket. Some—maybe all—of them wonder what it would be like to have even an ounce of this kid's talent. But they know they're just schlubs destined to be anonymous faces in the background.

I look around. I'm surrounded by Newmans. Some are full color, some are glorious black and white, and they're all contained in sleek black frames. I recognize a few—Fast Eddie Felson, Butch Cassidy, Frank Galvin—but not all. It doesn't matter; the point is, they're glimpses of a man at different points in his career. Pieces of a puzzle, like the kinds I spent hours making as a kid. Put together right, they tell a story.

That's the hope, anyway—that random scenes from a life will amount to something. In most of these shots, Newman looks elsewhere, but there are a few where his unwavering eyes look right into mine. I can almost hear his voice, gruff but not unfriendly. *What's your story, kid?*

When I stood at the Continental Divide a few hours earlier, the story was a surprising one, at least to me. I didn't realize until then that I never expected to get so far, never really expected to get out of Arizona. But there I was, at the rocky top of the country. I planned to get to Alamosa that night, but after I switched into some cold weather gear, hurtled down the eastern side of Wolf Creek Pass, and pulled into a little town called Del Norte after the road leveled out, I knew there was no way in hell I was going to make it.

Bikers talk about pain at the "points of contact"—hands, feet, butt—and nearly every article I've read on the subject lists obvious advice about how to deal with pain. Use padded gloves, make sure your shoes are the right size, buy a better saddle. But bike touring means riding day after day after day, and a fair amount of that riding includes grinding up hills with a lot more weight than what's carried by the aerodynamic racers who flash their perfect teeth on the covers of *Bicycling* magazine. For tourists, "points of contact" pain creeps into other areas, like the neck, shoulders, elbows, back…and knees.

My right one was worse than ever, and I hoped that the climb over the Rockies hadn't done it in for good. The ten or fifteen mile stretch after Del Norte was a painful blur even though I had a tailwind and a flat road. For part of the way, I unclipped my right leg and stuck it out to the side while I pedaled with just my left. It looked and felt ridiculous, and I couldn't move either leg without grunting. I reengaged my right foot, but every downstroke on that side felt like my kneecap was being pried off with a knife.

On the western edge of Monte Vista, a couple of hundred yards from a big building, I felt a sudden *twang* as something either shifted or snapped behind my knee—Ligament? Tendon?—and I yelped as my body clenched and I stopped pedaling.

With both feet firmly clipped and without the strength or awareness to unclip them, I tipped over and landed in the low weeds just beyond the shoulder. Two words formed in my mind: GAME OVER.

I lay there and watched a couple of stringy clouds drag themselves from the bottom to the top of my perfect blue field of vision, and I kept waiting for the sound of tires roaring on asphalt. But all I heard was my own panting.

By the edge of the shoulder was an empty Coke can and something black next to it that came into focus as a dead mouse covered in ants. I disengaged my left foot from its pedal and then, more gingerly, my right. Once I was out from underneath Rusty, I stood up on my left leg then carefully set my right foot down, toe-first. It held, kind of. I picked Rusty up and limped the rest of the way to the building ahead, which I now saw was a long, two-story motel. Out in back were two giant movie screens.

The Best Western motel chain likes to give its locations little names particular to that spot. In Ashland, Oregon, where a Shakespeare festival runs for eight and a half months each year, the motel is called the "Bard's Inn." In Gila Bend, Arizona, it's the "Space Age Lodge," and it features a giant flying saucer on the roof and a lounge named the "Outer Limits Restaurant." And in Monte Vista, Colorado, it's the "Movie Manor." The gimmick is that all the rooms have big windows where guests can watch either of the two drive-in screens behind the building. On the wall is a speaker and switch that toggles between #1 and #2. But the Movie Manor doesn't stop there; the concrete driveway outside of the main office holds the impressions of faux movie star signatures, and instead of numbers, the rooms are given the names of those same stars.

When I finally made it past the empty parking lot and into the lobby, the girl behind the counter let me know I pretty much had my pick of rooms.

"Which one's closest?" I asked.

She pointed to a map of the motel taped on the counter, her finger running between two rooms.

"Walter Matthau or Paul Newman."

"That's my choice?"

"Yessir."

I shook my head. "That's no choice."

Now, my knee encased in a plastic bag full of ice, I call my boys and omit a few details. I try to do the same with Shannon.

"Bullshit," she says. "How bad is it?"

"Well," I say, calculating how honest I can be. "Okay, it hurts."

"Is it you-need-to-fly-home bad?"

I think about those five minutes when I lay in the weeds. I had run through a scenario where I hitchhiked to Denver and caught a flight home. No way I'm admitting that, but clearly I can't get away with too much here.

I tell her the climbing, which was obviously a factor in all of this, is pretty much behind me.

Silence on the other end. I'm holding my breath while I look to Paul Newman for help, but he's got his own problems; in one still, his cheeks bulge and laid out in front of him are about twenty hard-boiled eggs waiting to be eaten. Shannon still hasn't said anything. She's either gearing up for a plea to come home or resigning herself to my stubbornness.

"I'm this close to calling the authorities."

In the morning I set out to cross the seventeen flat miles between Monte Vista and Alamosa. With the flat grade and a tailwind, seventeen miles shouldn't take longer than forty minutes, forty-five, tops. Instead, every inch of the way is agonizing, and I'm on the road for more than two hours, grimacing the whole time. At some point I face the unpleasant fact that I need to find a doctor.

I end up at the San Luis Valley Regional Medical Center, where there's an orthopedist on staff. I steel myself for a long wait, but instead, I'm sitting on a paper-lined examination table in about twenty minutes. For only about the second or third time on this trip, Rusty is out of my sight; he's propped down the hall where the receptionist promised to keep an eye on him.

Fidgeting and listening to the paper crinkle beneath me, I'm expecting the worst possible news. My suspicions from yesterday are back now and stronger than ever. Something's got to be torn in there. From my phone, Google is spitting out all kinds of possibilities—ACL, MCL, meniscus. I call my buddy Paul, who's an orthopedic surgeon, and he tells me I might need a cortisone shot.

"It's a pretty big needle," he says and explains there will be intense pain as fluid from the shot fills the affected area. In fact, there might be pain for the next few days that's worse than the initial symptoms. As I hang up and wonder why I called, I gently squeeze my right knee and try to imagine how it could possibly feel worse than it already does. Also, how big can that needle be?

The doctor walks in. She introduces herself as Dr. Candace, which I assume is her first name. She's young and trim and athletic, with long, sun-bleached hair. In fact, if not for the lab coat and scrubs, she looks less like she belongs in a hospital than on a beach somewhere, spiking volleyballs. She sets her clipboard down. "Okay, tell me about this knee of yours."

I do my best to describe what it feels like, how long it's been going on, and how the pain has been changing. I don't mention that I'm on a cross-country ride, mainly because I don't want to be told it's over. As I talk, she nods and moves my knee with both of her hands this way and that, asking if I'm feeling pain at various points and angles. She sticks her fingers behind my knee and runs her thumbs over the knee cap, shifting my leg from side to side. Then she pats my knee twice to let me know I can relax my leg. As she scratches out the verdict on her clipboard, I stare at a square of faded paint on the wall where a picture was taken down and never replaced.

"Well, everything feels intact," she says.

Pause. "Really?"

"Acute patellar tendonitis," she says, then describes the architecture of the knee, the tendons that run underneath it, and the various ways that they get inflamed. "I'll write you prescriptions for a strong anti-in-flammatory and a mild painkiller. Nothing that'll make you loopy."

"No Cortisone shot?" I ask.

She smiles. "Well someone's been on the Internet," she says. "Or have you had one before?"

I admit to phoning a friend.

"Well, I'd rather not go that way. If you're still in a lot of pain a week from now, it's something to consider."

She wheels a stool over and sits down.

"Okay, let's hear it," she says. "Your best one."

"My best one what?"

"I saw your bike out there. You've got stories."

After I entertain Dr. Candace, I worry she might ask me why I'm out here, so I ask a question of my own, the one that's been in my head since I fell.

"I don't see why not," she answers. "Those meds should help a lot. Just don't try to be Superman. Where are you headed next?"

"Fort Garland, then Walsenburg."

"That's a good ride."

"You bike?"

"I do," she says. "Mainly local. Someday I might do a deal like yours, but not anytime soon." She pulls a pad out of her lab coat and starts to scribble on it. "After Fort Garland, you'll go over La Veta Pass."

"What's that?"

"Last pass of the Rockies heading east. After that, you're done with them."

I kind of thought I was already done with them, and this disappointment must show on my face because she says, "Oh, don't worry about it. It's pretty tame from this side. Long, but not steep. I'm sure you've been through much worse."

# VOICES FROM THE ROAD

# 13

# Road Warriors

The relief that I haven't torn up my knee has worn off, and now I
need to muster the energy to limp down to the lobby of the Alamosa
Super 8 and grab whatever free sugar and carbs they're handing out as
a "continental breakfast," but instead I'm lying on the bed with said
knee wrapped in ice and watching the news about—what else?—the
Gulf spill. The broadcast is in mid-whiparound, first to a woman in
Florida who reports that oil is washing up on its western shores, then
to an environmentalist who talks about the long-range damage to the
food chain, and then to a few people in a studio who announce that
BP will set up a fund to pay for damages. One look at what's going on
is enough to know that whatever amount their team of accountants
comes up with won't be enough to fix what they broke, and it won't be
enough to keep them from breaking something else tomorrow.

I look around. Motels in the mornings are miserable places. When
you first check in, they're full of promise. The room is neatly packaged
and all its amenities are wrapped and waiting just for you. But come
morning, everything is used up. The unmade bed's slick bedspread
droops across the floor, tepid water fills the ice bucket, the garbage
can overflows with detritus from the previous night's dinner, towels
lie in damp piles like bodies at a crime scene. Then you notice the
yellow light seeping under the door, the hum of a vending machine

somewhere down the hall, the footsteps upstairs, the doors opening and closing on secrets inside, the cars driving away.

The scene in the lobby won't be much more inspiring. Cold tile floors, heavy scent of chlorine from the nearby pool, little islands of people speaking in hushed tones, a different television blaring the same bad news. I switch the one in my room off and stare into its dead eye. My reflection—green and distorted by the curve of the picture tube—looks like a bubble ready to burst.

The eastern Colorado morning is cool and clear, and I'm at a point where I can join the TransAmerica Trail and return to the route I mapped out months ago.

If the world of cross-country bike touring were ancient Rome, then the TA would be its Appian Way; it's impossible to say for sure, but ever since the over-4200-mile route between Astoria, Oregon, and Yorktown, Virginia, was inaugurated in 1976, it would not be unreasonable to estimate that the total number of bikers who have ridden all or part of it is in the tens of thousands. From where I'm at on Highway 50 between La Junta and Lamar, it lies a mere twenty miles north. Detailed maps of the TA sit in one of my rear panniers, buried underneath my clothes and sealed in a big Ziploc freezer bag. Why not take advantage of all that information gathered from all those bikers?

Then I remember John in Arizona. *Fuck guys on bikes. What are you gonna do?*

Less than a dozen miles from the Kansas border, I stop at a gas station to refuel with a Milky Way, two Hostess cherry pies, and a Gatorade. Then I feel myself reach for something else.

The clerk takes what I hand him. "Mappa Kansas too?"

I figured that if I somehow made it to Kansas, the trip was in the bag. In my mind, the state promised easy biking.

Turns out I should have done my homework. The name "Kansas"

comes from the Sioux and means something along the lines of "People of the South Wind." As in wind coming from the South. As in nasty crosswinds and headwinds, which I'm fighting almost as soon as I cross the border.

When I'm biking, I'll take cold, heat, fog, and even rain over wind. Who needs it, other than kids flying kites? With fog and rain, you expect to exercise caution; there's a reason for being slow. But wind? When you bike into it, you look down at the smooth road, expecting to find the asphalt has become sand, because that's exactly what it feels like. With heat, dehydration makes sense; you can feel sweat drain from your body and run down your face, arms, and legs. Wind, on the other hand, is a sneaky dessicator. As it blows over you, it steals your moisture, and you're left wondering why your lips are so chapped and your throat is so dry.

And wind is a special kind of nightmare for someone on a loaded tour. Forget the weight—that's obvious—and consider the design. A person on a loaded tour is going to have racks and bags over the wheels, and these will effectively cover up most of the open spaces, which means more wind resistance. Also, a typical touring frame seats the rider more upright and, therefore, less aerodynamic.

What all of this means right now is that a mighty, invisible hand is holding me back. Or trying to sweep me into the road. It takes barely a morning of this to completely unravel my expectations for Kansas. Given how long I've looked forward to this state, I can't help feeling a little betrayed.

Just past a town named Syracuse, I see something on the shoulder ahead. It's too big to be a biker, and it's moving, so it can't be an abandoned car or truck. When I get close enough, I can see that it's two guys with something between them. They wave to me and I stop. They're thin, unshaven, and probably in their twenties, though it's tough to say for sure because their bodies are hidden by wide-brimmed hats, loose shirts with collars, baggy shorts, and scuffed hiking boots. Between them is a big cart with handles at either end and piled high with a cooler, canvas-wrapped bundles, a rolled-up sleeping pad, blankets, and a couple of umbrellas. On top of this pile is a torn piece of cardboard, and poking out from under it is the head of a small brown and white dog. The two wheels of the cart are about the size of those on a child's bicycle, and one of them is wrapped with duct tape. Both men give me a firm handshake.

"I'm Brian," the shorter one says. "This here's my brother Glen." Glen dips his head so that the brim of his hat momentarily obscures his dark eyes.

"Glen don't say much," Brian tells me.

He also tells me that they're walking to California and have come all the way from Georgia, where they worked various jobs on farms, in restaurants, and even—in Glen's case—on a lobster boat. I'm left to imagine the details of that because Glen just nods solemnly when Brian mentions it. Their latest job was honey bees. They waited to hear from the keeper about being hired on again this season, but then one week stretched into two, then three, then four.

"Me an' Glen used to talk about going for a long walk," Brian says. "I suppose we had too much time to think on it, so we took off."

That was three months ago. They've been on the road since then, sleeping when they got tired and eating when they got hungry, like a pair of Forrest Gumps. Their dog, Tex, had been a real trouper, but now he's riding so that, as Brian says, "His feet can heal up." Most of the time they camp in fields; whenever the weather turns, they find places to hunker down.

"People been real nice," Brian says. "Been givin' us food and such. A few rides, too."

Glen finally speaks. "It's walkin' we prefer."

"Why California?"

"Seen pictures," Brian says. "Looks fine by us. Plus we hear they need grape pickers."

To get to wine country, they'll have to cross the Rockies, two big states' width of desert, and then the Sierras. Making it through all that with a cart is too much to think about, so I ask about the first of those challenges.

"We'll make it up, I s'pose," Brian says. "It's the comin' down that might be a problem."

Their plan is to stop somewhere and pick up a few lengths of PVC pipe to make a longer handle, one that can help them slow their cart on the other side of the mountains. As Brian outlines this plan, Glen studies my front brake. I can almost see the wheels turning in his head as he imagines what he could rig up.

Looking at Brian and Glen's weather-worn hats, their duct-taped wheels, their sad little dog, and their sun-bleached load of everything they own, I suddenly feel like I'm driving a Lexus SUV. Sure, there are many more expensive touring bikes than mine, but still, Rusty is rock solid, my racks and panniers are top of the line, and my communications system—that symbol of hip technology, the iPhone—is loaded with apps that deliver information about weather and directions and places to stay with the touch of a sweaty, tired finger. Plus, I'm not exactly sleeping under bridges.

"You be safe now," Brian says.

"Yeah," I say. "You guys do the same, you hear?"

"Wait a sec," Glen says as he leans over their cart and digs around, careful not to disturb Tex. Then he gives me something.

"Take that, case you get hungry," he tells me as I stare at a granola bar in my hands, and I can't help thinking of the man I handed food to a few days ago, the man gathering sticks by the River of Lost Souls.

Somewhere west of Garden City the next afternoon, a bright shape appears in the distance. Another biker. He spots me at about the same time and crosses to my side of the road. As we get closer to each other, I can tell he's on a mountain bike. Probably someone out for a pleasure ride.

But when we roll to a stop, tire-to-tire, I see that I'm wrong on a couple of counts. First, he's wearing a stuffed backpack and has an even bigger bag strapped to the rear rack. Definitely out here for a while.

And second, he's a she.

"You're the first woman I've seen alone out here."

She laughs. "Yeah, my parents are freaking out a little."

She tells me her name is Miranda as she removes her helmet, runs a gloved hand through her short blonde hair, and then wipes it across her fluorescent orange vest. The vest is striking; it's what I first noticed in the distance and is a nice piece of preparation, which makes it all the stranger that she's on a mountain bike. It's not meant for road riding of even moderate distances, let alone the trek she tells me she's on, from Ohio to San Francisco. Of course, she looks to be in her early twenties, and being young makes up for a lot of poor planning.

She graduated college with a degree in management about two years ago and landed an assistant director job at a local gym. The work bored her, but it allowed her to move out of her parents' house and into a one-bedroom apartment.

"Pretty crappy," she says. "Thin walls."

There was a boyfriend, too, but she felt the same way about him as she did about her job.

"I'm not even sure why we were dating." She tells me how all of her days started to look the same—come home from work, ignore the texts from her boyfriend, and collapse on her couch.

"Then I had a dream," she says, "right on that couch." In the dream, she was pedaling. On a bike, on a wide, flat shoulder, tall cornstalks waving at her from the right and left. It might have been just a few miles outside of the Ohio town where she lived, but she had a feeling that it was much further away. Iowa, maybe. Or Nebraska. She knew she was heading to the ocean.

"And I woke up happy," she says.

Until that moment, she never thought of biking across the country, didn't even know if people did that. She found out they did, and the more stories she read, the more she became convinced to do it, too. It made perfect sense. A complete U-turn, which is exactly what she needed.

"Did you tell them? Your parents?"

She laughs. "No way, not then."

She waited until she quit her job and broke up with her boyfriend. She figured there was no way they could talk her out of it at that point.

By the time she hit Illinois, she had been bitten by bugs, spooked by traffic, rained on, chased by dogs, and pestered constantly by texts on her Blackberry from her now ex-boyfriend.

"I thought about going back," she says. "But I would've had to eat some shit."

I could imagine. She would return to the 24 Hour Fitness or whatever it was, step through the double glass doors and into the climate-controlled coolness, walk up the metal-and-carpet stairway to her old boss's office, and watch his head nod slowly as she explained how she made a huge mistake and would do whatever it took to get her old job back.

I could imagine her try not to meet her mom's eyes as they moved her meager belongings into her old room, muttering *just for a few weeks until I can find another place.*

I could imagine her dial her ex-boyfriend's number to get together, thinking *just a drink, to show him I'm okay,* not to get together *together. Not right away, at least...*

"But then there was this truck," she says. On a little country road, an eighteen-wheeler thundered past on her left, sheared off the mirror at the end of her handlebars and knocked her off the bike.

"Asshole never even slowed down."

She lay in the long grass and checked for broken bones. Just a cut on her leg. Then she got up and stared down the road at the truck, which was just a speck.

"I figured it was a sign," she says. When she fished out her

Blackberry to make the inevitable call home, the screen was shattered, and she couldn't get a signal.

"I decided it *was* a sign, just not the one I thought."

"And here you are."

"Here I am," she says, taking a long swig from her lone water bottle. "I like *your* sign, by the way." She points at the back of my bike.

A couple of days earlier, I found a big yellow car magnet that said STUDENT DRIVER, and I lashed it across my rear bag as a kind of joke.

"So what's your story?" Miranda asks me.

# 14

# Bedtime Story

The San Diego fires of October 2007 scorched a half million acres of the county and threatened to burn their way right up to the ocean, but then the winds died down, the flames lost their fury, and firefighters wrangled the chaos under control.

I had been picking up the kids a couple of times a week and meeting with Elizabeth in sessions with different counselors that all ended the same way. The shouting wasn't productive and wasn't meant to be. Things hadn't worked out as we planned, and even though we had tamped down our feelings about this, there was no place left for them to go once they broke loose. For her part, she didn't like living so far away from friends and family and hadn't really wanted to come to California in the first place—but who am I to tell her story? As for me, well, what exactly *did* I blame her for? In those sessions it was easier to shout than to figure things out.

We dragged on like that for another week and a half until there was only one thing left to do, the hardest thing I've ever had to do in my life—tell eleven-year-old Nick and nine-year-old Tony that I wouldn't be living in the house anymore.

In addition to joint counseling, I was seeing my own therapist, and we talked about this moment. I tried to remember and focus on the points we discussed—it was my decision, I loved them so much and this was not about them, there was nothing they could do to change it. The whole time I spoke, I felt like I had stepped off the edge of something very high and was falling into another life.

Nick pinched his lips together. "Can I go to my room?" he managed to get out. His eyes flicked back and forth between me and Elizabeth as if unsure which of us to ask.

"Yes," she said, and I nodded.

"Me too?" Tony asked.

They disappeared upstairs, and I just stood there, staring up after them. What would go through their heads as they sat in their rooms? What would they think later as they lay in the dark? Or in all the Dadless nights to come? My mind raced through an endless loop. *What have I done? What have I done? What have I done?*

She leaned toward me.

"We're leaving for Memphis next Wednesday. When we get back Sunday, I want all of your stuff out of here or I'm putting it on the driveway."

And then I was gone. First from the house and later from the pictures that sat on the shelves and covered the walls.

Nick called twice that night to ask me something about the fantasy football team we managed together. Nothing important. He just wanted to talk.

On Wednesday, the three of them left for Memphis—where her parents lived—and I arrived at the house with a U-Haul truck on Friday. The Christmas lights were already up outside, and when I walked in the front door, I saw the tree to the left and lights with garland going up the banister on the stairs. I realized that this was the Friday after Thanksgiving—the day that all of us would normally spend decorating for Christmas. They must have done everything last weekend. And now here I was to take things away, a reverse Santa Claus.

I dragged empty boxes into the house and filled them with clothes, a few files, and some things from the kitchen. As I packed a pan, a spatula, and a baking dish that we got as a wedding present, I saw the kitchen table now had three chairs instead of four. I carted off our bed, but only because Elizabeth had taken it apart and left a note that read ALL YOURS—I'LL GET A NEW ONE. Most of what I took, though, were books. Shortly after we moved into this house, I built three eight-foot-tall bookshelves out of poplar, screwed them into the wall, and filled them with books. After about an hour and a half, those same shelves stood as they did right after I built them. Empty.

Packing and loading the truck took the whole morning. Driving to Daniel's apartment took about twenty minutes. Unloading everything into my new room took only a little longer than that. I leaned against the lone bare spot of wall and looked at all the boxes around me. The smart thing to do, I thought, would be to set up the bed and replace the camping cot I had been sleeping on.

But then I was in my car, telling myself I had to make sure nothing was left at the house, even though I knew I had taken everything that was mine.

When I stepped through the door again, I felt like a stranger. Worse, actually. An intruder. My name might have still been on the deed, but this was no longer my home.

I walked to the fireplace, over to the box that I spotted that morning. On the drive over, I promised myself I wouldn't look in that box, but there I was, crouched over it, my fingers pulling at one of the cards stuck between envelopes.

Elizabeth had worked extra hard the past week to get those Christmas cards finished and mailed. That year's photo wasn't like the others. Of course I wasn't in it, but beyond that, it wasn't by the bougainvillea as usual. The photo was taken in front of the Christmas tree. I unfolded the checklist that went out with the card and immediately saw the obvious difference in this, too. Like the fourth chair around the kitchen table, my name and column were gone.

I put the list aside and read the card. There was no handwritten note; this was an unaddressed extra. Affixed inside the card was a sticker printed with the words:

**Rocco has departed our family this October.
We are still reeling from the shock and suddenness of this loss.**

It seemed straightforward and simple to me. I used to be there and now I wasn't. Any other meaning—like the one tied to the fact I had cancer a few years earlier—was lost on me until a week later, when Cathy called to tell me our cousin thought I died.

I wandered upstairs. Not to do anything, really. Just to look. In the hallway, our family portraits were gone, replaced with pictures of only Nick and Tony. I wondered for a second what happened to the old photos. Tucked behind the new ones? Stuck in an envelope somewhere? Thrown in the trash?

Nick's room was a mess. I sat on his bed and stared at the light switch cover. On it was a photo of Cubs pitcher Matt Clement. I drafted Nick into Cubs fandom during the 2003 season when they made it to within five outs of the World Series, and he took a shine to Clement for some reason. I found the cover online and we added it to his room as part of his Cubs redecoration—Cubs sheets, Cubs blankets, Cubs logo painted on the wall. Now I stared at Clement and his silly little goatee. Clement, who wasn't even a Cub anymore. I couldn't remember where he had gone. St. Louis, maybe, or Boston.

Tony's room was a disaster, too. It was dark out now, and I knew I should be getting back to my little room with Daniel and his birds, but instead I stood between the two twin beds in front of me. Tony slept in one, and on weekends, we let Nick sleep in the other. To the side was a bookcase I built, and I ran my hand across the big picture books there. Then I stopped. Hiding among them was a copy of *The Phantom Tollbooth*—the ragged paperback that I read and reread in sixth grade.

I had an idea a year or so earlier to read the kids a chapter a night, but Elizabeth said no. She didn't like that the main character, Milo, was older than Nick and Tony, and she really didn't like his attitude, at the book's start, of unfocused boredom and restlessness. I flipped through the pages and remembered how—fueled by my affection for the book—I started to argue back, and the whole thing began to swell into a big fight. But then I backed down.

Holding the book, I climbed under the covers of Tony's bed and lay still. I could see the orange glow of the streetlight outside through the edges of the light-dampening shade I installed. Outside, I heard a dog bark and a car drive by every now and then. Inside my head was a low, steady drone, as if my ear was pressed against a large seashell. When I woke up there the next morning, *The Phantom Tollbooth* was on the ground, but the Christmas card and picture were still in my hand. For a long time I lay in that little bed and stared at my wife and sons, and I tried to will my image to appear in the empty space behind their heads, to see myself smiling with both arms wrapped tight around my family.

# VOICES FROM THE ROAD

# 15

# The Spirit of the Plains

Despite its classification, "Highway" 50 is for the most part a simple country road. It puffs itself up into a divided four-lane road east of Garden City, but after a few miles it settles back down into a narrow two-lane road with a shoulder the width of my foot, which is to say, no shoulder at all. I pass through one unincorporated area after another on my way east, and the only real signs anyone lives in these places are the gigantic granaries next to the railroad tracks. They're stark white except for the name of each place, painted in large, square-block letters near the top—PIERCEVILLE, CHARLESTON, INGALLS. Every so often near these granaries, a little shack appears with the faded words "Coca-Cola" on a splintered plank of wood.

My destination tonight is Dodge City, and as I get closer, soybeans and corn give way to beef. At some point I come upon a cattle yard that stretches to the south as far as I can see, and I pedal into a hot bovine stench that almost knocks me over. Markers on the side of the road let me know I'm on the Old Cimarron Trail, and I can't help wishing that Rusty was a horse so that he could be the one to deal with this wind, which blows as hot and hard as ever.

If possible, that wind picks up the closer I get to Dodge City. I'm still about fifteen miles out, and I seriously wonder if I can make it. I try to divert myself in a number of ways, like listing the dead animals

I see on the side of the road. *Bird. Bird. Snake. Bird. Prairie dog. Toad. Bird. What's up with all of these dead birds?*

When the road widens and traffic gets a little heavier, I'm still about ten miles from Dodge. I've reached that point that I often reach near the end of long days, where I talk to myself out loud. Sometimes I'll tell myself any jokes I remember or list foods that I like in the order I like them, but right now I decide that the thing to do is sing every TV theme song I know. The trick is not to swallow any bugs. I start with the easy ones first—shows that Vince and I watched while sprawled across that gold shag carpeting. *Gilligan's Island, The Brady Bunch, The Beverly Hillbillies, Green Acres.* After that, random songs that I know most of the words to. *WKRP in Cincinnati, Welcome Back Kotter, Laverne and Shirley.* When the words escape me, I make something up. Vince could get all the words to a song the first time he heard it, so he hated when I improvised. As I pedal into the wind and try to remember exactly why Chico shouldn't be so discouraged by the Man, I can hear my brother's voice cut through the whistling in my ears.

*If you can't sing it right, then don't sing it.*

Just west of Dodge on a sage-scrubbed hill stands a big stone wall welcoming my arrival. On its face are large rusted letters that spell out DODGE CITY, and atop that wall are gigantic rusted metal cowboys on horseback that appear as silhouettes. They're charging forward, a couple of them twirling lassos above their heads, taming the plains and whatever else they see there.

Dodge City took root in 1871, when Henry Sitler built a shelter out of sod and tarps down by the Arkansas River—pronounced Are-*Kansas*, some chuckling locals informed me two days earlier. This "house" was meant to be a base of operations for his cattle ranching, but it soon became a popular stopping point for travelers. Down a stretch from Sitler's house was Fort Dodge, one of several forts in the area meant to protect settlers on the Santa Fe Trail from the "Indian

Wars." When it was built in 1865, the cattle trade was in the eastern part of the state, a long, long way from Dodge.

One little thing changed all of that—a tick. When these disease-carrying bugs spread among Texas cattle, Kansas lawmakers imposed a quarantine line in the center of the state to protect its eastern end, where most people lived. So the cattle trade moved west. By the 1880s, this trade fed Dodge City, which grew around Sitler's little sod house. Hundreds of thousands of cattle passed through the city's borders each year, and before long, Dodge became known as the "Queen of the Cow Towns." Stores, bars, and brothels all flourished, so naturally there were gunfighters and lawmen, including legends such as Wyatt Earp and Bat Masterson.

In its present incarnation, Dodge City bears little resemblance to its myth. Moving toward the heart of downtown, I don't see any cowboys. In fact, it's clear this town is now meant for adventurers of a different breed—families in minivans or RVs and older couples in roomy sedans with white wall tires. So the main businesses are motels, gas stations, and restaurants, which are all I see for the first ten minutes I'm there. It takes a few blocks to get past the McDonald's and the Subway and the Taco Bell, all of which must seem like salvation to people traveling with young kids. Predictably, the lots are full, and behind the big "$1.99"s and giant decals of food on the front windows, people devour their paper-wrapped dinners. Then more expensive upscale chains like Applebee's start to appear, followed immediately by a few non-chains that seem out of place in this former cowboy town. Maybe one of these—Lu Chen's—is a nod to the thousands of laborers who helped build the railroads, but who wants a Chinese buffet in the middle of Dodge City? Beef is what's for dinner.

Just beyond the restaurants are Boot Hill and Front Street, Dodge City's original graveyard and downtown. I lock Rusty to a tree and pass through the Boot Hill Museum, a crowded, air-conditioned souvenir shop where today's traveler, hungry for the "Old West" can buy post cards, DVD sets of *Gunsmoke*, and cap guns of all sizes and shapes. While I'm browsing some books, one in particular catches my eye. It's big, heavy, volume called *The Spirit of the Plains*, and on its cover are two images, side by side—an old black and white photo of some settlers, and a color photo of present-day "cowboys." The men and women on the left look worn out; the men's beards hang low and the women's shoulders sag as they stand in front of wagons about to collapse under their own weight. The men on the right are on horseback, gathered together and posed with their arms crossed low in front of them. There's a hint of arrogance in their half-smiles. Given their immaculate duds, it's safe to assume they haven't suffered through many harsh winters. But as I flip through the book, the message is clear and without irony. The spirit of the past lives on today.

It's tough to leave the climate-controlled interior when there's still a hot wind blowing outside, but according to the whiteboard next to the exit, there's a gunfight scheduled in about twenty minutes, and I want to mosey around some before that.

The Front Street exhibit is largely an Old West strip mall. Connected to each other and sharing a weathered-wood boardwalk are some famous landmarks from Old Dodge City, like the Long Branch Saloon, G.M. Hoover's cigar and liquor shop, and J. Collar's Dry Goods. The museum's tourist information doesn't widely broadcast the fact that all of the original establishments burned down in 1885 and these buildings are replicas. I peek into one of the closed "saloons" and see it's actually an ice-cream parlor. I wonder what the proprietors back in the 1800s would think about the going rate for a scoop of ice cream in a waffle cone, which—according to the old-timey script on the wall—will set a cowpoke back $4.25.

One of the exhibits—the First Union Church—is still open. Like the shops, the church is a replica of the original, which stood a few blocks from here and was built to bring some religion to this wild spot on the prairie.

I open the front doors and find myself staring at a rifle about two feet away, pointed right at my face. It fires with a loud clap that makes me jump. The barrel lowers and I see my assailant—a twelve-year old wearing a souvenir shop cowboy hat and a chromed plastic badge.

"Gotcha!" he shouts, and runs down the middle aisle to the front of the church, where he dives behind a pew. Two other little gunslingers pop out from my left and follow him. They vanish for only a second, and then their three heads poke up from behind the pew. Their rifles follow, lining me up in their sights.

"Where are your parents?"

One of them says, "We're in charge here."

"Well, I want a picture, but not of you. Duck down."

Their heads disappear, but three rifle barrels are sticking up over the pew.

"Guns too, pardners."

The church is austere, with flat white walls that make the dark oak timbers on the ceiling stand out. I doubt if more than fifty people could fit in here, and I wonder what the congregation looked like on a typical Sunday morning in the late 1870s. I'm guessing that more than a few of the congregants might have spent some time the previous night at the Long Branch or the China Doll, a brothel that somehow didn't make it onto the tourist version of Front Street.

In front of the shops there's a big lawn bordered on one edge by long wooden tables and benches. It's a perfect for place for a picnic of three hundred, but an even better place to watch a gunfight. The choice seats in front are already taken, so I sit on a table in the back. Two actors dressed as lawmen stroll out of the Long Branch and head over to the crowd of in front. They're wearing headsets with microphones that feed to a few crackly speakers above us.

"I declare," the taller of the two men says. "Lookee all these folks!"

"Ayup," his friend answers. "Say, everybody, whatcher waitin' fer?"

The banter continues like this for a few minutes as if it's an ordinary day in old Dodge. Never mind that there's a guy to my right in a Hawaiian shirt and Panama Jack hat, and never mind that two kids to my left are elbows-deep in Happy Meals, and never mind that nearly every adult male seems to have a digital recording device growing out of his right eye. Seeing this, I check the batteries on my own camera. I wouldn't want it to crap out before I get some shots of my own.

Our story begins. The marshal and his deputy are making a well-intentioned effort to keep things calm in wild Dodge, so they're enforcing a new policy where visitors must surrender their firearms upon entry to the town. But today, three ornery cattle drivers aren't too keen on this rule, and they stir up trouble with both the marshal and one of the saloon gals at the Long Branch. Fights ensue—first with fists and then with guns—and after the smoke clears, the troublemakers are dead.

The marshal, however, is eager to restore a jocular atmosphere, so he approaches us again, this time with a pitch to buy some souvenir photographs. He assures us that it's a "one-time only" deal just for us, the honored guests of Dodge. A throng of people in the front two rows start forking over bills. I'm ready to call it a night, so I go through the museum/shop to get back to Rusty. I'm almost out the door when I stop. Might as well pick up a few postcards while I'm here.

Time to get the hell out of Dodge.

Kansas rolls by in an endless carpet of prairie, cornfields, and cattle. The wind never lets up and the temperature and humidity never go down. The sky is a big blue screen waiting for a movie to start. Something with Paul Newman, maybe.

It's a wide open land, these plains. Most people don't have a lot of regard for Kansas and the other states that cut a wide swath of prairie from Canada to Mexico. To them, it's just a Big Empty between the places where things *really* happen. After a few days on a bike out here, I find it hard to disagree. I wonder if all this blankness helped build the mythology of the Old West. Against a backdrop this bland, any exploit might seem heroic.

I wonder what the people of the past would make of this artificial heartland today. The land they knew is now bound and crisscrossed by two- and four-lane roads with conveniently-placed gas stations that sell conveniently-packaged food like "Nutter Butters" and "Mellowcremes." And in between these places are little stops that promise a glimpse into history for tourists with a video camera in one hand and a credit card in the other. Out here, you don't need to search too hard for the spirit of the plains; all you have to do is head to the Front Street gift shop in Dodge City, where it's on sale for $29.95 plus tax.

But who am I to criticize? My cache of junk food, precision-engineered bike with waterproof bags, and iPhone are hardly the kind of props that belong in an adventure story.

Just outside of one little town, there's a big billboard that reads, WE WILL REBUILD.

I stop at a grocery store, and while I'm eating a sandwich in the parking lot, a guy in a cowboy hat strolls over.

"Name's Don," he says, extending a big hand.

He asks me about Rusty, and I ask him about the billboard.

The "WE" on the sign are the people of the town we're in, Greensburg. In May of 2007, these people were hit with a class five tornado, the highest rating possible. The twister was gigantic. More than a mile and a half across and wider than Greensburg itself. It stayed on the ground for an unheard of distance of over twenty miles. After it lifted, Greensburg was almost completely destroyed and eleven people were dead. President Bush declared the entire county a federal disaster area, but the money that followed could only do so much.

"Everything, and I mean *everything*, was flattened 'cept for a few buildings," he tells me. "All the trees, their tops just shaved right off." He slashes the air with his hand.

I look around at the people coming and going in the lot. "Seems to be back to normal."

"Well, some folks left. Can't say I blame 'em none. Lotsa folks lost everything."

"How about you?"

"My wife and I rolled up our sleeves and dug in. Lotsa folks did."

Don tells me how all the reconstruction is using the latest environmentally-friendly methods and that Greensburg will set a gold standard for energy efficiency, but I keep thinking of that tornado. The sky turns green, the air goes still. An alarm cuts through the silence as a fat black column of clouds heads for town from across the plains. The wind howls like a freight train as it lifts cars, trees, and houses like toys.

And afterward? In the weeks that followed, the people who eventually left must have looked at the gashed, open land and seen more of the same down the line. They must have thought about the kind of life that would be, forever watching that flat horizon for signs of coming disaster.

Two days later and fifty miles past Wichita, I'm soaked through with sweat and ready to give up. Partly it's the wind, and partly it's the insane humidity of a state that has decided to choose this particular week for record highs. I stop in a place called Beaumont, which as far as I can tell is just a rest area on a wind-pummeled bluff above the prairie. According to my map, there's nothing on the road until Fredonia, which is another forty-eight miles away. That would make close to one hundred for the day. The most I had biked so far out here was a little under eighty.

The rest area lies at the end of a long, winding road that climbs above the highway. There are a few picnic structures around, and the people who designed them probably had the wind in mind when they gave each one three brick walls and a low-pitched metal roof. A sign near the bathroom says the state of Kansas allows people to camp at rest areas, and I figure this is what I'll do. If it gets too windy tonight, I can just wheel everything inside and sleep by the toilets.

My stomach's rumbling, so I dig through my handlebar bag to discover all I have is half a bag of pretzels. My Clif Bars are gone, even the one I stashed in a rear bag. I had some emergency tuna pouches, but I gave them to Chester back in Durango. I have about a pound of quarters with me, so I look for some vending machines but can't find any. It's not like I'm going to starve, but I'm already uncomfortable enough without the added hunger pangs. The night before, I stayed with a couple named John and Sharlene in Wichita, and now I'm thinking of breakfast this morning and those last strips of crispy bacon none of us could finish.

I sit as much out of the wind as I can for close to an hour. A few travelers come through, and they fall into one of two categories. They're either curious and come talk to me, or they think I'm crazy and keep their distance. I call Shannon, but there's no answer. She's teaching summer school and is probably in class.

Twenty minutes later my phone rings.

"Where are you and what are you doing?" she asks.

I tell her what's going on, ending with, "I'm in Prairie Limbo."

"Sounds like a song."

"'Should I Stay or Should I Go?'" I say, wondering if she'll catch on.

A pause. "'Ease on Down the Road.'" Then she starts to sing.

"Really," I say. "I go Clash and you give me *The Wiz*?"

She's still singing.

"I think I liked it better when you were worrying," I say.

She stops. "Look. You're gonna do what you're gonna do. Plus, you're a capable guy, so why worry?" She says this all very calmly. "It was a whole epiphany thing I had."

"You don't get to have an epiphany. I'm the one on a journey, I get the epiphanies."

"Then get one and quit whining."

After we hang up, I wonder where Miranda is, and if her boyfriend is still texting her to come home. I wonder where Brian and Glen and Tex are, and what field they're sleeping in tonight.

"Okay, Rusty," I say. "Let's go for it."

~

Later, I think about calling my dad. I'll see him and my mom in about a week when I drive up to Chicago for Jerry's wedding. That's the plan, but if this wind keeps up, I'm not sure I'll make it out of the state. I haven't called for a few days, mainly because I haven't wanted to hear my dad's worries or my mom ask, "How's Elizabeth?" When I decided to go on this ride, I waited until a month or so before I left to tell him. Between his bad hearing and initial inability to wrap his mind around what I was saying, our usually brief call stretched out for a while. Finally, there was silence. I could tell he was gathering himself.

"Whaddaya mean?" he said. "It's too far to bike!"

Lying here, my legs feel like bags of sand and every joint aches, but the fact remains that I made it to Fredonia. Ninety-eight miles for the day, my longest by far.

But he may be right yet. There's still a long way to go.

"Why do you want to do this?" was his other response, and I knew there was no way to answer that in a way he would understand. I didn't completely understand it myself.

•

One night during my sophomore year at the University of Illinois, a few of my buddies and I decided we'd had it with both the bars and girls on our campus, so we piled into a car for the hour-long drive to Normal, home of Illinois State University. What inspired the trip, naturally, was beer. We were drinking in someone's room when a theory emerged that—because girls at ISU had, on average, lower ACT scores than girls at the U of I—we would have a better shot at getting laid there. Those ladies would be unable to resist our big brains, we moronically concluded.

It seemed reasonable to my alcohol-soaked mind, but in actuality

I was less interested in hooking up with an ISU girl than I was to be someplace new. Our weekend rituals had settled into a parade of the same bars, the same people, and the same conversations. I was sick of it.

We hit the new campus and headed to the apartment of someone's friend, where we found people gathered, killing off a keg from the previous night. About half were getting ready to go to the bars and the other half were going to a party, but there was some kind of argument about where the party was and who was throwing it. I got pulled into a game of quarters, and by the time I got out, all my friends were gone. I headed out alone.

Wandering through campus and then to its edges, I stumbled into a cul-de-sac crowded with people holding red plastic cups. They formed a huge triangle that spread across a lawn and led into a house pulsing with light and a heavy bass beat. Someone handed me a beer, and before I knew it I was in the midst of a group of partiers who laughed and stumbled against each other. Someone asked me my name, and without really thinking I made one up. Then I said I was from New York visiting my cousin, but we got separated.

"You go to school in New York?" a girl asked.

I didn't, as it turned out. Back in New York I worked for my uncle, who ran a hotel. In exchange for living in a room there, I split time between the front desk and the kitchen.

When I found myself with a different group, I was someone else. A soon-to-be former student whose dad's copy machine repair business had gone belly up. There was no more money for school, so I had joined the army.

As the night went on, I continued to invent lives that seemed much more interesting than the one I had. The drunker I got, the wilder the stories got, and by the end of the night, I was an exchange student from Italy chattering in a thick accent to people even drunker than I was about my small fishing village on the Adriatic Sea.

At about two or three in the morning, I tied to make my way

to the apartment. The campus was quiet, and the only people out were a few staggering drunks like me. I cut across a park, and halfway through I stopped. The full moon hung low on the horizon and bathed everything in light. I sat on the damp grass and thought, *How did I end up here?*

Whatever else was going through my head that night is gone with the years. Maybe I thought about Peter Fonda and Dennis Hopper, or maybe I thought about gold shag carpeting, or maybe—anything's possible—what I thought about in the glow of that full moon was riding my bike as a kid, pedaling further and further from home and half-hoping I wouldn't be able to find my way back.

# PART II

---

# In the Heart of the Heart of My Country

"The map is not the territory."
—Alfred Korzybski

# 16

# Miss Fortune

I'm flying high above a checkerboard landscape that alternates between dark squares of dense trees and bright squares of wheat. Some of these squares are softened by water—ponds, streams, and the remnants of last week's flooding—and all of them are beginning to glow as the sun rises in the predawn blue sky to the east. It's a peaceful picture, but what interests me are the roads. They're pale lines carving out the checkerboard's rigid geometry, except for one that defies the pattern—a thick black curve through the grid that looks like a long garter snake sliding through grass. These roads look nothing like the ones I've been anchored to these past few weeks; they've become something new and strange in this dream of flight.

But it's no dream. Even through the heavy headphones I'm wearing, the roar of the engine and the plane's fluttering remind me that I'm about two thousand feet above Linn County, Kansas, in a two-person, single-engine plane built from a kit by a man who is right now asleep in his house somewhere below me, his body wrecked and ravaged by the final phases of malignant mesothelioma. When I left a few weeks ago on Rusty with a ton of gear and no idea what I was getting myself into, I imagined lots of things that might happen, but not this.

So what am I doing up here?

This story might begin in eastern Colorado with a German

woman at the front desk of the Fort Garland Motor Lodge. That was eight days ago, on June 14th. I rolled into town around noon and planned to stop there, but she told me that I would have to wait a few hours for a room. So I walked across the street to Marconi's Italian Villa to eat lunch.

Because I stepped into Marconi's at around 12:15, I stepped back out at around 12:45, and when I did I looked across the street at the Phillips 66 and saw a highway patrolman's car.

I walked over to ask its driver, an officer named Dan, about the road ahead. More specifically, about La Veta Pass, the last climb of the Rockies for me. It was the day after I saw Dr. Candace in Alamosa, and I didn't want to strain my knee any more than I had to. Officer Dan told me it was a gentle climb for about eighteen miles to the summit, and after that it was all downhill to Walsenburg. So I scrapped my plans to stay in Fort Garland, got back on Rusty, and hit the road, where something was waiting for us a little further on.

But maybe the story really begins eleven days before *that*, on June 3rd, at 9:30 in the morning at a Chevron station in northern Arizona. That's when I met John, the scary-looking dude who pulled a road atlas from the back of his Harley and showed me how I could shave a few days and a few hundred miles of hard desert riding from my original route. Without John, I wouldn't have gone through Fort Garland, I wouldn't have talked with Officer Dan, and I wouldn't have been on that stretch of highway mid-afternoon on the 14th.

And I wouldn't have met John if not for something that happened on June 2nd in Detroit, Michigan, over two thousand miles away from that Chevron station. With two outs in the top of the ninth inning of an Indians-Tigers game, umpire Jim Joyce blew an easy call that cost Tigers pitcher Armando Galarrago what should have been the twenty-first perfect game in baseball history. On the morning of the 3rd, sitting on the edge of my bed at the Arizona 9 Motor Hotel in Williams, I got caught up in the ESPN coverage and started biking later than usual. If I had left even five minutes earlier, John and I would have never crossed paths.

So how does all of this get me into a Kitfox plane, soaring high above Kansas farmland? These and a near-infinite number of other events that I don't even know about clicked together like the cogs of the most complicated machine ever to place me between mile markers 275 and 276 on Highway 160 at precisely 2:42 in the afternoon on Tuesday, June 14th. There and then, while climbing La Veta Pass and still about two miles from the summit, I saw a guy standing next to a pickup truck with a trailer carrying what looked like a gigantic bug.

•

"I wish you'd just go home," my dad says, for what seems like the thousandth time. "I can't understand why you want to do this..."

And for what also seems like the thousandth time, I have no answer. I'm still waiting for the hidden picture to emerge in this particular puzzle, and I'm a little scared that it won't.

I should tell him about Miranda and her question to me—*What's your story?*—because that's a question my dad would get. He's got stories of his own that he tells over and over again, and because he's my dad, they're kind of my stories, too.

One of them begins in the late spring of 1947. Discharged from the army the year before, he was trying to figure out what to do next. He lived at home in a three-story brownstone in the Greenpoint section of Brooklyn with his two grandmothers, his parents, his sister Dorothy, his Aunt Rosie, his Aunt Lily and Uncle Louie, his Aunt Lizzie and his Uncle Nick, and their two boys, Johnny and Angelo. It was a loud house on a quiet block, and my father had missed both while he was in the army. He missed the big Sunday dinners at his mother's table, missed the *frittata* and *cavatelli* and *calzone* that his mother and aunts prepared, missed the kids playing ball in the street or pitching pennies against the stoops, missed his best friend Guido calling to him—*Hey Tommy!*—to go down to the corner and get an egg cream. Now that the war was over, it was time to move on, but where? The notes of uncertainty greeted him his first few months home and had become a steady hum of panic, especially now that his membership in the "52-20 Club"—for 52 weeks he received $20 a week from the government—was almost over.

Since returning, Tommy worked mornings in a clothing factory run by a *paisan* of his father's. His job was on the suit-making line, where material cut into the shapes of suit parts would fall in front of him. Alone, these pieces didn't look like much. Long rectangles with slight curves and angles cut into them, a few narrow bands, a wide parenthesis. He had a bin of numbers he attached to these parts so that somewhere down the line, tailors could assemble them into suits that would make a guy feel like somebody.

In the afternoons he took mechanical drafting classes at the Mondell Institute, courtesy of the G.I. Bill. But he was just about finished, and he needed something to show for his time there. He didn't want to be like the *gavones* who hung around in their t-shirts during the day and shot dice at night. Tommy wanted to work.

But every morning, as he matched slips of paper to the steady stream of fabric shapes that dropped before him, Tommy worried. So many men looking for work. It was supposed to be a time of opportunity, but where was his? He would see big shots in their cars driving down the block, and he wondered how they got there. He didn't want much, just a job so that he could someday get married, have kids, and buy a home. His father told him that to get married, he needed about five thousand dollars for a ring, an apartment, furniture, and other odds and ends, and until then...well, what would he be? He worried so much about finding a job that sometimes he threw up. His mother and aunts diagnosed this as a "nervous stomach," and when it acted up, he was lucky if his father was in the garden looking at his cherry tree or in the cellar checking on how the wine was coming along. Tommy knew it bothered his father to see him this way. Men didn't get sick, curled up on the floor of the *bacchousa*; they looked the world in the eye.

Tommy's mother was more understanding.

—Something'll come along, she would tell him. Wait and see. Things work out.

•

The great thing about biking is the openness. In a car, you're hidden; speed, doors, windows, air conditioning, and radio all conspire to cut you off from everything and everyone on the outside. But you can't hide on a bike.

So when I saw that pickup truck with its strange cargo on the side of Highway 160 on the afternoon of June 14, I slowed down.

What I thought was a giant bug was actually a small black plane, its two wings detached and secured over its back with thick canvas straps. A lanky guy in sunglasses leaned against the driver's side of the truck. As I eased to a stop in front of him, he looked up from his phone and flashed a big set of teeth.

"Howdy," he said.

"Hey." I set my feet down on the shoulder.

"I passed you a little ways back there and wondered what y'all were doing."

"Biking cross country. San Diego to North Carolina."

He threw his head back and laughed. "No foolin'?"

"Yeah, pretty crazy," I said. "You need help?"

"Nope. Just waitin' on my son." With his thumb, he pointed up a hill that disappeared into thick forest. "Ain't never been outta Kansas before, so he wanted to get a look at some real country."

"Kansas, huh? Where at?"

"Girard," he said. "You prolly never heard of it."

"I have, actually. I'm planning to go right through there."

"No shit," he said. "Ain't that somethin'."

His name was Roy, and his son—a speck up on the hillside—was

Charlie. They were on their way back from Arizona, where they had picked up the plane on the trailer. He was helping a friend of his who couldn't make the trip himself.

"Been seein' some other riders," he said. "You with them?"

"No, those are RAAM guys."

"Whuzzat?"

"Race across America." I tell him about the annual event where bikers cross the country at breakneck speed. For a few days, my route overlapped with theirs, and I spent an afternoon in Colorado being passed by one rider on a superlight bike after another. Unlike what I'm doing, the RAAM is an exercise in *serious* self-abuse. Winning bikers pedal over three hundred miles a day and are trailed by big support teams.

"Where's your guys?"

"I'm it."

He took off his sunglasses. "All alone?"

"Yep."

He held up his phone. "I'm giving you my number. You need help or if anyone gives you a hard time, call me."

I wasn't sure what he thought might happen or what he would do if something did happen, but we traded numbers anyway. He and Charlie planned to drive the fifteen hours back to Girard that night, and he asked if I wanted a ride. I could just hear Nick's voice in response to *that* news, so I passed on Roy's offer but said that when I came through Girard sometime next week, he could put me up for the night.

"Hell yes!" he said, and nearly pulled my arm off when he shook my hand.

As I made my way through the rest of Colorado and Kansas, Roy called every other day. Each time he asked where I was, and each time I told him, he laughed and said "Unbelievable!" He had some big plans for my visit.

"We'll eat like kings and I'll take you flying."

I wasn't so sure about the flying part, but I said "okay" anyway.

•

My grandfather wanted my dad to become an engineer, but he had no love for math; his real passion was languages. One of his grandmothers spoke only Italian, and he learned it at a young age; as a result, he always did well in his language classes and had high scores on his Spanish and French exit exams from Boys' High School. Before the war, he enrolled at City College, where he likewise did well in those classes. He knew that the world was becoming a place where people all over the world would have to talk to each other more, and he thought that there might be a future for translators.

—Engineering is the future, his father said.

But at City College, Tommy struggled. While he liked the precision of his drafting tools, he didn't see how he would be able to overcome calculus. The letters and signs made no sense to him. He would see "a" as an exponent of "x," and his mind would focus on that "a," the ending sound to so many words that echoed through the walls and floors of his house: *cucina, pentola, insalata.* He would see "0"—the point that "x" approaches in many calculus functions—and it would transform itself into an "o," the resonant sound to so much of the Spanish he studied and loved: *bienvenido, mucho gusto, Yo soy.*

In the war there was no math, and that was fine with Tommy. He had done his jobs and felt like he was helping with the effort.

*Already a lifetime ago*, he thought, as he quickly attached another set of numbers to another collection of shapes at his spot in the factory. He looked at those pieces and tried to see in them the final design, and while he knew what suits looked like, the actual process by which those separate pieces became a whole remained a mystery to him.

When the Mondell Institute set him up with a job, the family celebrated. Tommy's mother picked an armload of zucchini flowers from the garden, dipped them in egg and flour, and fried them up—his favorite.

The next morning, he found his way to the address they gave him. The sign on the door read STEIN AND SONS, and he wondered if he would talk to Mr. Stein or one of his sons.

Neither, as it turned out. The man who stood and shook his hand was named Gray.

It wasn't clear to Tommy what Stein and Sons did; they appeared to have a number of interests, including the women's salon business, which was where he was needed. Mr. Gray wanted him to develop a series of plastic forms to help women decide on a hairstyle.

—Women like change, Mr. Gray said. This will let them see what's possible.

Tommy knew this was a rare opportunity. Ever since the war ended, there was a glut of draftsman looking for work. This job was a gift.

—You won't be sorry, he answered.

Later, he looked over the materials that Mr. Gray gave him—sheets of plastic of varying thicknesses, a book of sketches with different hairstyles, more sketches of round shapes that were meant to be face types. The plastic wasn't the problem; he could figure out some kind of a mechanism to hold it all together. The problem, he knew, were the sketches. Clearly, there was some way that the different hairstyles and different face shapes should come together. But how? What did he know about women's hair or faces? What did he know about change, other than he didn't like it?

He had his share of change in the last few years. First he moved from his home in Brooklyn to basic training in North Carolina, then from North Carolina to Texas, then from Texas to the Philippines, then from the Philippines back home. But home was different. The block was different. At the corner candy store, the bright soda fountains and the glass bottles of syrup were gone; now there was just one lever at the counter—a big red one that said Coke. It seemed like a long time ago when he ran to that corner store with Guido to get a Milky Way for a nickel, seven cents frozen; it seemed even longer ago when he served as an altar boy at St. Francis de Paola a couple of blocks away. The kids now, they just hung around on the stoops all day. Some of the older ones even called him "pops" before they laughed and disappeared between buildings.

Tommy could practically feel the acid eating away at his insides. Who in their right mind wanted change?

With everything spread out before him, he knew it was hopeless. Stein and Sons needed some kind of designer, not a draftsman. Someone with a better appreciation for change, someone who could make the whole idea seem elegant. Tommy could understand the problem but could not begin to come up with a solution; this was a calculus of a different kind, and if there was one thing that Tommy knew well, it was his limitations.

He returned a few days later and told Mr. Gray that someone with a more artistic background could do a better job, and Mr. Gray told him that he was an honest young man. He respected that, though not enough to offer Tommy a different job.

A few weeks later he ran into a guy from the neighborhood who lived over on Humboldt Street. Like Tommy, he served in the war and had looked for work when he got back. He was now at the Brooklyn Navy Yard, running the IBM machines there. When Tommy told him about his lack of prospects, his friend said he should head over to IBM, like he had done. They were sending people to their data processing schools and then setting them up with jobs. Good jobs, with a future.

—Pretty sweet deal, he told Tommy.

At the IBM office he met a woman named Miss Fortune. She was the secretary there, and she said they had ended the program his friend told him about.

My father's memory of Miss Fortune is not as detailed as I would like. He doesn't remember anything about her other than her name, which he says he'll never forget. But I wonder about other things. Like her age. She was probably older than my father, who was only twenty-one during their brief meeting. Did she get a job during the war years? Did she have a family? Was she an old spinster, living with her parents? There's no way to know for sure.

The problem is that so much of our lives is hidden, even from us.

I like to picture Miss Fortune in her thirties or forties, dark-haired, with black cat's eye glasses. She's wearing a smart black skirt and a starched white blouse that practically glows in the midsummer New York light. She never married. Instead, she lives with her mother and takes care of her. Her mother's friend Irene has a son named Paulie who comes to call every once in a while. Paulie works in a shoe store, and when he talks to Miss Fortune and gestures with his hands, all she can think about is how he puts them on strangers' feet. Still, her mother is hopeful, though not as hopeful as Irene. Sometimes Miss Fortune will walk in on the two ladies talking only to find the conversation suddenly stop as Irene turns to her, bright-eyed and full of news about Paulie's new suit or latest raise. On many weekends Miss Fortune and her mother will head out to East Rockaway to see her sister Anna's family.

The matchmaking, the visits—all of this Miss Fortune finds oppressive. It's only when she's behind the desk at work, sun streaming through the windows, stenographer's pad to her left and phone to her right, that she feels most herself.

I'm just guessing, of course. Maybe her job was just a simple way to earn money, and her real passion was art or writing. Or maybe she was a war widow. Or happily married. Or unhappily. I'm limited by what my father remembers, and what he remembers is governed strictly by the bare essentials of plot. Her name was Miss Fortune and she changed his life.

But I want more because, in a way, I owe my life to her. When I imagine more details in my father's story, I see Miss Fortune notice his bony shoulders slump inside of his suit jacket. His defeat is just too much for her, and she thinks, *We all deserve a chance.* So she tells him to wait, picks up the phone, and calls a man named Dick Ferguson.

— I've got a clean cut young veteran here who I think you should talk to, she says into the phone as she smiles at Tommy.

•

I made it to Girard eight days later. Roy lived a few blocks off the town square, on a dead end road next to a rail yard. The landmark he gave me was a hulking metal grain elevator flecked with red paint. I rolled into his driveway and was immediately spotted by a young girl who shouted, "The bike guy's here!" Roy quickly materialized, all smiles.

He gave me a hug that lifted me off my feet and then took me on a tour of the house he rented with his girlfriend Becca. The main room was a dark place where heavy wood paneling suffocated most of the available light. It was also a shrine to flying. Roy said that his love of flight was beyond his control, passed down through genetics. His father was a pilot, a decorated Vietnam veteran. He was also an alcoholic whose drinking got worse after the war, when he was prone to bouts of self-destructive violence. He never talked much about Vietnam, with the exception of one story. It was about a bombing mission with targets that included, he found out later, a school. He spoke of the incident only in cryptic, whiskey-soaked snippets that Roy was not able to completely decipher. Among the many pictures on the wall hung an austere frame with a few yellowed shots of a young man in uniform.

"That's my dad," Roy said, pointing to the picture. "That's how I like to remember him."

Later, when I got out of the shower, he was making some phone calls. "Got a few deals in the works," he said with a wink, and disappeared.

•

On my bookshelf at home is a long out-of-print book called *Three and Two*, the autobiography of former baseball umpire Tom Gorman. The copy is an old hardback, a discard from the Adams County Library in Hastings, Nebraska. I purchased it for one cent plus $3.99 shipping from someone on Amazon Marketplace, where there are over forty copies available from different used book dealers across the nation. The general reader would not consider this book valuable, but it's valuable to me. At least a couple of lines in it are, anyway.

Throughout the book, Gorman talks about his personal life, and at infrequent intervals, he mentions his wife, Margie. At the beginning of Chapter Five, for instance, he writes that in 1947 she worked at IBM in New York City. That same year, he took a job as an umpire in the Boston area, which meant that Margie had to leave IBM.

There's a story hidden in these lines, hidden even from the man who wrote them.

My dad, in the many times he's told me the story of Miss Fortune, always mentions that the reason Dick Ferguson—the man she called—agreed to give him an interview was that a woman just so happened to be leaving his office, opening up a space. And that woman was Margie Gorman, wife of Tom Gorman.

"Who?" I asked the first time I heard the story. It seemed like a reasonable question.

"Tom Gorman," my dad said, and waited. "Whaddaya mean? The umpire!" He stared at me as if I knew none of the world's essential information.

"Now I didn't take her exact job, y'see, but her leaving made it so they could hire me."

My father became a data processor on IBM machines used by

Montgomery Ward. He input cards in the first of four machines, and the data would move right on down the line until, at the end, a report about sales would emerge. Some of these reports went to the fashion department, and in them was information about the large-scale buying and selling of clothes nationwide. When he wasn't focused on doing a good job, he would sometimes think about how quickly the world was changing. His own father came to this country as a tailor, and now his son used huge machines to examine and arrange numbers that represented more clothes than a person could stitch in ten lifetimes. *What will my own kids do?* Tommy sometimes wondered.

He started work in August of 1947 and made eighty-six cents an hour for a total of about thirty dollars a week. Each day, when the elevator lifted him up to the eighth floor and into the world of the employed, his stomach was a little less nervous.

But this is only half of the story. A few floors below my father and his IBM machines was the shipping and receiving department, where a young girl named Nicholetta Tursi worked. She lived with her parents and three younger sisters on East 32nd Street in Flatbush and had been working full-time since dropping out of school at sixteen. Her father Rocco, like many of the other men who came to Brooklyn from Italy, delivered ice and coal. But refrigerators and oil heaters were becoming more popular, and his customers were vanishing. Nikki's mother Lucy was a dressmaker, but that, too, had its limits. A household with four young girls was difficult to maintain; the dandelion greens in the garden could fill part of their plates, but meat at dinner was becoming more and more rare. Getting a job wasn't a choice for Nikki, and it wouldn't be for her sisters, either, who would also have to drop out of school when their turns came.

For a girl of sixteen, the opportunities were limited. Nikki first worked at a laundry store, sorting and tying bundles of clothes for seven dollars a week. A few years later she got a better job, also involving clothes, at Montgomery Ward. There, she packed dresses into boxes, matched the shipping slips with the destinations, kept a list of prices, and affixed tags to the boxes. It wasn't very challenging, but it helped make sure that her sisters would have their slice of bread and milk every morning and maybe, on Sundays, a sweet roll from Brunetti's Bakery over on Quentin Road. Plus, the shipping and receiving department at Ward's was a lot nicer than the stifling back room at the laundry, where the roar of the machines and the rattling of the fans often made Nikki feel like she was drowning in noise.

The roads that Tommy and Nikki were traveling intersected at the Montgomery Ward Christmas party in December of 1947. Tommy stepped out of the elevator with a co-worker named Sam. He didn't know many others in the building, so he stuck close to Sam and took in the entire room and its islands of people laughing over their drinks, the garland-wrapped tree presiding over a pile of presents, the long table of food anchored by a giant punch bowl on one end and by a forest of colored bottles on the other.

He and Sam had been talking about the Yankees-Dodgers Series from a few months back. Sam bled Dodger blue and Tommy loved the Yankees, led by Joe DiMaggio, his favorite player. It had been a tough series—the Yankees won it in seven—and Tommy remembered that Sam had taken the loss hard. He steered the conversation to game six because he knew that Sam would retell how Al Gionfriddo robbed DiMaggio of a home run with an amazing catch. Tommy liked that Sam could take such pleasure in this small victory from the larger defeat. They were just getting started on the two teams' prospects for next season when Tommy felt someone grab his sleeve. It was a short blonde woman.

—C'mere, you, she said, and yanked him across the floor. My friend wants to meetcha.

The woman's name was Olga, and Tommy let her lead him to the bottle-end of the table, where he saw a black-haired woman with dark eyes. She was holding two cups. As they got closer, the woman held one of the cups out to him.

—Here's a drink, she said.

Tommy looked at it.

—It's good, she said. Pepsi and whiskey.

He took a sip. It wasn't for him. Too sweet. But what the heck? The woman who handed it to him was beautiful.

—Fer cryin' out loud, Olga said to Tommy. Tell her ya name.

—I'm Tom.

—Nikki, she answered, raising her glass. *Salud.* Drink up.

•

Shannon was afraid that Roy might be a serial killer, so she came up with a code word that I was supposed to use on the phone if he had a knife at my throat. I wasn't quite sure how I would call with a knife at my throat or why I would say "blueberry cobbler" instead of "Help, he has a knife at my throat," but I agreed anyway. After I spoke to her and was very careful not to say "blueberry cobbler"—or any other dessert for that matter— Roy took me out to his garage and showed me a small plane that he was restoring. The fuselage wasn't much bigger than my bike, and the wing, which was supposed to sit atop the cockpit, was leaning against the wall. The whole thing didn't look like it would be up in the air anytime soon, but Roy assured me that it was just about done as we drove to the G&W Foods to pick up a few things for dinner.

We pulled into the parking lot, and he left the truck running while we went inside. I tried to pay for the milk and butter, but he was having none of it.

"No sir. You're my guest."

I tried to find out what Roy did for a living, but he just smiled and said, "Oh, a little bit of everything and not too much of one thing."

He did tell me that at one point he lost "a bundle" investing in a strip club.

"Don't get me wrong, now. I don't go in for tittie bars as a general rule."

It seemed like there was a "but" coming.

"But," he continued, "I got bills, too, and if I can pay 'em while havin' a beer and watchin' girls shake their assets, well…"

The plan didn't quite work out, though. The bar flamed out before it even got off the ground, and Roy's account was suddenly a lot lighter.

"Thievin' sonofabitch stole my money," he told me. "Not much I can do, though."

Then he told me about his best friend Dave, a fellow plane enthusiast who was dying. Dave had worked most of his life at a shingle factory up in Kansas City before he retired to a little town about an hour north of Girard. A lifetime working around fibers and dust had taken its toll; Dave suffered from mesothelioma, and though he was a part of a big class action suit, Roy's description of his condition left little doubt about whether he would ever see any money.

"It's a Goddamned shame," he said, shaking his head. Then he looked up, as if he just thought of something. "I really want to take you up in that plane. When did you need to take off tomorrow?"

I wasn't ready for this. I was heading into the Ozarks, and I didn't know exactly where I would stop, but it looked like it was going to be one of my longer days. Maybe eighty miles or more, so I wanted to get going early. Plus, I've never really liked flying.

But Roy was adamant. As soon as we got back to the house, he got on the phone to arrange everything.

While he did, I hung out with his kids, Charlie and Heather. Roy had told me that after paying a "shitload" on lawyers, he had recently won custody of them from their mom, who apparently has some serious issues with crystal meth. The two kids were now in high school, but when they were younger, their mom would leave them alone for long stretches of time. Once, for over a week. They were polite kids who liked having a stranger in the house. Heather showed me some pictures she drew, and Charlie showed me his collection of survival gear. Canteens, lights, boots, and his most recent addition, a Bowie knife that was roughly the size of my forearm.

Roy popped his head into the room. "If we leave by five, you can be on the road by eight, eight-fifteen at the latest."

The sheer force of his smile was too much to fight. I nodded.

"Hot damn," he said, clapping his hands.

The dinner table was set for six, and Roy had given his kids specific instructions to put the two of us at each end. The fridge had crapped out the night before, so he moved the steaks to a neighbor's house, where Heather was sent to retrieve them. I watched him fire up two camp stoves in the kitchen.

"Oven ain't working right, either," he told me, then winked. "Good thing I'm a master camping chef."

I tried to help, but he shooed me away and went to work. The rolls, bacon-wrapped asparagus, and mashed potatoes all came out piecemeal. Becca and the kids had strip steak while Roy and I had two gigantic T-bones that spilled over the edges of our plates.

The food was phenomenal. While we ate, more interesting facts came to light. First, Roy had ruptured a few discs in his back while mountain biking with the kids and was now in nearly constant pain; second, he was taking several types of painkillers; and third, he had a homemade flamethrower.

I was wrapping my mind around fact number two when the word "flamethrower" sank in.

"Oh, it's something," Roy said around a mouthful of potatoes.

As scary as it was to watch Roy shoot a sixty-foot rope of flame across the gravel lot behind the house, it was nothing compared to the ride up to Dave's the next morning. He fidgeted in his seat to ward off his back pain, and I took this as a sign he hadn't popped a fistful of pills that morning. That was small comfort, though, as we hurtled north on a two-lane country road before dawn. I knew the area was full of deer; I had been seeing them ever since Wichita. Driving in the dark through deer-rich areas always made me nervous. I spent six years in downstate Indiana, where small highways often abutted forest. The local news once did a piece on hitting deer, and it included a little diagram that showed how braking—a natural reflex when a two-hundred pound animal suddenly appears on the road in front of you—is actually a bad idea; a sudden stop angles the nose of the car downward so that the impact is devastatingly aligned with the driver's neck. As the truck vibrated and hummed on the dark road, my eyes edged over to the dashboard. The thin red speedometer needle was stuck firmly at seventy-five. I gripped the door handle and pressed my legs into the floorboards, bracing myself for a deer that would leap out from the trees, shatter the windshield, and crush our skulls.

Roy drove down a series of smaller and smaller gravel roads until he pulled between two tree stands and into a huge grass field. Off in the distance to the left was a building that looked like a giant garage, and off to the right was a long, low-mown strip of grass that led to water. The building was Dave's hangar and house, and the grass strip was the runway. He parked the car, and while I took some pictures, he opened the hanger door. I offered to help with whatever needed to be done, but he told me he had it under control. Dave was still asleep, so Roy pushed the plane out of the hanger by himself.

It looked like a toy.

I asked how much it weighed and was sorry I did when he said, "Six hundred pounds, give or take some."

As he walked around the plane and wrote on a clipboard, I tried not to wonder how six hundred pounds of plane was going to lift over three hundred pounds of people.

"Just one more thing," he called as he jogged back to the truck. He came back with a can of Coke.

"Caffeine for the flight?" I asked.

Roy smiled. "Something like that."

He climbed into the plane and directed me to do the same on the other side. The opening was small and tucked under the wing. I bent over, climbed in, and arranged my feet around a blue metal bar on the floor.

"Keep your feet clear of that when we take off and land," Roy said.

I pulled the door down and latched it as instructed. I didn't like that I was the one responsible for it being properly secured. Once I fastened my seatbelt harness, Roy gave me a headset and we did a quick sound check. Then I made the mistake of looking at the notice affixed to the panel in front of me, which read

THIS AIRCRAFT IS AMATEUR-BUILT AND DOES NOT COMPLY WITH FEDERAL SAFETY REGULATIONS FOR STANDARD AIRCRAFT

A voice crackled in my ear, "You ready?"

I turned and there he was, all smiles. I gave him a thumbs-up.

And then we're soaring over Kansas farmland.

Roy points off in different directions, naming towns and their relevance to him. To let me see better, he opens his door and angles the plane to the side, but I'm distracted by the fact that I now have my seat in a death-grip. When my ass finally unpuckers itself, I hear him tell me that in one direction is his ex-girlfriend, who's raising their child. In the other direction is another ex-girlfriend and another child. And way back yonder is his ex-wife, the meth addict who used to raise Charlie and Heather. He runs out of exes and we glide along the wind currents in silence.

With the exception of the custody battle with his ex-wife, there seems to be little tension in his obviously extensive web of relationships. In fact, he's got such affection for all of the women he talks about, it's hard not to imagine them as one big happy family. I get the feeling that the ex-girlfriends might have a different take on the situation, but it's easy to get swept up in Roy's good nature. He's a guy who takes each day as it comes, who gets up and expects interesting things to happen to him. A new day means a new story, and today it's me. I can almost hear him telling someone—the bored cashier at the G&W Foods, maybe—about the biker he met and took up in his plane.

"I just love it up here," he says suddenly. "Down there," he gestures at the ground, "down there, ain't gonna lie, things can get a little fucked up. Bills come due, the truck won't start, Becca's on my ass about some shit."

I wait for him to go on.

"But Goddamn, I love to fly," he says. "I belong up here, know what I mean?"

I nod.

"Feeling brave?" he asks.

"What do you have in mind?"

"Some tricks," he says, smiling. "Just a few, and if you don't want to, I understand. Last thing I want is turn someone offa flying."

I'm about to say no when I think about the phone calls I've had with my dad these last few weeks. I'm like him in many ways, and when I was a kid, he must have seen himself in me. Everyone on his block sure did; every summer when we visited New York, all the old Italians who remembered my dad as a boy called me "Little Tommy." But somewhere in the crapshoot of genetics, I missed some key traits. My dad likes to say, "There are two kinds of people: the ones who get ulcers and the ones who give ulcers." As far as the two of us go, it's pretty clear who's who.

That much was clear when I stepped inside this homemade plane, and it's clear when I turn to Roy now and say, "Let's do it."

We immediately climb until there are cloud wisps between us and Dave's runway, which is now a tiny gash of bright green next to a thin band of water. Roy pulls a lighter out of his shirt pocket and lets it rest on his right palm.

"Keep your eye on this," he says. "And hold on."

We drop suddenly and my ass immediately re-puckers itself, but I manage to keep my eyes on the lighter, which lifts from his palm and hovers above it for a few seconds. We climb and drop two more times as I watch the lighter float magically in the air between us. Both times make me grateful I didn't eat anything this morning.

"Howzat?" he asks.

Not wanting to open my mouth, I give him a thumb's up.

"Want to see another one?"

I manage to nod.

He pulls out the Coke can he fetched from his truck and hands it to me.

"Open her up," he says.

I pull back on the tab, an act that's unsatisfying because my headset muffles the crack and hiss.

"Set her on the dash," he tells me, pointing to a flat spot between us. "Right there."

I set the open can down.

"Hold on."

We break into a barrel roll that again has me clutching my seat while my organs are slammed against the left side of my body. They arrive back in place a second or two after we come out of the roll and bank briefly in the opposite direction. Once my brain lodges itself back in place, it occurs to me that I should be covered in soda. Roy is laughing, and when I look over at him, he's pointing to the Coke, which is sitting in roughly the same spot where I set it down. There's no residue of spilled Coke anywhere, and when I lift it up, it has the heft of a full can.

Later that morning, I load up Rusty and get ready to go. Roy stands behind me, and I realize he's been quiet for a few minutes. Even though I've been around him for less than twenty-four hours, I know this isn't right.

He finally breaks his silence. "Can I ask a favor?"

*Oh shit*, I think, and remember a story he told me on the ride home, about how his back's in so much pain that he can't even carry on a normal sex life. He didn't elaborate, and I didn't ask, so now I'm imagining a strange scenario involving Becca.

"Uh," I say. "Sure."

"Can I ride your bike?"

My eyes widen out of relief, but Roy interprets the expression as a signal that he's crossed some kind of line and he quickly struggles to explain himself.

"I know your bike's real personal and all and why you'd say no…"

"No, no," I say. "Yeah, of course you can."

"I'm just kinda curious what it feels like for you out there."

"You want me to take the bags off?"

"Nope," he says. "I want the whole enchilada."

He wheels Rusty across the driveway, hops on, and wobbles up the street. Riding a bike is easy, but the first time on one that's completely loaded down in front and back can be tricky. Roy moves slowly at first, the front wheel unsteady until he builds up a little speed and begins to move more smoothly. He turns at the end of the street, and he knows enough to take the turn wide—something I learned the hard way my second day out. On the third pass, he's got the hang of it, and he starts whooping and hollering. I get the feeling that if he had a cowboy hat, he would be waving it in the air.

As he rides, I imagine one of his neighbors hears us and pulls her curtains aside to get a better look. And what does she think she sees? Probably two guys who should be working but are instead farting around, one of them riding a bike up and down the street and hollering like an idiot while the other one just stands there with a stupid grin on his face. But what she's witnessing is actually the rarest of things—two very different people who have come together through an improbable and complicated web of chance.

•

Less than two years after meeting at that Christmas party in 1947,

Tom Versaci married Nikki Tursi. At that point, their story together was a blank page. They didn't know it would take twelve years for their first child—my brother—to be born, and then six more years for their second one—me. They didn't know these two sons would one day give them seven grandchildren. They didn't know my father would stay with Montgomery Ward for many years, accepting a transfer to Baltimore in 1962 and then another to Chicago in 1968. They didn't know he would work with the company up until 1982, when he would be forced into early retirement. In 1947 my father's stomach would have shredded itself if he knew that at the age of fifty-six he would have one son in college, the other on the way there, and no job. They didn't know their younger son would get and survive cancer, leave his eighteen-year marriage, climb onto the seat of a bike, and step into a plane somewhere in Kansas with a complete stranger who flies homemade planes and builds flamethrowers. And they certainly didn't know how the final chapters of their own story would be written.

At home I have a file folder where I keep a timeline of my parents' lives and a family tree that goes back three generations before me. All the events are linear, and all the relationships are indicated by short, straight lines with ninety-degree angles.

But those neat, precise lines are an illusion; after all, how do we know the people and experiences in our lives were meant to be? Everything might be completely different if only we had stopped for lunch a little later, gone to the post office *before* the gas station instead of *after*, or woken up ten minutes earlier. It's scary to think we're all subject to chaos, like puzzle pieces dumped on a folding table or like cells multiplying and dividing uncontrollably.

But if we look hard enough into this chaos, we might find something hidden there we can hold onto, even if we're not sure what it means. Maybe it's a delicate chain of meetings on a cloudless day in a little town named Fort Garland. Or maybe it's the symmetry of two umpires, one who takes a job in Boston and one who makes a bad call in Detroit sixty-three years later. Or maybe—and this is the one I prefer—it's a dark-haired woman named Miss Fortune who picks up a phone and dials a number.

# 17

# Not in Kansas Anymore

On the side of U. S. Highway 126, about two and a half miles east of Pittsburgh, Kansas, there's a sign that says

Welcome to Missouri
The Show-Me State

and as soon as I read these words, three more take shape in my mind. *About. Goddamn. Time.* Wind-whipped beyond all reasonable limits, I've had enough of Kansas, so I make a ceremony of the moment. The grass is damp and scarred by two long, curving streaks of mud. From the width and shape of the marks, I'm guessing it was a truck, whose driver lost control but somehow managed to swerve back onto the road without hitting the sign. Camera in hand, I've got one foot on the grass and the other in a tire rut as I frame my bicycle between the sign's metal posts. For the last several days I've been dreaming of this moment when I'm finally delivered from the heat and winds. *Missouri*, I think. *Now this is more like it.*

I'm at Flo's Market, a little white box of a convenience store that sits behind two gas pumps, both out of order. There's a pile in front of me on the counter. Milky Way, Three Musketeers, Little Debbie Cherry Pie, pint of chocolate milk. I've also got a Vitamin Water courtesy of a local named Clyde. He came in, asked about Rusty and the bags piled high on top of him, and felt like he had to do something for me when I said I rode from California. "Never heard of such a thing," he said, laughing. He didn't ask me why I was doing it, so I didn't have to tell him.

Another sign. I can't see much up ahead; the road bends into woods. According to my map, the most likely place for the construction is still a ways off. According to my map, I can follow the detour by riding three sides of a giant rectangle around this area. According to my map, this detour will take an extra ten miles and close to two hours at the rate I'm moving. The sign seems pretty sure of itself, all tall and wide and orange, but I'm not sure if I really believe in signs. Or maps.

●

I do believe in detours, however, like the lump in my chest that turned into nine weeks of being slowly almost-killed by chemotherapy. Like most detours, it had piss-poor signage, and by the time I got back to the road I had been on, nothing looked the same. Not nearly.

●

I'm creeping through a construction zone. A bulldozer, small in the distance, hangs onto the side of a hill like a beetle on a turd. The road crosses over a highway up ahead. As I make the final crest, a pickup truck with a flashing yellow light appears in front of me. *Goddamn it*, I think. *They're going to send me all the way back.* As we pull up alongside each other, I brace myself. The driver doesn't even look over. Just drives on by.

Ten miles to Golden City. I imagine shining spires reaching up into a cloudless sky, roads paved with bars of gold, waterfalls and fountains overflowing with shimmering coins. I look ahead for the glow, but all I see are ripples. The road is a sine curve, undulating up and down as it disappears into the horizon.

I'm in Cooky's Café in Golden City, a definite contender for Most Ironically-Named Place on this trip. No shining spires, no gold bars, and most definitely no glow.

I'm peeing in the bathroom at the Pennsboro Farm-n-Feed. On my way out, I see a row of four glass-walled offices, each with an identical scene: a man in a short-sleeved shirt at a desk, phone to his ear. I blink to see if it's some kind of weird trick with mirrors, but they're all real.

East of Pennsboro, the sine curve metastasizes into an ECG read-out for someone in cardiac arrest. Steep climbs in my lowest gear followed by sharp drops where I hit thirty miles per hour or more and then back uphill again where I'm shifting for all I'm worth. The climbs and drops turn sharply through wooded hills, occasionally leveling off but not for long before I'm climbing or dropping again.

Welcome to the wonderful world of the Ozarks. Back in the desert, I felt small amid sprawling, wide-open landscapes and ageless rock. But there were clear skies and long lines of sight. Here, trees shoot up on either side of me and clasp their leafy fingers together to hide the gray sky. The road ahead and behind me disappears into hills and curves. I don't know where I am. I'm Dorothy, crash-landed in Oz.

●

It's after dinner, and as Nick and Tony's bedtime approaches, I feel unfocused dread, like the night before the first day of school. My day is done—hitting tennis balls to them in the street, wrestling with them in the playroom, making puzzles and reading comics—and all that's left are a few empty hours of *American Idol* or *Survivor* and the search for something to say.

•

In Everton, and I want to sleep. The heat's been stoking my saddle sores, the climbs have drained my legs, and the constant shifting has numbed my wrists and fingers. I was warned by a biker going the other way that Everton was "pretty empty," but it's not. I pass a white shed that says FIRE DEPT and a bar with no windows called "The Shaved Beaver."

In Ash Grove, the sun is dropping and I need to find somewhere to camp. A woman at a gas station directs me to the city park, which I miss even though the town is only about four square blocks large. A guy trimming his hedges points back the way I came, and when I pedal around a corner, the park is right there. A long expanse of grass anchored by a pool on the near side and bordered by a curving row of massive picnic shelters. How did I miss this?

Teenagers hang out at the park at night. Two of them—Gordon and Tucker—tell me that this is what everyone does come summer. They're from an even smaller town up the road. Gordon's graduating next year and plans to get his truck operator's license so that he can work in his uncle's construction company. "Them drivers make some sweet cashola," he tells me. I ask Tucker what he's going to do, but he just shrugs and watches his right foot push a rock through the dirt.

At a bait shop, I sit in one of the two booths by the window, dividing my just-bought food into two piles—the crap I'm going to eat now and the crap I'm going to save for later. In the other booth is a lady with gray hair pulled up in a bun. She's been studying me, so

I smile at her, a small act that breaks the silence. After she finds out everything she needs to know, she shakes her head and says, "Son, you got grit."

*Tell it to the road.*

There isn't a yellow brick road that leads from here to there. There are many roads, all lettered. No numbers. No names. No logic. U becomes BB, which later changes to CC or Z or even ZZ.

On the wall behind the toilet in a bathroom at a feed store on one of these lettered roads, someone has carved into the paint *X Country, April 11 2009* and next to it a crude scratching that resembles a bicycle. I grab my pocketknife and add *June 2010*. I'm not sure what day it is.

•

Biking home from work in the middle of the day, the kids still at school. I turn up our street and see our open garage and in it both of our cars. Something sinks inside of me before I know what it is or what it means. Then I do. I wanted the other car to be gone.

•

On a hill, on the other side of the road, a flood of bikers. Young and buff and riding wispy bikes with no baggage. Of course, as we pass each other, I'm sweating my way up and they're coasting down. "Where's all your stuff?" I manage to wheeze as we pass each other, and one of them shouts, "Using credit cards, bruh!" A few minutes later their support van rolls past, packed high with bags and towing a trailer, empty except for a couple of spare bikes. I want to beat them all with my bike pump.

Dead possum on the side of the road up ahead. I hear a truck behind me and glance quickly back. A pickup, red and rusty, mean-looking. It rumbles past, and I make my move to the left. There's a shriek of brakes behind me, and my head jerks to see another truck behind the first one. It wasn't there a second ago, was it? I lurch back to the right and navigate between the dead possum and a weedy drop into rocks and woods. As the truck shoots by, its motor growls and so does its driver. "Fuck you doin', dumbass?"

When I sleep, I sleep the sleep of the dead.

●

I look in the mirror but I don't know who it is. Sunken eyes. Gray skin. Slack mouth. My chest feels like it's being gouged with a knife, and in a few minutes I'll be on the way to the ER, but right now I just stare at the man there and think *This is me. This is all real. My life.*

●

Dogs. Not the fetching slippers kind, not the doing tricks kind, not the obey your master kind. These dogs crash through weeds, leap over and squeeze under fences, materialize out of the very dirt and mud around me. They're unleashed and angry. They rush at me with an explosion of noise and I can't stop my muscles from taking over, swerving into the possible path of speeding vehicles that will make a dark stain out of me and barely pause. Worst are those dogs that announce themselves from a long way off, letting me get a good look at their terrible trajectory across a low-mown field, set to intercept me at t-minus three, two, one—

Humidity drops over me and presses into my lungs. There are no shoulders out here, but bugs are everywhere. Even when I'm tired—which is always—I can't stop because they descend on me in a whistling, biting fury. Rain, too. Lots of rain and no shelter.

~

Two kids are beating a mailbox with sticks. That was yesterday. Or was it the day before? At some point I pass a man dragging a huge garbage bag across his driveway. I wave, but he looks away. *That* was yesterday. The two kids were sometime before that. More hills, more heat, more angry drivers. Still no shoulders.

The wall of trees on one side of the road clears, and I glimpse the countryside. I'm up high, overlooking the land. All the way to the gray horizon and to either side are tree-covered mounds. A man can wander into the dark, leafy folds and never find his way out.

At the end of a long gravel driveway, a hound dog with a patchy coat pants and turns his head as I creep by. I'm expecting the worst as he starts to move, but it's not a chase he's after. He trots alongside for about fifty yards. "What do you need, pal?" I say. "Food? Water? Some courage?" Just when I think that I've found a fine companion, he turns and heads home.

I hit my slowest and highest speeds on these roads. The climbs are never long; no mountains here. So how can so short a climb be so Goddamn hard? At the brink of exhaustion almost immediately into a climb, I work my way up to the top, where there's a crazy fast downhill waiting for me. I can't lose focus. Hit wrong, even a pebble could mean sliding headfirst into a tree—or worse, down the embankment to be swallowed whole by the forest.

•

There's no trick to getting lost. Just step outside what you know, take a few lefts, take a few rights, and you're there. The real trick is finding your way home.

•

I'm at a picnic table under a corrugated plastic cover and drinking pink lemonade at Lazy Lee's One-Stop, a drive-up burger place in Hartville. It's been raining all morning. An industrial-sized fan blows behind me. It does nothing for the heat, but its hum sounds like an airplane and makes my head hurt. A cloud of bees pulses over a 55-gallon garbage drum. A few vibrate above my lemonade, and when one drops onto the straw, I flick it off. A guy in a tank top leans against his pickup while his girlfriend sits inside, watching the end of her cigarette burn between her fingers. They face opposite directions, neither looking my way.

The clerk at a bait shop tells me about a guy who killed his girlfriend with a wrench and hid out in the woods here for months. Cops on foot, in cars, and in helicopters looked for him, but no dice. A different girlfriend who brought his food in and hauled his trash out finally gave him up. All I said to him was, *It's easy to get lost out here.*

•

I'm grocery shopping. I have to do this now, for the first time in my adult life. I unload my cart and see the frozen pizza, the ice cream, the cookies, and the chips through the eyes of the girl ringing me up, and I wonder if she's thinking what I'm thinking. *Weekend dad.*

•

I'm up and I'm down and I'm up again. After each crest comes another. There's always another. My arms shine with sweat that beads and rolls down to soak my gloves. Between this sweat and all the rain, Rusty's handlebar tape is unraveled, exposing the metal beneath. I keep trying to twist and push everything back into place, but it won't stay.

•

Dispatches from the road:
"What'd you see today?"
"Lots of rain, lots of trucks. Got chased by a dog."
"You get bit?"
"Nah, your old man's too fast."
Pause.
"You being careful?"
*Sure.*

•

It's my 40<sup>th</sup> birthday and I've been gone from the house for a month and I'm sitting on my bed in my buddy's apartment and I'm trying not to think about why my brother won't call, won't even talk to me.

•

Other than the gravity that drags me back on climbs and yanks me forward on descents, the normal laws of physics don't apply out here. Take sound. Vehicles appear without warning, their motors' laboring breath deflected by a stand of trees or swallowed whole by dense thicket. Sometimes I hear an engine, but no car or truck ever comes. And when they do, I can't tell what it will be. The thick, wet air and soft hillsides amplify a compact car's motor so that I imagine a pickup roaring behind me. Other times, they dampen a truck's rumble so that I pedal along with a nice cushion of space between me and the weeds to my right and am totally unprepared for the wallop of wind on my back that might send me sprawling into those weeds, which is exactly what happens near Road DD just west of Yukon.

•

The roads have letters, but I think about numbers. Like eighteen. Four years after my last chemo treatment, my eighteen-year marriage came to an end. Lots of other numbers packed into that eighteen. Five degrees, three states, six jobs, seven cars, two apartments, three houses, at least fifteen family trips, two major illnesses, and two sons. Beyond us, two sets of parents, four siblings and their spouses, four nieces, and three nephews. Almost twenty aunts and uncles and cousins. Numbers upon numbers of things and people more or less captured in twelve to fifteen photo albums that took up nearly three full shelves on a bookcase. I didn't take any of those albums. I left with two suitcases. And one bike.

•

The native tongue out here is the horn. Short taps are meant to be encouraging—"Way to go!" or "Hang in there!"—and are almost always accompanied by a thumbs-up or a wave. These are rare. Long blasts—usually delivered right as the vehicle pulls alongside and scary-close—mean "Fuck you, queer!" I know this because some drivers, afraid I won't get the message, lean out of their windows and translate for me. This happens a lot. Response to either communication is optional. I wave at the former and never respond to the latter. People who would torment a biker in the rain, on a blind turn, going uphill no doubt have truly miserable lives and are capable of anything. Instead of shouting back, I let myself imagine the truly miserable details of those truly miserable lives.

A dark shape moves across the road. As I pull closer, the gray-green glob becomes a turtle taking ponderous steps. I pick him up by the home on his back and watch his stumpy legs search for ground. After I move him out of harm's way and to the other side, I decide to become the Helper of Turtles. That afternoon alone, I stop a half dozen times, always the same. Pull over, look both ways, lift a turtle and deposit him in a bed of weeds on the side of the road. I watch until he crunches through the long stalks and disappears into the dark. What do they feel about their sudden weightlessness, their rapid transport to someplace else? Freedom or terror?

●

I drive but have no place to go. I park on a bluff by the ocean and watch the surfers below. Little black shapes sprinkled across the water. In my rear view mirror I see new hair poking up across my scalp. Everything slowly coming back to normal.

●

I want to impose shape and order on this chaos of the Ozarks, but how? My maps are no help. The one tucked inside the plastic sleeve on my handlebars focuses only on the road I'm on; there's no larger context. I can't find my place in this place. I get a state map from a yet another bait shop and unfold it on top of the gravel lot in front. The road I'm on is nowhere to be found. According to this map, I'm floating free in a field of green and white. The spots on the map where my hands are planted are already soggy from the sweat dripping down my arms. I need a map that has yet to be drawn—or better yet, a comic— that will help me untangle the roads that crisscross like arteries and veins over the heart of the heart of this country.

More rain. More turtles, dead long before I can get to them. The smell of something bad—mammal, for sure—off to the right in some trees. A rumble from behind, getting louder as it approaches. Pickup? No, RV. Has to be. Wrong again. A big truck hauling logs. I brace myself for the blast I'll get when the truck passes, and then it comes. I'm shoved forward as it roars past, floating through a cloud of mist where its tires meet wet pavement.

Near a town—Summersville?—I see a flash of brown to the left and suddenly there's a slobbering Boxer bearing down on me. This is how it goes. A house every few miles with dogs on the loose. And always big ones; meekness has no value out here. The *clacketyclack* of his nails on pavement grows louder. The road was level but now it's starting to head downhill. He isn't slowing down, but with all of my weight I'm picking up speed, and the distance between us starts to grow. I'm pedaling as hard as I can. A pickup comes up behind me in the road. He has to have seen this little chase unfold, and as he passes me I swear he's smiling.

•

Near the end of an awkward conversation. My dad asks where I'm living, how often I see the boys, am I coming for Christmas. My mom asks, "How's Elizabeth?"

•

When you're alone on a road that's worse than you ever could have imagined and you've been in the saddle for five hours and your skin is puckered up because it's been raining on you for four of those five hours and all of your joints—knees, shoulders, elbows, wrists, even your *knuckles*, for Chrissake—ache and throb and your heart is racing because you've just been chased for a quarter mile by a black and gray dog with yellow eyes, then it's easy to believe that when the clouds part and a bright shaft of sun pushes through, it's a sign, just for you, of better things to come, but the problem with believing that is you must also accept the reverse—that all of the shit you've come across is likewise meant just for you—and what do you do with that?

Rain again. Thunder. Lightning, too? I look for some kind of shelter other than trees, which is all I can see. Rain gear is a number one priority for long-distance tourists, but the truth is that if you bike in the rain, you will get wet. The deeper truth is that if you head out on a bicycle into the unknown and for unknown reasons, you will encounter trouble. Hills, drivers, heat, rain. Memory and imagination. Guilt. Your bike may break down. You will break down.

●

Why couldn't I just ride it out? In the months after I left, I asked myself this question a lot. Sometimes, on Sunday nights, after I hug my boys and watch them walk through the garage that's now filled with new tools that I didn't use to build or fix anything inside that house where we all used to live together, I'll still ask.

●

Exhaustion settles all the way down to my heels as the chain clicks its slow, steady mantra—*there's no place like home there's no place like home there's no place like home*—but the words fade as soon as they appear, the same way a dream evaporates as you try to remember it, and you're left wondering if it was really there to begin with.

# VOICES FROM THE ROAD

# 18

# Welcome to Springview Farm

**"WHERE THE CATTLE ARE CALM, AND THE CALM ARE EATEN"**

THESE ARE THE OWNERS, BILL & JAN:

SPRINGVIEW FARM IS FILLED WITH STRANGE & WONDERFUL CREATURES...

"UNDERFOOT," THE INVISIBLE BARN CAT...

"GOOSEY" & "GOOFY," TWO LLAMAS...

A POND BRIMMING WITH KOI...

TO BE CONTINUED...

# 19

# Operation Iguana

With Rusty safely tucked between a hoe and some bags of fertilizer at Jan and Bill's farm, I drive north on Interstate 55 toward Chicago in a gigantic Chevy Silverado—"The only vehicle that's clean," according to Jimmy at the Budget Rental in Springfield, Missouri—surrounded by air conditioning, FM stereo, and memories of a girl named Cindy that my mom watched after school when I was in the fifth grade.

I don't remember her last name, but I do remember that she was in kindergarten, had a bowl-cut of blonde hair that was almost white, and was impossibly cute to everyone but me. Fact was, I hated Cindy. I hated the way she leaned up between my mom and me in our car and slung her arms over the bench seat. I hated the way she called my mom "Nikki." I hated the way she asked my mom for candy and comics at the store and *got* them, while I had to beg and whine and wheedle—all skills I had honed to perfection. Didn't this kid know that *I* was my mom's little buddy?

The only thing that made the situation remotely tolerable was that my brother didn't like her either. He wasn't as invested in hating Cindy as I was; his orneriness came from being a bored high-schooler. Still, I took what I could get, which turned out to be quite a lot when summer came and my mom—who couldn't watch us during the day because she worked—put Vince in charge.

Cindy scared easy, and he had some pretty good stories to get her there. The best was "Johnny, Give Me Back My Liver." In it, this kid Johnny is given some money by his mom to go buy a pound of liver for dinner, but he spends it on a kite instead. As he's looking at the liver he can't afford in the grocery store, he sees an old woman buy some. He follows her out of the store, and when no one's looking, he bashes her on the head with a rock and takes her package of liver.

As someone whose idea of high art at the time was best expressed in movies like *Gamera* and *Attack of the Mushroom People*, I had no trouble with this kind of plot development.

That night, as Johnny lay in bed, everything is quiet. At first. But soon he hears something on the other side of his door. Footsteps. And a voice, meek but insistent—and done expertly by Vince—that calls, "Johnny, give me back my liver..." The voice gets louder and more forceful as it makes its way through the house: "Johnny, I'm coming up the stairs...give me back my liver...Johnny, I'm at your sister's room...give me back my liver..." He could draw out the approach for an excruciatingly long time, his voice rising in volume and menace until the end, when he would grab the listener by the arms and shout, "GIVE ME BACK MY LIVER!"

Whenever he told the story to Cindy, my heart would beat faster as I waited for the grab, the shriek, and what always came next.

Cindy's tears.

She cried easy, too, and my favorite way to make that happen was Operation Iguana. Vince always started it; whenever I tried, which was often because I loved to make Cindy cry, he would narrow his eyes, stick out his lower lip slightly, and give a quick shake of his head, all of which meant *Nope, not the right time*. So those times when he would turn to me and mutter, "Iguana," I got a thrill. A double thrill, actually. We were going to punish Cindy, and my brother and I were on the same side, teaming up.

Operation Iguana would start slowly and then build. Cindy would say something to us and we wouldn't respond. That could be normal, so she let it slide. After this went on for a while, Vince would say something like, "Too bad Cindy couldn't come over today."

"I know," I would reply.

"I'm right here."

We would keep watching TV.

"I'm here, you guys," she would say again, standing up.

No response. She might tap one of us to make her presence known, at which point we said that we needed to close the window because there was a breeze. Things would escalate as Cindy became more and more frantic and Vince and I became more and more aloof. The game always ended the same. Cindy burst into tears, and we would suddenly "see" her again. There were two strict rules that Vince and I never actually discussed but always followed. We didn't stop until she cried, and we always calmed her down before our mom got home.

I wonder now if she really thought she had faded away. If she did, it must have been terrifying.

Driving through rural Illinois reminds me of the trips we made down to the University of Illinois to visit my brother. I looked forward to those trips for weeks because when Vince left for college, things changed. He had a vivid presence, and without it, the house was subdued.

I already hated Sundays, but they were worse with him gone and worse yet after my dad lost his job and had to look for a new one as a fifty-six year old man with no college degree. My parents never talked about this in front of me, but I heard whispers on the other side of their closed bedroom door before breakfast and after dinner. Once a week we trudged to church and there was no doubt what they prayed for. Some Sundays we would go to the movies, and my parents always let me choose what we saw. Perversely, I picked movies that amplified the way I felt. One Sunday was *Prince of the City*, and what I remember most about it was the main character's tumble into one shitty situation after another when he rats out his crooked cop friends. Another Sunday was *The Verdict*, which my mom loved for the courtroom drama and which I loved for the dreary, dimly-lit scenes in empty bars and stark offices. Whenever I'm channel surfing and come across a movie that we saw on one of those Sundays—*Kramer vs. Kramer, My Bodyguard, Ordinary People*—I slip right back into that gray mood.

If asked about my parents' favorite movies, I wouldn't even know where to start with my dad. Probably something with Frank Sinatra. My mom, however, is another story. Her favorite movie, which I heard about all through my childhood, was the 1939 version of *Wuthering Heights*. One Saturday night a few weeks before I left on this trip, I came across it on Turner Classic Movies. It had just started, and I watched as Merle Oberon called eerily from the beyond for her true love—*Heathcliff! Heathcliff!* My mother would imitate these calls whenever she talked about that movie, which was often, and she did it with such energy that until I saw the scene I thought the voice was a much bigger part than it turned out to be. As the film ended and Robert Osborne strode back into the faux sitting-room set, I found myself tearing up. It certainly wasn't because of Osborne or his one last factoid about the movie, and it wasn't because of any specific scene from the movie, either. It was because I knew that when I called my parents the next day and told my mom that I saw *Wuthering Heights*, she would have no idea what I was talking about.

About a year and a half earlier, just past midnight, my phone rang. It was Vince, who was with my dad. Earlier that night, my mom had fallen and couldn't get up. My dad couldn't get her up either, so he called Vince, who drove them both to the ER. The doctors checked her out and ran tests, and other than the fact that her arms and legs weren't very strong, she was all right physically. The real problem was her responsiveness. After a neurological consult, more tests that stretched over a few days, and another appointment with a different neurologist the following week, she was diagnosed with dementia.

Since then, the life that my parents have built together for over sixty years has been rearranged. Sometimes in small ways, like phone calls. My mom always made them and would talk through the main business before handing the phone over to my dad for his brief turn.

Once upon a time, her big Brooklyn voice came through the phone so loud that I had to hold it away from my ear. Back then, it was "Hello, Mistah Rocco!" Later, after I finished my Ph.D., she promoted me—"Hello, Doctah Rocco!" Now, on those rare occasions when I talk to her at all, I get a subdued "Hello, Son Number Two" after my dad passes the phone to her and I hear him say, very clearly, "It's Rocco."

"What did you do today?" I'll ask.

"What did we do today?" she'll repeat, louder, as if she wants to clarify the question. I can just make out my dad's muted reply, and then its bizarre echo in my mother's voice.

"Went to lunch, went to church."

"Where?"

"Where?" she'll repeat.

In the background: *Bnnabff.*

"Buona Beef," she'll say. When I'm lucky, she'll quickly add "Hold on" and hand the phone back to him. But most times she'll ask the question she's forgotten is embarrassing.

"How's Elizabeth?"


Like most Chicago suburbs, Downers Grove is undergoing constant metamorphosis. In the downtown area, several buyers—attracted, no doubt, by the town's relatively high standard of living and excellent schools—have razed the 1950s-built white clapboard houses with detached garages and erected in their place giant brick-and-glass structures.

But unlike the surrounding area, and unlike my parents' lives, the townhouse where they've lived since 1974 hasn't changed. Stepping through the front door is like entering a giant time capsule from that era. They have a portable bar tucked into the corner of what's supposed to be a dining room, metallic brown and silver striped wallpaper in that same corner, and the original shag carpeting—rust upstairs and gold downstairs. Back then, decorating in burnt oranges and dark browns was popular, but now the dark tones, low-wattage bulbs, and heavy lampshades all work together to choke out the light.

My dad greets me at the door with a pair of binoculars.

"Here he is!" he says, unlocking the storm door and pushing it open for me. Despite the volume of the welcome and the hug that follows, he looks a lot older than when I last saw him. For one thing, he doesn't stand completely straight; the top half of his body bends forward at a sharp angle. He's always had problems with his back, but it's been getting worse since he's taken over most of the household chores like hauling groceries, lugging laundry up and down two flights of stairs, and helping bathe my mom. His hearing isn't the best, either. On the phone, after he's catalogued that week's medical appointments, he'll give a half-laugh and say, "I'm falling apart."

My mom gets up from her seat at the end of the couch. She has to try a few times to build enough momentum to rise.

"Ya know who this is?" he asks her.

"Should I?" she answers.

"It's Rocco!"

"Rocco, Rocco," she repeats in a little song. I'm not sure if she knows me, but she gives me a hug just the same.

Before I left, I mailed some clothes here so that I would have things to wear at Jerry's rehearsal dinner. My dad tells me the box is in the kitchen, so he sets down the binoculars and leads me to it while my mom turns back to the couch. From where we're sitting at the table, I can hear the sound of the television shifting as my mom clicks the remote. Fox News to the Weather Channel to something about dogs to an opera concert. Not too long in any one place.

When I pull out my camera and start showing my dad pictures of the trip so far, he calls out to her.

"Nikki, come look at the pictures."

She gets up again after a series of attempts and shuffles into the kitchen, where I help her sit down. As I hold out the camera and explain the different photos, my mom's only response is "Mmm-hmm. Very nice."

My dad, on the other hand, makes faces. When he sees photos from my plane ride with Roy, he shakes his head.

That night, just before I fall asleep in my old bed in my old room, I hear footsteps. They stop right outside my closed door. For a second, I expect to hear an old woman's voice, dry and reedy, say "Johnny, give me back my liver…" But it's quiet on the other side. I let out the breath I didn't realize I was holding when I hear them fade back down the hall.

The next day, I sit with the two of them in the living room and find out why my dad had binoculars yesterday. Even though his chair is about eight feet away from the screen, he watches television through them. My mom clicks from one channel to another until my dad lowers the binoculars and says, "Pick something, willya."

"Nothing's on."

"How about some music?"

"Yeah."

They have a rack of CDs perched next to an old boom box. Both sit atop a cabinet stereo that hasn't worked since I left for college. He puts on a Dean Martin disc, and by the time Dino has crooned through "That's Amore" and "Ain't Love a Kick in the Head," they're both asleep, my mom at the end of the couch and my dad in his chair.

I wander into the kitchen to read that morning's *Chicago Tribune*. Before I was in high school and holed up in my room most of the time, I did my homework at this table. I would face the living room, my back to the mural of an old Japanese village that's been on the kitchen wall for as long as I can remember. My mother used to sit across from me and do her own work.

Sometimes this work was making the photo collages that cover nearly every square inch of the upstairs hallway. She was the family archivist, arranging the pictures in large frames with pre-cut mattes. I used to ask her about the people in them. The man who was holding a two-foot long pipe was my dad's grandfather. The man with the magnificent moustache that curled up at the edges was my mother's grandfather. And the black and white photo of a kid wearing altar boy robes who looked exactly like me? That was my dad.

Sometimes her work was writing letters. She would gather family news from all over the map, which was an enormous task; our clan was filled with aunts, uncles, cousins, and cousins' kids emanating like spokes on a hub where the hub was Brooklyn. She was the one who knew that her nephew Billy had just bought a house in California, or that her cousin's daughter Martha was engaged to a "nice young man with a good job," or that her sister Annie's heart was acting up again, and when these updates reached critical mass every few weeks, she lugged the big tan case that housed her Royal typewriter down from the den and into the kitchen, wrote them all up, and sent them back into the world.

She lived for this news and didn't have a lot of patience when the flow of information was interrupted. When I was in the third grade, we had to plan a pretend driving trip somewhere. The project was supposed to teach us some basic geography and math because we had to figure mileage, estimate costs, and make a budget. It seemed beyond me, especially since I couldn't get past the first and easiest step—picking a place to go.

"Go to Spokane," my mom said as she shuffled through the stack of letters to answer that night.

"Where's that?"

"Washington, I think," she said. "Yer cousin Luciann lives there."

"What's it like?"

"Who knows? When ya get there, tell her to write her Godmother once in a while." She said. "She's on my shit list, that one."

She didn't type in the traditional sense, but you would never know that from the rapid clacking, the bell, and the mechanical *whrrrr* as she slapped the carriage back into position. Confronted with story problems or mindless exercises in my spelling workbook, I got caught up in the steady rhythm of that keyboard, the spell broken only when two tiny metal arms clunked together and my mom had to stop and pry them apart.

Later, they're both awake, and Fox News is blares at an ear-drum-rupturing level. It gets even louder when a commercial comes on and William Devane starts talking about how we should put all of our money into gold. For some reason he's on horseback.

"Thomas," my mom says.

"What?" my dad answers.

"Who'd we name Rocco after? My father?"

"Huh?"

"Turn the TV down," I say, but the volume is only part of the problem.

"Who'd we name Rocco after?"

"Whaddaya mean? Your father!"

"Oh," she says, and nods.

That night, I hear footsteps again. They creak down the hall and stop outside my door. I sit up in the dark. I know my mom is on the other side, staring at the door and wondering why it's closed. Or maybe she knows someone is in there but can't quite remember who. *Should I open it?*

Before I can decide, the steps fade down the hall, and I lie back down.

My parents have a routine. Church on Sundays, Dunkin' Donuts for a free senior coffee and old-fashioned doughnut on Tuesdays and Thursdays, shopping on Fridays, Buona Beef for lunch on Sundays, Wednesdays, and Fridays. Today is Wednesday, so we're off to Buona Beef. I ask my dad for his car keys.

"Whaddaya mean?" he says. "I can drive!"

I look at the binoculars by his chair. "That's okay," I say. "I've been biking so long that I miss driving. I'll do it."

With my dad's bad back and my mom's walker, they move slowly, and I hover between them, ready to catch either if they stumble but pretty sure I won't be able to if they do. The girl at the counter already has their order rung up before we make our way down to her. Two "Turkey Deliziosos," two fruit cups, free senior drink, and free senior coffee.

"See, they know me here," my dad laughs. Then he tells me for the third time that they serve pepper and egg sandwiches, too, but only on Fridays.

"Just like the ball games," I say. "Remember that, Mom?"

"What?"

"The pepper and egg sandwiches that we'd take to games," I say. Every so often when I was a kid, we would go to a White Sox game. Vince and I were Cubs fans, but parking at Comiskey was much easier than at Wrigley, and ease of parking has always been very high on my dad's priorities for any outing. Before we left, my mom would fry up eggs and green peppers, pack them into French rolls, wrap them in foil, and stuff them in a bag.

She shakes her head and looks at my dad.

"He's talking about the sandwiches you used to make," he says. "The peppers and eggs!"

"Oh," she says, nodding.

I take a few detours after lunch. First stop is the nursing home where my mother worked for twenty years and where I worked during high school and summers when I was home from college. Both of us were on the kitchen staff. Back in the 1980s, the nursing home was a three-story building at the end of a long driveway on a large piece of property, but the old age business has been thriving, so that driveway is now lined by at least a dozen little assisted care apartments, and the main building is no longer visible from the road.

"Do you remember working here?" I ask my mom.

She doesn't answer.

"Nikki!" my dad says.

"What?"

"Your son's talking to you!"

I try again. "You remember working here, Mom?"

"No," she finally answers. "I forget things."

I don't want to let it go. How could twenty years of something that was a central part of her life could just vanish? "Remember Jesse?"

There's a pause. "Our boss," she says.

"That's right."

"'Mistah Rocco,' she called you."

And then she says, to no one in particular, "Hello, Mistah Rocco."

When I first started there, I had a hard time hauling the meal carts to the second floor three times a day. It wasn't the physical labor; it was seeing all those people who couldn't come down to the dining room and who, in some cases, didn't even realize they were supposed to eat. Some would bang their trays and shout at the aides. Others would call me over and say that people were stealing things from them or ask me if I had seen so-and-so—names I never recognized. Still others would cry, or curse, or just moan.

And then there was Stanley, the youngest resident at just over sixty. He was a tall, thin man who wore glasses. I heard he used to be a math professor somewhere, but now he had Alzheimer's. Stanley wandered around on the second floor, not because he was infirm, but because he had nowhere else to go. Or maybe because he thought that's where he was supposed to be. More often, I saw him down on the first floor, asking questions about some meeting he was supposed to go to or some papers he had to prepare.

Every two weeks, his daughter and her husband visited. They would sit in the library, where they worked hard to wrench Stanley back into the present, telling him exactly where and when he was. Stanley took it all very pleasantly; for his family, however, it was much tougher. One time I was punching out at the front door as they left after a visit. I held the door for them, and even though Stanley's daughter pressed her face into her husband's shoulder, I could see her eyes, red and moist.

My co-workers had a very specific way of dealing with Stanley. They would tell him he was living at Fairview Baptist Home and he had to go somewhere else until dinner was ready. Whenever I was setting up the dining room for lunch and dinner and Stanley walked over to ask me some question from his new reality, I simply told him I needed his help. After I handed him placemats and show him where they needed to go, whatever scenario had been playing in his mind adjusted itself to this new task. When we were done with the placemats, we moved on to plates, then saucers, then cups. The two of us would move slowly around the dim space, the only sound the *clack* of ceramic dishes on wood tabletops.

Next up is our old apartment, where we lived before my parents bought the townhouse. I'm not hopeful about this stop. The memory it holds is probably too small for my mom. Besides, it's my story, really.

We move down the road that runs between the long, two-story buildings. Even though they've been re-shingled and repainted several times over by now, these apartments still look like tired places for tired people. I find our old unit, on the bottom floor at the end. White curtains are drawn tight over the glass sliding doors, and the only evidence that someone lives behind them is a plastic lawn chair and little round grill on the slab in front.

But I didn't come to see that. I came to see the pool. It's a weekday, so most of the parking spaces are empty. The pool is empty, too. From the stacks of lounge chairs and the yellow "Caution" tape wound around and between them, it looks like it's going to be empty for a while.

I stop the car and we sit there. I'm about to ask, "Remember this?" when my mom interrupts from the back.

"Ya fell in the water," she says.

"What?" my dad asks.

"She's right," I say.

My eyes find her face, reflected in the window. She's staring at the empty pool.

I was young. Five, maybe six. Something was going on. Lots of people, lots of decorations. Fourth of July? I sat on a towel by my parents' feet and watched other kids pluck balloons from the water.

*Go get one*, my mom said, pointing. *G'head.*

A big red one bobbed by the edge. I walked up to the water so that I stood on the cool tiles that bordered the pool. I bent over and grabbed at the balloon, but my hands were too small to close around it and instead pushed it further away. I reached out, tumbled forward, and went under.

Everything was blue and quiet and pressed tight against me. The sky vibrated overhead, but it was far away. I could see a few legs in front of me by the corner steps. They were moving, kind of, and then I was, too. Floating toward those stairs. Was I really walking or just drifting with the pulse of water? For years afterward, I was convinced that I breathed water down there, just like Aquaman.

Then I rose up into the light and sound, my mother's hands tight on me, her eyes wide. She knelt with me at the side of the pool and repeated, over and over like a prayer, *Oh fer heavensake.*

It was just the shallow end, but back then it was deep enough to swallow me. Once I got bigger, I'd kneel with my head just above water, the blue concrete scraping my skin as I'd fight to stay balanced. Later, when I was even older and expected to do more in the water, I stopped going to pools altogether. Somehow I made it to my forties without ever diving off a board or swimming in the deep end.

"I was so scared," she says.

"How old was I?"

"I forget."

"Was it a party?"

"I forget," she says, then shrugs. "I forget things."

I look at her in the rearview mirror. She's waded out to that place where she spends most of her time now, that place where memories and names and faces float untethered around her. Is she in 1940s Brooklyn? Playing Mah-Jongg with her girlfriends? Talking with her dead father at a party?

Wherever she goes, it's a mystery. And as she goes, so much goes with her. Years ago, I interviewed the two of them about their early lives and took some notes, but when I look at those notes now, they seem pretty thin. A few dates and places, names of long-dead relatives, random details about the jobs she held at Montgomery Ward right before she met my dad. Other than that, all I have are my own faulty memories of stories she told me back when I was too young to care, and now it's all fading away, like a Polaroid in reverse. I want to reach into my mom's new world with both hands and pull her back to me, but all I can do is put them on the wheel and drive us home.

# 20

# Family Album

It's Friday night at Jerry's wedding. The toasts have been delivered, dinner has been served, and dessert is on its way. I lean against the bar, a gin and tonic in hand. It's not my first. I can see into the dining hall, where the floor is crowded with dancers. The band—near deafening inside—is muted out here to the point where I can't even identify the tune. It's a long, long way from rain, hills, and eye-watering body stink to tuxedos, prime rib, and an open bar.

"So is this a mid-life crisis thing?"

Someone's standing next to me. It's one of the guests—the fiancée of a bridesmaid, I think—and he seems so impossibly tall that for a second I think I might be sliding down the side of the bar. The stack of dark curls on his head and his horn-rimmed glasses combine to make his height even more strange, and I have to stifle laughter. It's really not that funny, but things just seem funnier when you're on your sixth—or is it seventh?—drink of the night.

"I heard about your ride," he says.

I steady myself against the bar. His question catches me by surprise; word of my ride has gotten around, but most people have asked me things like what did I pack, what do I eat, and did I bring a gun. Lots of questions about a gun. This one, though, is trickier. I try to think of an appropriate response, but most of my energy is focused on not spilling my drink. I turn his words over in my mind, and they come to me in slow motion.

*Is. This. A. Mid. Life. Crisis. Thing?*

It's too big a question, and I'm in no condition to take it on. Yet this guy—Craig? Chris?—seems earnest, and I want to respond. Before I can, he tilts a bottle of beer to his mouth and then tries again with something he thinks is easier.

"You married?"

The next day I try to sleep in before we all go to Vince's house for the twenty-fifth anniversary party that he's been planning for the last few months. I haven't seen him since the divorce.

The whole thing didn't sit well with my Catholic family, but Vince was especially upset. For a time, he wouldn't talk to me. A conversation about it would have been awkward and unpleasant, and in my family, things that are awkward and unpleasant quickly become THINGS WE DON'T TALK ABOUT.

What we do talk about is neatly packaged in short, weekly phone calls that are simple and safe and padded with neutral information. My parents' doctor appointments. Their regular trips to neighborhood restaurants. Updates of my brother's kids, cars, and methods for dealing with lawn grubs. Questions to me never stray far beyond *How are the boys?* and *How's school?* and *How are you feeling?* They don't venture into the new details of my life—living in a different house, with a different woman, with Nick and Tony only part of the time.

After I pack my parents into their car, I try not to think about a potentially awkward and unpleasant reunion, so I think about the trips we took every summer when I was a kid.

We didn't travel much; my dad had only two weeks of vacation every year, and we always spent it visiting relatives and friends in New York City. The trips were the same, right down to where we stopped. Clarion, Pennsylvania, on the way out and Youngstown, Ohio, on the way home. In the succession of cars that carried us there and back again--a 1969 Oldsmobile Delta 88, a 1977 Chevy Impala, a 1983 Chevy Citation—the radio was strictly AM. Because the airwaves were a lot less cluttered in those days, we could stay tuned to Top 40 all the way to New York, so as soon as one song would begin to fade into static, there was a new one waiting, bell-clear, somewhere else on the dial. On any given trip, we heard the same hits over and over again, and whenever one comes on the radio today, I'm right back in our car, leaning over the front seat and watching the miles roll by as I butcher the lyrics to Andy Gibb's "Shadow Dancing" or listen to my dad complain about how many times Bob Seger repeats the title at the end of "Against the Wind."

On the nights before we left, I couldn't sleep. My dad insisted on waking up at 4 am, and I did too. I liked being up with my dad while it was still dark, the two of us responsible for getting the journey underway. I helped lug everything out to the car and watched my dad put it all in its place—suitcases, toolbox, miscellaneous bags, cooler, and a box or two from Foremost Liquors that was filled with bottles for people we planned to visit. When he was done and there wasn't a spare cubic inch of space, we nodded approvingly and then went inside, where Vince and my mom were still getting ready.

Despite the fact that I was the early riser, Vince rode shotgun. I was too young, and my mom couldn't read a map, not that we really needed maps on that trip. Vince didn't do much up there other than dispense change for tolls and torment me whenever we approached a state line. He would lean far over the dashboard, extend both hands to the bottom of the windshield, turn to me in the back seat, and shout, "First one in Ohio!"—or whatever state we happened to be entering. Every time he did this, I wanted to stab him with one of the dozen or so pencils I packed. My dad once tried to help by sticking one hand over the dash and telling me to grab his shoulder, but my brother and I exchanged narrow-eyed looks. We both knew electricity didn't count.

We stayed with my grandparents in the same Brooklyn three-flat where my dad grew up. When we arrived, we climbed up the creaky stairs and hugged everyone along the way—Aunt Lizzie on the bottom floor, Aunt Lily and Uncle Louie in the middle, and then my grandparents at the top. Those little women were the first adults I grew taller than, and I measured my growth by those trips.

My grandmother's kitchen was stocked full of roasted peppers, veal chops, pig's feet, Canada Dry ginger ale for my brother and me, and Piels beer for the adults. The table was large enough to seat everyone who lived there, as well as my aunt and uncle, who lived in Queens, and a few cousins, too, and there would be one big dinner with everybody while we were there.

The menu for this dinner was always *cavatelli*. While my grandfather watched his afternoon "stories," a big pot of sauce simmered on the stove and filled the whole house with the smell of garlic and tomatoes. It wasn't safe by the television when Grandpa was watching; if I made any noise, he would bark at me in Italian. So I sat in the kitchen and watched my grandmother and aunts work. They started with a giant mound of flour that was hollowed out at the top to receive a few eggs, and then their hands kneaded and turned the mound, sprinkled it with salt, and kneaded it some more until they had a huge lump of dough. From this dough, they would spin off long tubes about the width of a pencil, cut them into short pieces, and run these little stubs through the inside of a grater to give them texture. Their tiny hands moved quickly and surely over the dough as they kept up a constant chatter. My grandmother always reserved a few strands of dough, slapped them a few times to flatten them out, and cut them into strange, misshapen figures. These were "monsters," and she made them just for me. Later, at dinner, anyone who found one would pass it over. Except Vince, of course. He ate them and grinned at me through marinara-stained teeth.

They made cookies, too, called bows. They were flaps of dough that were twisted and fried so that they looked exactly like a bowtie. Once they cooled, my grandmother drizzled them with honey and tiny sprinkles of all different colors. After meals, she brought out cof-fee and a plate heaped high with them. The adults had one or maybe two while my brother and I devoured the rest. I haven't had a bow in thirty years, but just thinking about them makes my mouth water and my jaw go tight.

My grandmother kept them in a big, plastic-lined cardboard box on a chair in the back hall. Vince and I would sneak back there and eat them in between meals. Ten, maybe twelve cookies at a time. As we reached in over and over, our arms grew sticky and freckled with sprinkles. Honey collected at the bottom of the box, and the best cookies were the ones that had been soaking in that thick pool of gold. They were translucent from the honey that had seeped into every pore, including the little bubbles that formed in the dough as it fried. These cookies were heavy and didn't crunch so much as dissolve as we bit into them. At the end of the hallway, where the light filtered in through the small window and lit up the dust motes in the air, the bows were sugary hosts at our secret communion.

When we get to the house, I'm swarmed by my five nieces and nephews, who all want to hear all about my bike ride. Vince appears and gives us a quick status report: food is on its way, drinks are in the kitchen, tables and tents are set up in back. We make our way through the crowded kitchen.

When my brother was in college, his roommate and a few friends on their dorm floor had a game they liked to play. They would move things around on his desk while he was at class. Nothing dramatic; maybe slide the desk lamp an inch to the right, reverse the direction that his pens were facing, shift his note cards from one side of his blot-ter to the other. He would return from class and immediately notice. His friends watched him put everything back in its proper place and waited for him to miss something, but he never did.

That's as good an anecdote as any of my brother. He's been look-ing forward to throwing this twenty-fifth anniversary party, and I suspect that the pleasure he'll get out of managing its several moving parts is a secret little gift to himself. There's a lawn to mow, tents to set up, tables to arrange, pool water to be chemically balanced, and food to stage.

His and Jean's wedding album is out on the dining room table, and I steer my parents over in that direction while Vince answers the telephone. It's startling to see how young we all look in the photos. My mom's hair is thick and black, my dad's glasses are smaller, and he stands up straight. They're both thinner and their eyes—especially my mom's—know what they're focused on. And there I am, too, in my best man's tuxedo. I recognize my smile. It's the smile of someone who can't wait to leave for college in less than a month.

My dad points to someone in a group shot and asks my mom, "Do you know who this is?"

She shakes her head.

"That's our nephew Gene," he says. "Dorothy's son."

"Oh," she says, nodding.

He frowns, makes a little sound, and points to another. "How about this one?"

My mom studies the picture and shakes her head again.

"That's your sister!" he says.

She nods again, and he looks at me. "She forgets."

He's smiling, but it's a helpless kind of smile. It's the same one he gave me earlier in the day when he told me about my mom's neurologist appointments. She's asked simple questions to gauge the progress of her dementia, but she's not so good at answering them. Before her appointments, my dad will fire these questions at her—*What day is today? What month is it? What year is it?*—as if she's studying for an exam and if she can just memorize the material, she'll be fine.

My parents find a shady spot in the back yard, and once they're settled, I look for my brother to see if he needs help. But as is typical for any Vince Production, everything is operating like clockwork. He hands me a beer and grabs one for himself.

"I have to have a talk with Dad that I know he won't want to have."

I'm not sure what he means.

He answers my look. "About what if he goes first."

I wonder if I should be a part of that conversation, too. It's hard not to feel like I'm just a visitor here, that I'm not an actual functioning member of this family because I live so far away. Or because I'm still the little brother. Or because I've made some questionable decisions in my own life. Or maybe it's because they've just never quite known what to do with me, and I've often felt the same way about them.

The doorbell rings.

"Gotta be the food," he says. "We'll talk later."

I know we won't. And even though I complain about their tendency to repress and deny, I'm just as responsible for the silence. I want to tell my dad that I know it must be hard for him with Mom in her current state. I want to tell him that when I'm not irritated by the way he keeps everything bottled up, I'm kind of in awe of his refusal to complain about anything. I want to tell him that I've always respected—but not always followed—his example of honesty, even in little things, like returning extra change at a store, an act that I witnessed more than once as a kid. I want to tell my brother that I know he does a lot for the two of them, running them to Dad's eye appointments, sitting with Mom. I want to tell him that he's built a nice life and family for himself. I want to tell him that I loved growing up with him and having him for a big brother.

But instead I'll appreciate the moments that were.

A quiet half hour during the party when Vince sits with me and our parents to eat, and there we are, just the four of us around the dinner table for the first time in twenty-five years.

A longer hug than usual from him when we leave. Him telling me that he likes my blog updates about the ride.

My dad, on the ride home, asking, "What's your lady friend's name again?"

When we get back, my dad heads to his chair and my mom heads to the couch to watch television. Because I'm not really interested in O'Reilly or Hannity or whatever other Fox News clown happens to be on, I shuffle through the photo albums lined up underneath the TV and wipe away the top layer of dust on each with my finger. There's not much order to them; the one I pick first is from 1980, when I was thirteen. That summer we painted the rooms upstairs a slightly lighter tan over the tan that was already there, and my parents decided to immortalize the event in pictures. Naturally, I'm either looking sullen or away from the camera because I would rather be doing anything else. Then I see one of my mom. She's holding up her paintbrush with a huge smile on her face, and it's only then I realize she doesn't smile anymore. I look over at her. She's sleeping now. I slip the photo from the album and set it by my arm.

The albums end with Nick and Tony's early years. Like most parents, Elizabeth and I documented nearly every minute of their lives, and then she sent the evidence off to both sets of grandparents every few weeks. I remember these shots. Nick in his car seat on the ride home from the hospital, Nick asleep on my chest, the two of us on the floor surrounded by toys, Tony in his car seat on the ride home from the hospital while Nick glares at him, the three of us making faces and wrestling in the playroom. It's been years since I've seen them, though; the copies we kept are lost to me, tucked away in albums somewhere in my old house, along with most other pictures of my life from about age twenty-one to forty.

These are coming with me. One by one I pull them out of their sleeves and stack them up. Rusty's bags are packed tight, but I'll find room.

That night, I hear the footsteps again, coming down the hall and stopping right outside my door. I imagine my mom on the other side, standing in the dark, not sure why she got up or maybe even where she is.

I get up, put my hand on the knob, and turn it.

My mom's eyes widen.

I wait for a shout—loud and scared—the most reasonable response to a stranger in your home.

But she just blinks a couple of times and says, "Oh. It's you."

"You okay?"

She nods and turns away. "G'night."

Later, I lie in bed and think about those words, *It's you*. Who did she see? Maybe her "baby," as she liked to call me, even into my thirties. Or maybe someone else, someone with a familiar face whose name she can't quite recall. As I wait for sleep to drop over me, I remember Cindy and that awful trick we would play on her, and I wonder if I'm the one who's fading away.

# 21

# Leaving Springview Farm

...LEAVING

# SPRINGVIEW FARM

THE NIGHT I GET BACK FROM CHICAGO, JAN AND BILL TAKE ME OUT TO DINNER. THEY TELL ME THAT IT'S THEIR ANNIVERSARY.

I WANT TO TREAT, BUT THEY WON'T LET ME.

THE GOOD FOLKS AT LAMBERT'S ("HOME OF THE THROWED ROLLS") KEEP BRINGING THE FOOD.

I SLEEP WELL THAT NIGHT.

IN THE MORNING IT'S RAINING. JAN WATCHES ME PACK UP RUSTY...

WHILE BILL MAKES EGGS AND LISTENS TO THE WEATHER REPORT.

JAN WANTS ME TO STAY...

*Just 'til this next patch of clouds go by?*

BUT IT'S TIME TO GO.

SHE & BILL DRIVE ME BACK OVER GRAVEL ROADS TO A NEARBY GAS STATION.

WE STAND THERE IN THE RAIN, WAITING FOR SOMEONE TO SAY SOMETHING.

FINALLY, JAN BREAKS THE SILENCE.

*Well, I just feel like I'm never going to see you again...*

Jan's classic "worried" face, according to Pat.

I CALL THE TWO OF THEM THAT NIGHT FROM FURTHER DOWN THE ROAD. JAN TELLS ME THAT THEY FOLLOWED ME FOR A COUPLE OF MILES TO MAKE SURE I WAS OKAY.

THE SOLITUDE OF THE ROAD HAS BEEN WEARING ME DOWN, AND I'VE BEEN FEELING AS EMPTY AS EVER. BUT AFTER I HANG UP THE PHONE, I FEEL FULL...LIKE I'VE JUST EATEN A BILL-SIZED SERVING OF HIS STRAWBERRY-LEMON ICE CREAM AND WAITING FOR ME IS A SOFT BED BENEATH THE WATCHFUL EYES OF MAMA OWL.

# VOICES FROM THE ROAD

BENDAVIS, MISSOURI

WAKE'S
/// FEED ///
&
SUPPLY

"Lotsa bikers come through here."

One gentleman...
an older fella...camped
on the lawn out back,
and the next morning,
I watched him take
several pills...

He did not
seem well.

SLI
JI

Another time,
a group of six
came all the way
from New York.

The city,
that is.

They sure liked
to talk their
politics.

English professor, huh?

Well, I imagine you've
heard all sorts of variations
of the King's English on this
adventure a yours.

# 22

# The Great Imposter

During a break in the rain, I fight off gnats with one hand and press my phone tight to my ear with the other so that I can better hear the thick German accent on the other end. The voice belongs to a man named Herman, whose house I'm hoping to stay at tonight. He gives me a complicated set of directions involving local businesses and secret signs he's posted along the road, but I can understand only about half of what he's saying. Then the rain kicks up again, so I stow my phone and get back on the road in the Ozarks, which means being chased by dogs, drenched by rain, and harassed by drivers.

After another two hours of this, I'm in Ellington and scanning ahead for the landmarks Herman mentioned. Like nearly every other Ozark town I've seen, Ellington looks to be not much more than a bar, a gas station, a grocery store, and a church. Just after the gas station, I spot what I'm pretty sure is one of Herman's guideposts. It's a small, hand-lettered cardboard sign that's duct-taped to the base of a telephone pole. The bottom piece of tape has peeled loose, so the rain-soaked sign flops lazily in the wind. I can barely make out the words BIKERS WILKOMMEN above an arrow and an address.

I follow the arrow to a narrow road that winds among several tiny ranch-style houses in various states of disrepair. Each homeowner has his or her own idea about where and how to display an address. The bold black numbers on white clapboard are easy to spot, but others are more subtle—painted numbers on a few weathered rocks in the lawn, faded reflective stickers beside the door. At one house, any posted address is overwhelmed by the spectacles on display. There's a large replica of the Ten Commandments in the front yard with the words JESUS IS LORD above them, there's a hand-painted sign reading CHRISTIAN FELLOWSHIP lashed to the chain link fence with zip ties, and there's a van in the driveway covered in "Praise Jesus" stickers.

Naturally, this is Herman's house.

•

There's been no shortage of God on this trip. Back in Arizona, just outside of Grand Canyon National Park, I stopped at a Shell station to grab a quick snack, and I couldn't have picked a worse time or place. The station doubled as a massive souvenir shop, and to get to the checkout counter, I was forced to navigate a maze of glass and metal shelves.

I stepped out from between two of these shelves and found I was at the end of a long tail of people curling outward from the one open register. Everyone's arms were filled with glittering objects.

Many of the people seemed to be together, bound by t-shirts that identified them as members of some church. The fronts were all the same—sitting squarely atop each person's left breast like an official badge was the outline of a dove over the church's name. The backs of the shirts varied. In front of me, a father wearing cargo shorts and black socks had one that read

SEVEN DAYS

with

NO PRAYER

makes

ONE WEAK

*Clever*, I thought, but then I saw the back of his son's shirt. On it was a drawing of Christ on the cross from the waist up. His hands, bloodied at the end of the cross, spanned the boy's back and lent meaning to the accompanying words

How much does Jesus love you?

THIS MUCH!

The line's progress was glacial, but eventually this kid got to unload his bounty of miniature moccasins, two glasses etched with an image of the Grand Canyon, a wooden circle adorned with feathers and beads, a keychain attached to a pebble of turquoise, a bear and a wolf carved out of rock, a leather coin holder, a tiny pocketknife with "Grand Canyon National Park" silkscreened onto its case, and a box of Junior Mints the size of a Prius. Grand total, eighty-five dollars and change, which Dad paid for with a crisp $100 dollar bill.

More people with similar shirts fell into line behind me, and out in the parking lot they flocked around a luxury bus. I wondered if they were going to stay at the park lodge, where rooms cost upwards of $400 a night. I also wondered what Jesus would think about this. I tried to picture how he might react to having the good word spread via t-shirts while his devoted dropped serious change on disposable crap that would eventually resurface in a garage sale, right between the Happy Meal toys and a few paperbacks from the *Left Behind* series.

•

Herman is a small, round man with close-cropped white hair that stands straight up. Now in his late sixties, he came to the U.S. from Germany as a young man and has lived in Ellington for nearly twenty years. In his garage—where I'm told to wheel Rusty—are large workbenches, racks of tools, and a glass case displaying metal candlesticks, sconces, and crosses with tiny price tags tied to them. Herman tells me he's a welder and shows me his latest project, held upright on one workbench by two stout vises. It's a sign for the local historical society. Right now it's a jaggedy-edged rectangle that Herman has constructed from steel tubing. It's in the shape of the county we're in—Reynolds—which has a lot of angles in its borders. When I look at them closely, I'm impressed by how smooth and perfect the welds are. If any bikers show up at Herman's place with a cracked steel frame, they're going to leave with it stronger than ever.

He escorts me to a back room in his house where three cots are lined up, shows me the bathroom, and then dashes out to the grocery store to pick up a few things for dinner.

While the garage is devoid of any Christian symbols, the story inside is much different. Here, Herman has covered his walls with framed quotes; one of these—GOD DOES NOT CALL THE QUALIFIED; HE QUALIFIES THE CALLED—stares at me from the back of the living room wall. Beneath this is a comfortable chair, in front of which is propped a music stand made of heavy wood. There's a big book open on top of it, and before I walk over to see what it is, I already know that it's a Bible. Several bookmarks sprout from the pages, and on the seat of the chair is a spiral notebook filled with pen and pencil scribbles in what I guess is German. In front of the big living room window is a magazine rack filled with "Chick Tracts"—mini-comics used to spread the word of Christianity by revealing the supposed satanic underpinnings of things like Halloween and tattoos and Catholicism. Living in an area filled with evangelical Christians and being interested in comics, I've seen most of these before, but there are a few titles that are new to me. I'm flipping through some of these when a book at the top of the rack catches my eye. On its cover is a picture of a winking Santa. The book's title is *Santa Claus—The Great Imposter.*

Herman gets back about an hour later. I help him carry in the bags, and he gets right to work on dinner. As he does, he tells me about some of the bikers he's hosted. He's not far into the stories when he says, "Wait a moment," disappears into the living room, and returns with a thick spiral notebook. For a second I think that it's the one that was near his Bible, but it's not. It's what he calls his "Biker Book," and it's filled with signatures and notes by the people who have stayed with him. Nearly every entry has a picture taped next to it.

While I write a little note and sign the book, he tells me about the churches in town. This part of Missouri is considered the South, and the people of the South take their religion seriously—but not, as it turns out, as seriously as Herman does. He tells me how the ministers in town are "out to get him" because he challenges them on points of scripture. He liked to do this in the middle of services, so the ministers suggested he not attend those services. Politely, at first.

"They say one thing," Herman says, his eyes wide again, "but I tell them, that's not what it says in the Lord's book. And what do they do? They tell me I'm not welcome!" He snorts again and starts chopping onions. "In God's house!" he adds, shaking his head.

I keep expecting to be told that the only true path is the path that leads to Jesus, but Herman doesn't want recruits. He wants to tell his story, and after dinner, he does. Many years earlier, Herman, his wife, and their daughter—who was one or two years old—were living in a tiny apartment in St. Louis. While he was a mechanic's assistant at a nearby garage, his wife stayed home with their daughter. One afternoon, Herman got a call from God, who told him that he wasn't going home that night.

Herman climbed into his truck, put his hands on the wheel, and listened to God tell him to get on Interstate 70 and head west.

As he talks, I try to imagine how a young man heading away from his family and into the unknown might be part of some divine plan. But obviously the divine lies well beyond my understanding, because all I can come up with is a young immigrant from Germany who finds things in his new country to be not quite what he expected. The paucity of job opportunities. The too-small apartment with rusty water, thin walls, and loud upstairs neighbors. The precarious bank balance at the end of each month that's been tilting more and more toward zero since the baby came, and the doctor's bills *still* arriving in the mail each week. If I'm trying to understand what might have led Herman to head west in his truck that afternoon, those are the details that take shape in my mind.

Herman pauses in his story, closes his eyes, and nods slowly. Then he opens his eyes and tells me that—as he approached Kansas City— he tried to steer his truck onto an exit ramp, but he couldn't turn the wheel. It was locked tight.

"The Lord wouldn't let me," he says, hands on an invisible wheel, trying to jerk it to the right but having no luck. "I tried to force it, but I couldn't. I said right then and there, 'All right, Lord, you're driving.'"

The Lord directed him further west, then south. He refused to let Herman stop at either Topeka or Wichita. At Oklahoma City, Herman saw a sign for Las Vegas, and for a moment he thought the Lord wanted him to go there. But no, there was another plan.

"Where?" I ask.

Herman holds up a finger.

"Dallas."

He saw a rainbow in the distance, and God told him that this was the sign, to exit here, to go down a series of streets that led to an apartment across the street from a restaurant.

"He told me that I would live here," Herman says, pointing to the right, "and work there," he finishes, pointing to the left.

I ask about his wife and daughter. God sent Herman back to get them a week later.

The next morning I'm still thinking about Herman's story. I get that life can be disorienting, and when we feel like Dorothy, spun into a bizarre world on the spine of a tornado, it would be nice to believe that a carefully-laid brick road leads to a deity who gives us all the answers. Call it God, Jehovah, Allah, Yaweh, Shiva, or even Oz the Great and Powerful. The problem is, you can't fake belief. You either have it or you don't, and I don't.

But I'll be honest; sometimes I wish I did.

It's all so reassuring. Take confession. If you break God's commandments, your soul is tainted. If your soul is tainted, you don't go to heaven. At least not right away; it all depends on how "tainted" we're talking. So you confess and are absolved. Until you screw up again. It's a convenient solution to the difficult job of understanding our weaknesses and failings.

For Mistah Secrets, confession was a kind of kryptonite. We had to go every eight weeks. It was roughly the same period of time that my dad allotted between haircuts, and my least favorite Saturdays were those when both chores came due. Every time we went to confession, I carried with me the memory of my first one. I must have been in the first grade, but I can't remember for sure. It was something we had to do before our first communion. In CCD, one of the older nuns told us when we stepped into the booth and talked to the priest, we would be talking to God.

"There is no keeping secrets from God," she said. "He knows and sees everything."

*Then why confess?* I wondered. She went on to say that whatever we confessed would stay between us and God. I heard someone whisper, "Even murder?" and the nun closed her eyes and pinched her mouth to show how it pained her that we might make light of this sacred rite.

But we spent most of our time on the procedure. Where to wait, what to say to the priest, where to go afterward, and how there was to be absolutely no horseplay. When we finally made our confession, we were in the nave, which during the week doubled as the St. Mary's school gymnasium. One side of the gym had two small confessional rooms, and we were broken up into lines stretched in opposite directions. As other kids emerged from behind those doors, I tried to read their faces. Had they been transformed somehow, now that their souls were clean? It was hard to say. The girls all looked solemn. Some of the boys flashed goofy looks to their friends. A few looked relieved. I moved steadily forward. Soon it would be my turn. I raised my hand to catch the attention of the teacher in charge of the lines. She waved me over with a look of impatience.

"What is it?" she asked.

"I forgot what I was going to say," I told her. "In there." I pointed to the door ahead. Shannon O'Connor had just walked out, and the teacher looked over my head and motioned to David Ryan, who was next in line.

"You confess your sins," she said.

"I know."

"Haven't you been thinking about it?"

"Yeah," I said, defensively.

She shushed me. "This is the house of God."

"Yes," I whispered. "I had some stuff but now I can't remember it."

She didn't have time for an irresponsible kid messing up the careful order of things, so she bent close and whispered, "Just say that you haven't honored your mother and father. All children are guilty of that." Then she sent me back to my place.

A few people later, it's my turn. I move toward the door.

It's heavier than I expect. Heavy enough to hold all the sins inside. I step into the little room, and the lights behind me cast a weak glow that dies before it can reach the far corner. The door closes with a solid *thunk*, and I'm alone in the dark. There's nothing here except a tiny bench to kneel on beneath the window. Not a window, really. This is a small square covered with thick dark fabric. I run my fingers over it. There's a little bit of give before I'm pushing against something hard. The priest's sliding door. I hear mumbling on the other side as I kneel. The priest is talking to someone through the other window, dispensing the penance that will cleanse his or her soul. It's a her, I remember. Mary DiPestini went in before me from the other line. I wonder what her sins are. What a great job, this priest business. Knowing everyone's secrets. Much better to be in that center room than in this one on your knees in the dark.

I hear a muffled thump on the other side. He's slid the other window shut. It's my turn. I go cold.

My window slides open. We can't see each other through the curtain, but I can just make out the shape of his head on the other side. *God's head*, I think. *And the power to cleanse my soul.* He's breathing heavily. I start.

"Forgive me father, for I have sinned…"

# 23

# Confession

I had an affair.

It was the worst thing I've ever done in my life, by far. I want to be clear about this because it's a hard story to tell and I don't want the details—the ones here or the ones missing—to seem like I'm making excuses.

There isn't much reason to go into those details that crop up in every adultery narrative. They're sordid but ultimately standard. Secret email accounts, furtive phone calls, remote locations to hide the car. Kid's stuff for Mistah Secrets. Of course, the stakes were much, much higher than with sneaking books or skipping church, but he was up to the challenge. Overseeing something like this was what he lived for.

The worst part was how guilty I didn't feel. It was like someone else was betraying my wife, not me, and the depth of my performance scared me. When I stepped back into my house, I felt I was the same husband I had always been. Where was I? Working out or taking care of some things at school or running errands…where else would I be?

It's also a hard story to tell because there's no easy drama. I didn't abandon my marriage because of drugs or alcohol, or emotional abuse, or any kind of trauma. The drama lay in the lack of drama; it lay in the silence that we both agreed to at some point, though I'll admit that this silence was a place I preferred and didn't work very hard to escape. What happened then was the mundane realization that I was unhappy. But even the word "realized" implies something big, like the explosive force of a pipe bursting under too much pressure. My realization was more of a slow leak somewhere deep inside the walls, one that's easy to ignore despite the feeling something's not right—a faint hiss, a periodic drip, a spike in the water bill. And even when it becomes obvious, it's a small puddle seeping from a baseboard in the corner of the bathroom. By itself, it doesn't look too bad, but there's no way to fool yourself about what that puddle means. Stretched out behind it, behind that wall, is a wide trail of sheetrock and wood, soaked and unsalvageable.

But maybe I'm just hiding behind a metaphor. The truth is, I was unhappy and too much of a coward to say so.

I can't even blame the affair on cancer. The diagnosis came after.

It went on and on. And on. I let things build until I couldn't live with the secret anymore. A few years earlier, when I told family and friends I had cancer, I caught a glimpse of the true face of secrets, of their awesome power to disorder someone's world. I would feel a little sick just before I opened my mouth to say "I have cancer," and then I felt even worse when I saw the person's face. This new secret—new, yet not new—was a fist curled tight inside of me and ready to knock down Elizabeth and the life we built together over eighteen long years, a life that she had not doubted in any serious way.

We had been giving each other a wide berth for a while, spending more time alone with the kids than with each other. Our conversations focused mainly on daily tasks and schedules. Our nights in front of the TV found us immersed in our own projects—she sorted coupons and I read. But for the days leading up to that night, I felt that fist thumping inside my chest and working its way out. Then one Saturday night in early October just before San Diego County burst into flames, she asked me a question.

"Why don't you like me anymore?"

I couldn't breathe. When she said that, I knew where it was going to end. I tried to talk around things, tried to find out if she was as unhappy as I was, tried to fool myself into believing there might be a soft landing here, but it was all just talk that went nowhere. Mistah Secrets was telling me to shut up, to just stop talking, but even he couldn't hold back that fist. Everything was about to come tumbling down because of me.

I opened my mouth and spoke.

The rest of that night, like the weeks and months that followed, is a puzzle where the pieces don't and won't fit together into a coherent whole.

Somehow our yelling doesn't wake the kids, and at some point I flee the argument. When I come back it's two or three in the morning and I'm so exhausted I can barely climb the stairs. The house is dark. I don't see Elizabeth. Upstairs, the bed is empty, and I crawl in.

The next thing I know is a voice, a hiss.

*How can you sleep?*

I open my eyes, but everything is black. And then the hiss again.

*How can you sleep?*

It's almost two weeks later, a few days after Tony's birthday. I listen to her shout at me on the phone until it goes dead after a final, exasperated shriek. I drive over. As I walk through in the front door, I hear the door to the garage slam and then the van pulls away. The boys are upstairs, sitting on a couch in the playroom. Maybe they want to know if I'm coming back, but they don't ask.

I have no idea where she went or when she'll be back. After I read to the boys and put them to bed, I go downstairs to call her friend Ellen, but I can't find the phone. I hear a noise behind me.

It's Tony on the stairs.

My heart is beating hard, like he caught me doing something.

"You know where the phone is?" I hear myself ask.

"I think Mom threw it in the back yard."

Later—both boys asleep for real this time—I hear the garage door. Elizabeth walks in, her jeans soaked to the knees, shoes caked with sand. She looks at me, says "Get out," and goes into the bathroom. I shouldn't leave, but I do.

We're in my office at school, yelling. Then one of us or maybe both of us is crying. Then more yelling. Then silence. Then she wants to leave and I open the door and one of my students stands waiting against the wall, her eyes wide.

I'm reading an email from my sister-in-law Jean to Elizabeth. She tells her to change all the locks and take the kids and move far away from me. Vince won't call, and he won't return my calls.

*I saw you through cancer. I watched you throw up.*

In early December Nick has his first middle school concert. I get there early and sit in the empty gym. As the other parents filter in— some arriving late in their work attire, others marshalling younger siblings and chatting with each other—I try not to feel conspicuous, alone on a metal folding chair. News has wormed its way through the Starbucks and soccer sidelines and PTA meetings, and based on the handshakes and brief waves and tight-lipped smiles I receive, I can gauge who's heard what. Soon, the lights dim to signal the end of social hour. Just before the concert begins, parents with cameras rush the stage and retreat again like the ebb and flow of a crazy, flashing ocean.

I spot Nick's head at the back of the stage, poking up above the drum set. I wave, thinking he won't see me, but he must have been looking for me, too, because he waves back with one of his sticks.

This small gesture makes me remember the day he was born. We planned a natural childbirth with midwives, but when Elizabeth's labor failed to progress and there were signs of fetal distress, we were rushed to the hospital for an emergency C-section. I followed Nick out of the delivery room and stood next to the incubator, watching his little body contract with each breath and waiting for his blood oxygen to normalize. Later, we held him in her hospital room. We went through this again with far less drama almost three years later with Tony. Who imagines at those moments that one day you'll sit alone at your son's school event and then return to your apartment and answer an email about custody?

When Vince finally breaks his silence, it's to tell me what my cancer meant. He says it was God giving me a chance to correct some mistakes, which I didn't do, and even though I don't say anything, I'm madder at him than I've ever been. Madder than I was at the weeks of nothing that preceded this statement, madder than when he came up with his "test" to show me I couldn't hack the Peace Corps, madder even than when we were kids and he would pin me down and dangle a big rope of spit over my face.

I'm at lunch with my friend Jack, and I tell him everything. Maybe the Catholic church knew what it was doing when it stuck confession in a little dark room; it's a hard thing to look at and doesn't get any easier after the first time. But it was the only way to keep Mistah Secrets at bay.

Jack takes it all in. Tall and broad-chested with a graying beard, he was the patriarch of the English Department when he retired a few years earlier. When he was a younger man, he raised two boys with a woman he later divorced. After I describe some of the fallout, he just shakes his head and says, "Not one damn thing will make this any better except time."

In the months that follow, it becomes clear that our split—like all splits—is a war of stories, and I'm going to lose. Whenever I try to tell part of mine in a phone call or in a joint counseling session or even to myself, I hear Elizabeth's voice say it's unconvincing, a cliché. But it's all I have.

Maybe not all.

It's bedtime. Nick and Tony just started spending the weekends with me, and they want some stories. I don't have any picture books—didn't take any from the house, didn't buy any new ones—but then I remember. A few minutes later, I'm wedged between their little bodies on the bed and reading them the first chapter of *The Phantom Tollbooth*.

•

Outside the sun is shining, but it won't be for long. Lots of clouds, their edges glowing in the morning sun, are gathered to the west, planning something for later. After a breakfast of eggs and toast, Herman and I head outside, where he tinkers with his camera as I load up Rusty. Looking down his street at the modest houses perched quietly on their generous swaths of lawn, I'm struck again by how Herman's property, with all of its holy ornaments, stands out from the others. Where I live in San Diego, his ideas wouldn't be that far off the map, but the landscape is different there; instead of rolling wooded hills and isolated outposts, there are scores upon scores of neighborhood streets that weave a comfortable blanket of middle-class suburbia. Mine is a land where HOAs put limits on how people festoon their yards, and the close proximity to neighbors makes one's central desire *not* to stand out. Here, though, deep in the hidden heart of this country, people are a little more free to be what they are. I'm glad I didn't follow my first instinct to keep right on going when I pulled up in front of Herman's house, like his estranged, grown daughter did when she came to visit him several years back.

I shake Herman's hand and thank him for everything, and when I finally start to pedal down the road in front of his house, I hear his camera click behind me. Another snapshot for his Biker Book. He's alone out here, but he seems content, and I don't get the feeling that he's lonely, not so long as bikers continue to struggle through this punishing terrain and find with him a haven where they can rest and gather themselves. And while Herman may put his faith in God, I won't be joining him. Instead, I'll take my chances with Oz, who made sense when he told Dorothy and her friends that what they were searching for was inside of them all along; they just needed to look hard enough.

Soon I'm alone on a lettered Ozark road that will twist and dip and climb its way toward Illinois. I scan the sky for a rainbow. With all the moisture in the air and the sun burning clear, it wouldn't be out of the question to see one. It would be a nice touch, that rainbow. If one were to arc down in the distance, its seven-hued arm reaching toward some unseen spot on the road ahead of me, I might have to believe that it's a kind of sign—maybe a promise that the days ahead will amount to something.

But all I see is sky.

# VOICES FROM THE ROAD

# 24

# Man of Steel Bridges

When most people think of Illinois, they probably picture sky-scrapers looming above bustling crowds or wind-caressed fields speck-led with cows. Maybe they think of our sixteenth president, or a cer-tain hapless baseball team, or a tradition of corrupt politics. What they probably don't imagine is water, but the truth is that the Land of Lincoln is almost completely surrounded by the stuff. If we could fly high enough for a God's-eye perspective, things would be clear, but we'll have to settle for any map of the area, where one look tells us that aside from the rigid vertical slash that forms the top half of its border with Indiana and the flat-top that seems to support Wisconsin like a juicy beef patty holds up a slice of cheese, the shape of this stately state is carved and bounded by water—Lake Michigan to the Northeast, the Wabash and Ohio Rivers to the East and Southeast, and the mighty Mississippi to the west.

I lack this perspective, too; even though Illinois was my home for twenty-three years, and even though I've crossed these rivers in vari-ous cars, and even though I've seen countless maps of the state, I never thought of its watery borders until this very moment, as I roll slowly toward the Chester Bridge, a steel-truss structure that spans 2800 feet over the Mississippi and connects the Missouri floodplain to the little town of Chester, Illinois.

The bridge's narrow two lanes are even narrower than usual. Construction has shut down one of them, and lines of cars are amassed at both ends, waiting for the green light that will let a small caravan through at a time. I decide that the wait doesn't apply to bikers, so I pass the line of cars, pull into the closed lane, and stop halfway across. As vehicles rumble past, I can feel the bridge bounce under my feet. The sun is just beginning to peek through the blueblack clouds, but it's going to be a long time before I'm either warm or dry.

Less than fifteen minutes after I rolled out this morning, drops fell softly, then landed harder, and then multiplied exponentially until I was pounded by bucketsful of water. All I could hear was the angry hiss of the storm and the *slosh* of Rusty's tires cutting through the soaked road, and all I could see was a gray screen that was further distorted by droplets on my glasses. I took them off, but this exposed my eyeballs to the sting of driving rain. When it hurt too much to keep them open, I steered into the driveway of a farmhouse that appeared around a bend and parked underneath the empty carport in its front yard.

I was lucky to find shelter. On most Ozark roads a person can travel for miles without seeing anything but hills, trees, and roadkill. I was also lucky that whoever lived in the house didn't mind my stopping there. The kitchen window flickered from a television set inside, and I caught a glimpse of a hand on the curtain—probably someone checking to see what their dog was yapping at—but nobody came out. They probably decided that I was harmless enough to sit outside but too strange to invite inside, which meant that I spent the next hour and a half shivering on a concrete pad while rain pounded the fiberglass roof over my head.

Once the storm lightened to the point where I could ride without putting my life in too much danger, I pedaled through the tapering foothills of the Ozarks to midway across the Chester Bridge, where I'm now paused between two states and thinking about water. Somewhere below is the border between Missouri and Illinois, not marked in dots and dashes like on a map, but buried deep in the Mississippi, which right now is a wide expanse of churning, muddy soup that the last few days' rain has swelled onto the flatlands of the western shore. Down there, clusters of branches detached from trees upriver spin, twist, and tumble as they journey downstream.

Something from my recent detour in Chicago has been chewing at the corners of my memory, and it comes back to me now. It was at Jerry's rehearsal dinner, and I was talking with one of the bridesmaids when she tossed a question to me over her wine glass.

"What have you learned so far?"

Caught off guard, I tried to deflect it with humor—"Watch out for dogs," "Don't eat sandwiches from gas stations," that kind of thing--but we both knew that there was substance to her question and I was ignoring it. Hadn't I learned anything in the desert? On the Rockies? Somewhere in Kansas? In the face of such directness, my thoughts tangled up like the spare bungee cords in one of my rear bags. I had no excuse for not having a single intelligent thing to say about what I was getting out of this trip—a trip that I was, incredibly, more than halfway through. I didn't admit this, of course; I just shrugged and shifted the subject to something else. She was content to let it go, but I hadn't been able to. After all, I had more at stake in the answer than she did.

*What have I learned so far?*

On the outskirts of Metropolis—a little town hiding on the bottom edge of Illinois—I see a huge factory ahead and a lot of activity going on in front. In addition to the clusters of people, there are cars, canopy tents, lawn chairs, a big American flag or two, and a large gray shape that looks to be one of those gorillas that car dealers use to advertise "King Kong-Sized Savings!"

But what I thought was some kind of party or picnic turns out to be something else entirely.

As I get closer, I see people with signs, and as I get closer still, I read the words on these signs.

HONEYWELL

USW Local 7-699

LOCKED OUT

CORPORATE GREED

I slow down.

Before I left on this trip, I had just wrapped up a two-year stint for my faculty union as both lead negotiator and grievance officer. Those two years capped a nearly unbroken streak of eight years of union service, and when I think of that work, a few images develop.

Talking with a reporter about unjustified budget cuts to the student literary magazine.

Arguing with the administration that our exploited part-time teachers should get *some* kind of health benefits.

Sitting with an older colleague whose deep grief after losing his wife made it impossible for him to teach anymore.

I knew that the work was important, but along with everything else going on in my life, it had worn me down.

The members of United Steel Workers Local 7-699 are happy to have someone to talk to. They're all employed at the Honeywell plant—the gigantic, chain-link-enclosed compound behind them—which happens to be the only uranium-conversion facility in the country. I don't understand the physical or chemical principles involved, but I understand enough to know it's potentially hazardous work and the people who do it should have some health protections, which is the very issue that stalled labor talks between the workers and Honeywell a couple of weeks ago and led to the lock out.

The shape that I thought was a gorilla is actually a giant inflatable rat. It's got a sign around its neck that reads "SHAW," a company that's provided scab workers to Honeywell. While business more or less continues at the plant, the locked-out workers and their spouses, sons, and daughters have to make do on savings and whatever support the USW or local residents can provide. Mainly food, a guy named

Sam tells me.

Lockouts and strikes are awful things. They're weapons of last resort that test each side's will and resolve, and the longer they go the more reluctant the warring sides are to blink. I look at this group of people in front of me and I know that they represent just a fraction of the total workers; if a union is going to pull off what might turn into a long-term standoff, its members need to protest in shifts. I can also see by the t-shirts and jeans and work boots of these people that they're going to be harder hit than the Honeywell executives. No one on the other side will go without meals or water or electricity during this struggle, but I see a future of letters from banks and first- and second-notifications from utility companies in the mailboxes of these workers. I see boxes packed with loaves of white bread, macaroni and cheese, and cans of soup being dropped off door-to-door or handed out at some parking lot.

One of the kids asks about my bike, and when I tell them I rode here from California, I'm bombarded with questions while a couple of people take pictures of me with their phones.

"Where to from here?" one man asks.

"Paducah."

One woman in the back looks at me with wide eyes. "You're not taking 45 over the river are you?"

I think I am, and I tell her so.

A couple of them exchange looks while she shakes her head.

"You need to flag down a truck and have them drive you across that bridge," she tells me. "It's dangerous."

"Someone got hurt real bad out there just last month," another guys adds.

I tell them that I've been through some pretty rough terrain already, and even though a few nod and one guy says "I'll bet you have," the woman in the back looks unconvinced.

"You get a truck to stop for you, hon."

~

A half mile past the workers, letters on a tall chain-link fence spell out WELCOME TO METROPOLIS, and posted above is a big picture of Superman in flight. I follow the signs to the town square, and when I round a corner, I see the Man of Steel himself.

He's about twenty feet high. As his cape billows out to the left, he stands with legs spread and hands on hips. I ride past the "Super Museum"—a massive shrine to all things Superman, which I plan to visit right after I get a closer look at the statue. The sky is gray; rain's on the way again, for sure, so there aren't too many people milling around outside. I ask one guy standing there if he'll take a picture of me in front of ol' Supes. I stand between his massive legs and strike a similar pose. I thank the guy as the air starts getting misty, and then I wheel Rusty into the museum across the street.

It's a funhouse of relics and kitsch. I have a hard time taking it all in, mainly because every square inch of space is packed with Superman memorabilia. It doesn't help that a tinny speaker plays a looped recording of the intro to the 1940s Fleischer cartoon series— "Look! Up in the sky! It's a bird, it's a plane…"—followed by the somber narrator who chronicles Superman's journey from tragic loss to triumphant embodiment of the American Way.

Within glass cases and behind roped-off areas sit props from the movies and television shows, including costumes that for some reason they've put on mannequins resembling child molesters. All sorts of items are on display—action figures, board games, lunch boxes, and cups.

During one hot summer in the 1970s, 7-11 had a promotion where they gave out big plastic cups with comic book characters on them. Vince and I would beg my mom for Slurpees, and we fought bitterly over the best cups. I always lost. He walked away with Mr. Mxyzptlk, Braniac, and Clark Kent tearing off his suit to reveal the big red and yellow "S" beneath, and I got stuck with Ma Kent, Jimmy

Olsen, and Perry White. Those raw deals are made even more clear by the arrangement of cups. The ones Vince had stand front and center, and mine cower—hidden and ashamed—in the back.

A little further on I spot a collection of puzzles, and toward the back is the one that was my favorite as a kid: Superman held tight by the tail of a giant T-Rex. I wonder which of Nick and Tony's toys will lodge themselves in their memories. I hope it's something like that, or the games we've played, or the places we've been, or the books we've read together that they carry with them into adulthood and not something else, like the way their Christmas cards changed when they were eleven and nine.

The final stretch of the museum showcases still photos from the Christopher Reeve movies. In one—from 1978's *Superman*—he's saving a train that hurtles toward a gap in a bridge. One of the rails is bent down and the other is gone completely. In the photo, the Man of Steel holds one rail up with his arm and lets his back serve as the other. Everyone is saved.

The streets are slick with a hard rain that's fallen and passed while I was in the museum. I'm sure more is on the way, but before I go, I make one last pass in front of Superman. I don't look too long, and I'm not sure what it is, but until I turn right off of Sixth Street and put some buildings between the two of us, the pedaling is tough and Rusty feels heavier than normal.

Several blocks later, I find another giant.

Big John Foods sits at the east end of town, and in front is a statue of Big John himself. Like Superman, he has a costume—red shirt, white apron, and blue pants—but his beefy arms don't rest idly on his hips; instead, they hold two bags stuffed with groceries. Even though it's late Sunday afternoon, the number of people pushing carts in the parking lot says this is the place to shop. With the on-and-off rain today, it's going to get dark early, and I still need to cross the river, but I'm not leaving without a picture of this other guy who also stands watch over the good people of Metropolis.

When I finally make it to the bridge, I know why the woman at the Honeywell plant was so worried. From where I'm stopped on the shoulder in front of it, the bridge looks narrow, and I don't see any lanes painted on it. What I do see is a sign warning motorcyclists that it's not safe to cross. There aren't any trucks to flag down for a ride; the few people who need to cross the river at this time are probably doing so on nearby Interstate 24. I take a minute to look it over. Known informally as the "Brookport Bridge" and more formally as the "Irwin Cobb Bridge," the long blue structure stretches out high above the Ohio River for over a mile before it hits Kentucky soil. Aesthetically, its ten steel trusses aren't fancy, but they look strong and solid, just like the people I met back in town. I take a deep breath, start across, and immediately understand the sign. If the people who posted it thought for a second that someone would be stupid enough to cross on a bike, they would have expanded the warning. But they probably assumed no biker in his right mind would ride over a bridge whose floor is made of steel grates large enough to reach an arm through and touch the girders beneath. The sound of my tires over this surface is an angry hum that sounds like an engine belt about to break, and I expect at any moment for one of those fierce metal squares to clamp my front wheel tight and throw me from Rusty.

Even though the drizzle is now gathering itself up into something more, and as much as I want to get to Paducah—which lies just on the other side of the bridge—I stop halfway across. It's soupy and humid out, and there's little activity on the water except for a couple of long barges that creep across the brown surface. Looking downriver, I can see the edge of Metropolis poke into my line of sight. Metropolis, home of Superman.

He was never my favorite comic book hero. I always thought he was too good, too perfect. Sure, there's Kryptonite, but that's really a plot device that has nothing to do with flaws or frailty or any of those inconvenient traits that make us human. And I guess that's the point--Superman isn't human. Staring at his face back in the town square, a generous onlooker might describe him as searching the distance for some wrong to right, but I saw something else. Resignation. It's the look of someone who thinks that this is not his world and we are not his people. It's the look of someone who has wondered more than once if his fall to Earth was some kind of cosmic punishment. It's the look of someone who wants nothing more than to retreat to his Fortress of Solitude and stare at his bottle containing Kandor, the shrunken capital city of Krypton and last remnant of the home he lost.

I can't imagine what the United Steel Workers of Honeywell think as they look at Superman's body, stretched mythically in flight on the town's several signs. He isn't going to make the Honeywell executives do the right thing; he's not big enough to combat greed. Hell, he's not even the biggest guy in town. Even though Big John lacks Superman's classic good looks—his eyebrows are way too thick and his nose looks like it's been broken a few times—he stands almost ten feet taller.

John is a hero to get behind. He's a *real* member of the community, helping out with the mundane but necessary job of grocery shopping. Superman, on the other hand, is exotic, a destination for tourists and curiosity seekers; if possible, the "Super Museum" has an even bigger gift shop than Dodge City. While Superman uses his arms to strike a pose, John's are busy delivering food, maybe to a neighbor in need. If you're a locked-out worker wondering where the next meal is coming from, would you rather see Superman with his x-ray vision at your door or Big John with ground beef, bread, apples, and milk?

The rain's picking up, but I don't move. This bridge may be scary, but because of it I can head into Kentucky whenever I'm ready. Before bridges, rivers were major obstacles. Native Americans and then pioneer explorers would have had to cross the Ohio by canoe. Looking at the current below, I wouldn't want to have been them. Later there were ferryboats, and before the steam engine, those ferries were towed by rowboats. It was a group effort, and even with several hands helping out, I'm sure that people died. Building this bridge was a group effort, too, from the people who designed it to the miners who dug the ore to the millworkers who forged the parts to the workers who riveted and welded it into existence. Anonymous faces working together so that I can cross this river in a few frightening minutes.

*What have you learned so far?*

I'm wet, my legs are tired, and as soon as I hear that awful sound of bike tire on steel grate, I'll wonder if I'm going to make it to the other side. Wouldn't it be great to be able to fly? After all, what's a river to Superman? If he didn't feel like flying, he could still leap over the wide expanse without breaking a sweat. Or maybe alter the water's course with otherworldly strength.

But nobody is more powerful than a locomotive, or faster than a speeding bullet, or invulnerable to everything except a made-up element. We owe a huge, un-repayable debt to all of those anonymous others who grow our food and build our bridges and develop the medicines that save our lives. And we—I—owe just as much to the not-so-anonymous others who hand us a water bottle at a gas station or welcome us into their home or answer the phone when we call from the side of an empty desert road because we're tired and alone. Superman may soar alone across the sky, but that's a fantasy. It's a Big John world out here, and no one can make it very far on his own.

# PART III

---

# The Road Home

"My guide and I came on that hidden road
To make our way back into the bright world;
And with no care for any rest, we climbed—
He first, I following—until I saw,
Through a round opening, some of those things
Of beauty Heaven bears. It was from there
That we emerged, to see—once more—the stars."
—Dante, *The Inferno*

# 25

# X the Unknown

It's raining in Paducah and I'm holed up at the Budget Inn, a skeevy, low-rate motel that's been par for the course on this trip. Instead of a simple window looking out into the parking lot, the wall next to the door is made entirely of glass, and the floor-to-ceiling vinyl drapes won't close all the way. The rain pounds the parking lot, its many craters overflowing with water. I tug the drapes together and jam a chair against the seam. It holds, more or less, though a weak stream of light seeps in at the top, illuminating the droplets on the glass. Like a lot of the places I've found myself at night, nobody is around and the frills are few. The motel promised free wi-fi, but I've learned this means the office has a little router, and if you're not in one of the rooms right next to the lobby or standing in the lobby itself, you're out of luck. The manager—a heavy-lidded guy in a white tank top who took one look at Rusty and grunted—said I wouldn't have a problem. But I can't get a signal.

It doesn't matter. I'm too tired to do much more than lie on the itchy bedspread and stare at the peeling flecks of ceiling paint.

This is the eighth state of my trip.

This is the seventh straight day of rain.

This is my sixth week on the road.

"You sound tired," Shannon tells me five seconds into our call.

"I am."

"So you just biked through rain?" Nick asks me. "That's sick."

In this context, sick is a good thing. Sick is cool, sick is boss.

"I don't like this," my dad tells me, yet again.

And in this last phone conversation of the night, I find myself once more wishing that he and I saw the same world more than we do.

"You wanna talk to Mom?" he asks.

"Sure."

If she has any memory of my being there a week ago, she doesn't say, and she doesn't ask her usual question. Could be my married life is now one more thing that's slipped away from her.

After we hang up, I picture the two of them in that house, my mom on the couch in front of the television and my dad at the kitchen table, shaking his head over his younger son, who always seems to make things more difficult than they have to be. What else can he do with this worry? A few years ago, he might have talked to my mom, but not anymore. I'm guessing that right now he's as alone as I am, and imagining this to be true, I feel a little bit closer to him.


Outside of a Kroger the next morning, I'm trying to set up a place to stay tomorrow night in Clarksville, Tennessee. On the sixth ring I'm about to hang up when my potential host answers. His name is Lawson Mabry, and his voice is a smooth pour of Southern Comfort.

"Whatever you need, be glad to help you out," he tells me.

After we hang up, I pass through Paducah's array of muffler shops and tattoo parlors and head into the country, where long, straight driveways appear with the irregularity of broken teeth on a comb. At the end of each lies a cozy house and a tree-lined plot. Gas stations and fast food restaurants sprout up around Interstate 69, and after that, I cross the Tennessee River and ride into the Land between the Lakes, a hilly nature preserve nestled between Kentucky Lake and Lake Barkley.

It's late afternoon and growing overcast by the time I get to the park headquarters, which is not quite halfway through the preserve. Nobody is on duty, the food I bought that morning is gone, and the only vending machine has drinks. As I dig a few quarters from the dark corners of my handlebar bag, I eye the picture of a blue PowerAde on the machine.

Of course, that one's sold out. So is every other flavor of PowerAde. I resign myself to a can of Mello Yello, which I drain without blinking.

In the few minutes that I've stopped, the rolling clouds have darkened the sky even more. According to the map outside the ranger station, I've got ten miles to go before I hit the Tennessee state line, and fifteen more after that before Dover, my destination tonight. I toss the can in a recycling bin, get on Rusty, and head back to the hills.

Five miles from Dover, the sky drops on top of me. It's not one of those gradually building rains; it's an instant storm, and it's followed quickly by night. There's nowhere to stop, no kind of temporary shelter, just some bison in a field to my right and a drenched coyote that skulks across the road in front of me. No cars, fortunately, so all I have to worry about are the heavy gray sheets of water.

Following my little headlight through the rain, I eventually hit Highway 79 and see a motel about a half mile up the road. Of course the highway bends uphill, and of course the motel—the Dover Inn— sits higher still, atop a steep circular driveway.

When I wheel myself into the lobby, soaking wet and barely able to stand, some giggling women are checking in at the counter. They and their matching suitcases look as fresh as spring, and I know if I touch any of their arms, I'd feel the chill of their air-conditioned car.

"Ladies," I say. "I'm telling you right now that if you get the last room, I'm gonna fight you for it."

They giggle even louder.

Turns out there are rooms enough to go around, and when I finally get to mine, I stand in the doorway, hovering between the icy air in front of me and the muggy breath at my back. I reach up to take off my helmet, and when my hands get close to my face, I get a whiff of ammonia. *What the shit?*

I look at my palms, covered by faded red biking gloves. When I bring them closer, I immediately pull back. Both have been collecting my sweat all afternoon, and they reek of ammonia.

I'm not too tired to realize this isn't normal. A quick Google search on my phone—"Why does my sweat smell like ammonia?"—results in a lot of hits. I can't wrap my mind around the chemistry, but what I do understand is that my body isn't getting enough fats and carbs and water, so it's starting to consume the proteins in my muscles.

I am, literally, eating myself.

As soon as I change, I walk across the street to the Piggly Wiggly and then back again to scarf down a whole roasted chicken, a bag of rolls, a half pound of strawberries, a can of pineapple rings and the juice, a half bag of pretzel sticks, a half pint of Ben and Jerry's Chunky Monkey ice cream, a giant Gatorade, and pint of chocolate milk.

I stare at the empty containers and cans and cartons that now overflow the tiny garbage can next to the television and realize I'm still hungry.

Later, on the balcony, I study the Dover night as it's laid out in front of me. The rain has stopped, but the heat combines with the soaked ground to create a layer of mist that looks like a white, moving carpet. It's quiet except for the occasional hiss of car on wet pavement, the soft murmurs of people downstairs, and the hum of the AC exhaust, which blasts hot air on my arm. Across the street, the Piggly Wiggly is closed, but the neon pig's grotesque smile still glows over the empty, rain-slick parking lot.

I figure that I'm a little more than a week away from Atlantic Ocean, but when I try to form some picture—any picture of what the end of this thing might look like—nothing comes into focus.

•

When I was a kid, Saturdays meant two things. The first was

chores. My dad organized the work detail, but the assignments were pretty much the same every week. I dusted and Vince vacuumed. It was a drag but a small price to pay for the second thing. Monsters. *Scooby Doo* in the morning, *The Monstrous Movie* right after lunch, and *Creature Features* at night. The latter two shows played on Channel 32—one of those old UHF channels that you adjusted with a dial like you were cracking a safe—and they introduced me to Gamera, Ghidorah, the Wolfman, Frankenstein's monster and his bride, and the Mushroom People. They also introduced me to the most troubling letter of the alphabet—the letter X.

X was the radioactive mud creature in *X the Unknown*. X was Ray Milland in *X: the Man with the X-ray Eyes*. X was also Monster X and Planet X, home of hostile aliens bent on conquering Earth by kidnapping Godzilla and Rodan.

There was Dr. X, a movie villain, and Professor X, a comic book hero.

Speaking of comics, X abounds. The rest of the X-men, for example, and also "X—the Thing that Lived!" from *Fear #2*, a comic I read until either it fell apart or my mom threw it out; I can't remember.

X as in Racer X, Speed's long-lost brother.

X as in "solving for x," which was the bane of my existence in seventh grade algebra.

Used as a cartoon character's eyes, X means drunkenness, delirium, or death.

From an illiterate's pen, X is an identity.

X closes a window on a computer; X marks the spot on a map.

X is a blank, a mystery. It's what we don't know, or maybe what we're afraid to know.

●

In the morning I'm tired even before I get on Rusty, and once we're on the road, I have to will my dead legs to keep pedaling. It's more than the predictable exhaustion that comes with long distance biking. It's the blanket of wet that hangs over everything. It's the thick air, the gray, featureless sky, the fog. It's the shoulder littered with dead animals—frogs flattened as if by a steamroller, a pile of dead fish with mouths agape, eyes bulging, backs torn open to reveal browning flesh pierced by tiny pin bones. It's the Jesus billboards, like the one up ahead of me now that reads JUDGMENT DAY IS AT HAND.

Highway 79 broadens as I enter the Clarksville metro area, and as the traffic picks up, I move to the far right of the garbage-strewn shoulder. Years ago, some developers thought it would be a good idea to machine-scrape all available land and put in rows and rows of strip malls. Cracked store signs in the parking lots preside grimly over a few shoppers who trudge across the asphalt.

Further on is the heart of downtown Clarksville, which is much older but not nearly as exhausted. The roads get steeper, the blocks get shorter, and the buildings morph from industrial ugly into stately brick-and-stone structures. Clarksville is the Montgomery County seat, so the most impressive of these old buildings is the courthouse, where spires rise on either side of a clock tower and a statue of Lady Justice. A few turns later and I'm in a residential area where ancient yellow poplars shade the roads and grand columned houses stare down imperiously from rolling lawns. And a few turns after that, I'm in front of Lawson's place.

A manicured lawn surrounds a massive red brick house capped with brown shingles. I walk Rusty up the winding driveway to the back, where there's a two-story garage attached to the main house by a covered walkway, and a smaller structure—maybe a pool house?—off to the left, both clad in identical brick and shingles. A stone patio fills the space between all three buildings, and beyond that is a yard that's an explosion of flowering bushes, shade, and trees.

I've got just a few seconds to register all this before I hear a door open behind me.

"Well, I expect you're Rocco."

Lawson approaches, hand extended. He's tall and lean, somewhere in his late fifties.

"That's quite a setup," he says, bending over to study Rusty. "How much're you carrying there? Fifty, sixty pounds?"

"Closer to fifty," I say. "I shed some weight back in Colorado."

"I'll bet," he smiles. "And not the only weight you been shedding, am I right?"

This reminds me how hungry I am. And that I'm a mess. The day is still humid, but it's clear now, and under the sun's yellow glare, my still-damp clothes are creating a pocket of steam around my body.

"We'll set you up in the carriage house if that's all right."

"All right" doesn't quite capture how all right it is. The carriage house is the entire second story of the garage, and it's got a sitting room, a bedroom with a four poster bed, and a bathroom with a stone tiled shower that's so big it doesn't need a door. I can barely keep up with the features that Lawson describes as he shows me around. He turns to me and claps his hands together.

"So what's your pleasure, Professor?" he asks. "Shower or food?"

After a hot shower, my body no longer smells like it's been housing marine life, and I feel fit for the company of others. Down in the kitchen, Lawson has laid out sandwich fixings, and he invites me to make one, and then as many more as I want after he watches me devour the first in seconds flat.

"I imagine you get hungry as a bear out there."

"It's a little hard to keep up," I say around a mouthful of smoked turkey and cheddar.

I'm polishing off my third sandwich when Lawson's wife and kids burst through the door. A little dog appears to greet them, and the kitchen is suddenly alive with chatter and barking. All three kids are younger than Nick and Tony, and after Lawson makes introductions, I'm struck by how the kids extend their hands to shake mine. Their little fingers are dry and cool, fresh from an air-conditioned minivan, and their smiles hint at the fine men and lady that they will someday become.

•

X is what Nick and Tony will be in five years, ten years, and beyond, all of it shaped in unpredictable ways by biology and circumstance. The biology part isn't too hard to figure; they reflect a bizarre Jekyll and Hyde split of my own personality. While Nick plans, makes lists, and wears his watch to bed, Tony has less fun creating order than disrupting it, and what he usually disrupts is his brother's carefully ordered world.

The "circumstance" part is another story. When we were still a family, the X of my boys' futures was uncertain enough, but now that one house has become two, how will their X be shaped? How will it be shaped when they're old enough to understand more than they do now, assuming that they haven't already pieced that part of the puzzle together?

Maybe I'm destined to play out with my kids the uneasy, disconnected relationship I have with my own parents. Or maybe our connections will erode slowly as the two of them move into exciting new spaces of adulthood. Or maybe they'll break dramatically when certain mistakes come into full view. Or maybe one or both them will develop into their own version of Mistah Secrets, deciding through biology or circumstance that the best identity is the one that's kept hidden.

Alone and far away, it's easy to imagine X the Unknown in the worst possible terms. It's easy to imagine my boys as older men and maybe with kids of their own, studying the map of my life—the summer I rode my bike across the country being just one section. It's easy to imagine them shake their heads in disbelief and think, *How could he be so irresponsible?*

X is the road that leads into a country whose contours are dark and where there are no reliable maps.

•

Lawson sells real estate in Clarksville, where he's lived all his life, and he has to be the most well-read real estate agent in the city, if not the entire state. His degree from Austin Peay State University is in English, and every year he attends the Clarksville Writers' Conference. As he takes me on a driving tour of the area, he fires the names of his favorite southern writers at me, and they aren't the obvious ones like Faulkner or O'Connor. Instead, he tells me about William Gay, who's a regular at the conference; Ward Dorrance, who cowrote a collection of stories called *The White Hound* with Thomas Mabry; and that same Thomas Mabry, who happens to be a cousin of Lawson's.

We head downtown to Riverside Drive, which runs along the Cumberland River. Lawson is craned over the wheel, squinting into the corners of the windshield and pointing out different buildings. One was destroyed by a tornado, rebuilt, and then ruined in a flood. One was a tobacco warehouse, the largest in this part of the state. One used to be a nicotine factory but is now a nightclub. And another one—a red-brick mansion with wrought-iron balconies and carved cornices—is known as the Forbes-Mabry House.

"How long has your family been here?" I ask.

"Since about eighteen hundred."

"In Clarksville?"

"Yessir."

"You must know a lot about your past," I say.

He winks at me. "Wait'll we get home. I got some things you might find interesting."

Back at the house, we sit in Lawson's office. Two big banker's boxes lie on the floor between us.

"I've become the unofficial historian of our family," he tells me.

"Find something old, send it to Lawson."

Before he shows me these old somethings, he describes the thicker branches of his family tree. These, it turns out, are fairly long, reaching out of Clarksville and pointing east and south toward Virginia, North Carolina, Alabama, and even Colonial Haiti. Affixed to these branches like nests are old homes, farmland, and plantations of mainly tobacco and sugar.

I don't ask the question that's formed in my head. It's a reasonable question, given that we're in the South, that his family has lived here and elsewhere in the region for generations, and that a lot of them were landowners.

As if hearing my thoughts, Lawson says, "There're some skeletons."

He reaches into one of the boxes, his fingers shuffling through the tightly-packed pages until he finds a stack he wants, extracts it, and hands it to me.

"My ancestors owned people," he tells me, his voice dropping the cheerful tone I've been hearing since I arrived. This sentence is strange to hear, no doubt stranger to say, and stranger still to think about in terms of the limitations of language. How can four simple words possibly carry the weight of something like slavery? The fact that they can't is clear from the careful way that Lawson steps through his narrative.

What he knows is that one set of ancestors owned slaves in Virginia and freed them before the war, while another set of ancestors owned slaves in Tennessee and freed them after the war. A third group of slaves were owned and then freed by an Alabama doctor whose niece, Anna, married into Lawson's family, bringing with her an inheritance built, in part, on the toil of those slaves.

Lawson understands that our ties to history are complicated and sometimes demand more than intellectual curiosity or abstraction, especially because the burden of the past isn't abstract; the documents Lawson has scrupulously maintained make sure of that. One of these documents is a will from 1845 that splits a large farm in Clarksville and divides the slaves—listed along with other property—among the surviving heirs. Another is a letter written by one of Lawson's ancestors in 1859. In it, he offers to sell a blacksmith named Harry for two hundred and fifty dollars on the condition that he be "allowed a reasonable time to visit his wife."

Also bringing the past to life have been the descendants of these slaves, a few of whom have contacted Lawson. One was a man named Jackie, who organized a family reunion several years back in nearby Fort Campbell. Like Lawson, Jackie lives in Clarksville, and the local paper wrote a story about the two men—one a descendent of slaves and the other of slave owners—coming together to understand their shared and troubled past.

Another descendant, a woman named Sharon, doggedly pursued details about her history and traced her family line to the slaves owned by the Alabama doctor. When Lawson's name kept appearing in her various genealogical searches, she thought she found some distant relative, and in a way, she had. They weren't blood kin, but to Lawson's way of thinking, they weren't exactly unrelated, either. Lawson was a link to her past, and he helped her fill in some of the bare branches of her own family tree. His help is part of his natural kindness, a quality I picked up on from our first brief phone call. But it also comes from a desire to address the past he inherited.

And then there's X the Unknown. Lawson knows how troubling blank spots can be and how satisfying it is to watch them take on form and substance.

•

My sons have said more than once that they wished "Kid Rocco" could go with them to school for a day. Kid Rocco. I liked that. Made me feel like a boxer. When I asked why, Tony shrugged and said, "I dunno. It'd be cool to see what you were like as a kid."

I've felt that about my dad, too, but his past is marked by X. He can recall some of his days as a young man, but they all crystallize into a few stories that he tells and retells—returning from overseas, meeting Miss Fortune, working at different jobs over the years. The problem is that his memories lack details.

Even less clear is the time he spent in the army.

When he talks about that time, his answers are vague, typically ending with a little laugh.

"Whaddaya want? It was a long time ago!"

"You wrote letters to Grandma, right?"

"Yeah, sure."

"Are they still around?"

"Nah. That stuff, they threw it all out."

His parents, his grandmother, and his aunts were all unsentimental when it came to memories. Gone are those letters, my father's army uniform, and his old stamp collection.

"I had stamps from some countries, they don't exist anymore."

In their house on their block in 1940s Brooklyn, space was at a premium. Twelve people on three tiny floors. There was a small cellar and attic, but city fire inspectors were known to cite residences that let things accumulate in these spaces. Plus, there was a war on and a future to build and plan for. Why hang on to the past?

I can piece some of my dad's military service together from what he remembers and what I've researched. He arrived at Leyte, in the Philippines, in April of 1945 after having spent forty days at sea. The trip from California was supposed to take a little over two weeks, but there was an accident near Midway Atoll. Out at sea, transport ships would zigzag as a safety precaution against torpedo attacks from enemy subs. During one of these maneuvers, two vessels collided, and my dad's was left with a hole torn in the hull above the water line. They had to wait weeks for a repair ship; in the meantime, up on deck, there was nothing to see except water and an escort destroyer left behind to protect them. When the ship finally showed, its crew pumped concrete into the hole to seal it up. My father finally set foot on the shore of the Philippines about six months after General Douglas MacArthur did, and about four months after the Battle of the Leyte Gulf decisively put an end to Japanese occupation in that island nation. He was stationed there in July of 1945 when the *U.S.S. Indianapolis*, just after delivering the atomic bomb to the island of Tinian, was torpedoed and sunk on the way to his base. Almost 1,200 men on that ship had hoped to see Leyte, but the Japanese and the sharks reduced that number to a little over 300 in one of the worst naval disasters in U.S. history. My father was still stationed there a few weeks later, when the U.S. bombed Hiroshima and Nagasaki, and later still on September 2nd of that year, when the Japanese surrendered.

In the handful of his pictures that survived that time, he's young and seemingly removed from the weight of the history unfolding around him. In early 1945 he was barely nineteen years old, the same age as many of my students, but because he's my father, I can't quite think of him as fresh and adventurous. Who is this young man, shirtless, hands on hips, standing behind three water buffalos? Or on the beach, shirtless again, behind a canoe? I've never seen my father around either animals or water. When the boy in these photographs tries to imagine what's ahead for him, what does he see?

•

Lawson hoists the second of the two banker's boxes onto a low wooden table that lets out a tiny creak as it absorbs the weight. He sets his hand on top of the box and looks at me.

"Now this here's really something," he tells me. "Crown jewel of the collection."

The box holds nearly four hundred letters, notes, receipts, and bills that belonged to Anna, the niece of the Alabama doctor who freed his slaves. She was born in 1842, grew up in Tuscaloosa, and married into the Mabry family in 1868. The earliest documents begin around 1860, when Anna was eighteen years old, and end with her obituary in 1913.

"We'd heard Anna's name before, cropping up every so often in family stories," he says, lifts the lid off of the box, and looks through his reading glasses at the file tabs sticking out. "She was like a ghost that haunted our past here in Clarksville." His hand caresses the tops of the exposed documents. "What's in here brought her back to us. Otherwise she'd have gone the way of most folks…forgotten."

"Your family saved all these?"

"My cousin was cleaning out her attic a year and a half ago and found them. Had no idea they were there."

He pulls out a stapled packet of papers from the front of the box and hands it to me. It's a nearly thirty page overview, written by his mother. The first line reads, "Every life is a story," and the rest reflects on the importance of the written word, which to a certain class of people in the 1800s was the main means of expression.

Like the other documents, these remnants of Anna's life are protected by plastic sleeves. Each one encases thin, yellowed sheets covered in slanted writing. Before reading the words, I study the sheets themselves. The writing extends to nearly all four edges of paper that's so thin the words from the back appear, ghostlike, on the side I'm reading.

"She was a real southern belle," Lawson says, leaning back in his chair. "All kinds of suitors. Notes sent back and forth. Wordy invites to go on walks and the like." He reaches over with a long finger and taps the corner of the stack in my hands. "Those are something special."

I'm holding letters to Anna from a man named Oliver James Lawrence. He was a forty-four year old lawyer in Tuscaloosa when he left his practice and joined the army, making him—Lawson guesses—one of the oldest privates in the Confederacy. As a member of an Alabama artillery unit known as Tarrant's Battery, he saw a good deal of action. In one letter he tells "Miss Anna" that the conditions are "cold, gloomy, showery weather—a noticeable fact in this land of perennial verdure." Nevertheless, the soldiers are in high spirits because they're expecting to rebuff a "yankee raid." He writes, "The glee & alacrity manifested in our having to obey Gen. Clanton's order to march gives assurance that a meeting with the vandals will be accepted with great satisfaction and eagerness."

As I read these words, I can hear in their wonderful verbosity the richness of the Southern drawl. They're careful sentences, thick and dense like the Spanish moss on the trees outside. It's also clear that this is no simple correspondence between friends. When Private Lawrence switches from affairs of men to affairs of the heart, he writes in a letter from July of 1864, "I never expect to be married while you are single, and I yet hope that you will smile on my suit and make me the happiest of all men."

"So what happened with them?" I ask.

"He never made it back."

In January of 1868, Anna married a farmer from Clarksville named John Elliot Mabry, a widower twenty years her senior. A little over four months later, he committed suicide. For the next two years, there is no record of correspondence either to or from Anna. Given the penchant for members of this particular family to write, it seems unlikely that everyone remained silent. The more logical answer is that Anna couldn't bear to keep any of the letters. What went through her mind is impossible to know.

There's a second period of silence that begins in 1903, but unlike the first one, it's never broken. Instead, it extends over what turns out to be the last ten years of Anna's life. Her obituary sheds a little light on the silence, announcing that she "died of senility after a gradual decline." I wonder about those last years. I wonder if Anna ever sifted through these notes and letters and tried to remember the faces of the people who wrote to her and to whom she wrote. I wonder if she tried to recognize her own face in those words, or if her life had already slipped across the border and into the land of X the Unknown.

•

For my mom, X marks a spot on a map that's worn and faded. I can't double-check facts or ask questions to get the details I need. There's no treasure chest of documents waiting to be unearthed.

But X extends beyond my mom; it's a broken link to more past. X is my mom's father—my grandfather, my namesake—who died nine years before I was born. Because he was the grandparent I never knew, he is the one to whom I am most drawn. He was the one I never had a name for, so now he stands in my mind simply as Rocco Tursi.

What I know about Rocco Tursi can be covered in a paragraph. He was born in Bari, Italy, came to America at age eighteen, and was a baker in the American Army during World War I. He worked as an iceman until refrigerators put him out of a job, a coal man until oil heaters put him out of a job, and a laundry man until washing machines put him out of a job. Eventually, he caught up with the times and worked in a television factory, and he did this until his sixty-one-year-old heart gave out. He married Lucy Milillo, and together they had four girls that he made go to church every Sunday. He loved to cook, loved to sing, loved to listen to his records of Caruso until two of his daughters—my mother and my Aunt Angie—sold them for a dollar one Saturday to the junk man because they wanted some spending money. He loved to garden and especially loved his fig tree. He was careful to bundle it before each winter, and it rewarded him with figs as big as plums. He loved his daughters but wanted a son, and when he heard the news about the Lindbergh baby—about how someone climbed a ladder in the middle of the night and snatched the sleeping boy from his crib—he cried.

But when I think of Rocco Tursi, he remains an iceman. That's the picture I know him through, the picture framed in my parents' hallway, the picture I saw every day growing up. In it, he wears a short sleeved white shirt and dark pants. His right arm hangs down at his side, and his left hand rests on the bridle of his horse, *D'humbrid*. The horse, who liked to run away, is tied to a rickety-looking wooden cart that reads "Rocco Tursi" on its side. This was the cart he used to haul ice and coal to the people of Flatbush. Rocco Tursi's eyes squint at the camera. Whether that squint comes from the weariness of hauling ice, or from the strain of raising four high-spirited girls, or simply from the glare of the New York summer sun is hard to say.

About the past, it's always hard to say. Even my own memories from childhood. What actually happened and what's been changed and misremembered over time? Do I really remember falling into that pool as a five-year-old, or am I just retelling the story that my mom told me?

X is a washed-out bridge that we need to carry us across the murky water between the shores of what's known and what's unknown.

•

The next morning Beth cooks up a big breakfast of pancakes and fruit, the perfect biking fuel. When the dishes are cleared and my offers to help rebuffed, Lawson and I look over my map. I'm not sure how to get through the rest of Tennessee and into North Carolina, but he's got some ideas, starting with back roads out of Clarksville that will keep me far from Nashville-bound traffic. He charts a course that runs parallel to Interstates 24 and 40 and then connects with a road that will take me through the Appalachian Mountains and into North Carolina.

As the carbs from breakfast seep into our blood, Lawson leans back and asks me why I'm riding across the country. I tell him what I think I know at this point, and then I ask him why he's been collecting all this history. In response, he tells me a story that makes me reconsider everything I just said to him. Before I go too far down that road, though, he claps me on the shoulder.

"Well, Professor, this is a heck of an adventure you're on," he says.

•

This is the story my mom told me more than any other.

In 1957 my parents had been married for almost ten years and still had no children to show for it. For two Italian-American Catholics in the 1950s, this was unusual, the subject of conversations. Around Christmas of that year, someone on my mother's side of the family was throwing a party. There was no shortage of family get togethers. Holidays, of course, but Sunday dinners, too, all filled with in-laws, brothers, sisters, and cousins.

Rocco Tursi had grown tired of these festivities. He would go to this party, but he took his time getting ready and grunted as he walked down the cement stairs outside the house, taking extra care to guide his and Lucy's way over the ice.

—*Sprigati!* she called. We'll be late!

—Yeah, yeah.

Didn't he see these people enough during the year? Why couldn't he spend a nice Saturday night alone with a glass of wine? Why ruin a perfectly good evening with his *ugatz* brother-in-law Bozo?

Rocco couldn't remember how his sister's husband had gotten that nickname, but who cared? All Rocco knew was that he couldn't stand him. He never let up. Like with Rocco's youngest daughter, Toni. When Bozo found out that her fiancé's family had changed their name from Bennedetto to Bennett, he raised his thick eyebrows and brought it up every chance he got. *What are they ashamed of, Rocco? Who changes their names? I'll tell you who—criminals!*

At the party the topic of conversation was Bozo's own daughter. Bozo refused to attend her wedding because she married a Sicilian. Now he wasn't talking to her because she and that Sicilian husband of hers hadn't named their second son after him, as was custom. Rocco listened to as much of this as he could, but every get together was the same thing. Bozo's endless complaints. He knew he should just keep his mouth shut, but he could feel his insides boiling. He saw his daughters begin to gather close to each other with looks on their faces. They recognized the beginning of a storm. It was a sign to stop, but he couldn't.

—*Lo spirito di contraddizione!* It's always complaining with you!

Bozo waved his hand, but Rocco kept talking.

—Look at you, he said to Bozo. You have a good business, steady work, my beautiful sister as your wife. And you still complain?

He could feel Lucy's frown from across the room.

—And look at me, Rocco said. Four daughters I got. No one's named after me! Do I complain?

He stomped out of the room, careful to avoid Lucy. He would face her, but not right then.

He went through the kitchen and out onto the back patio. It was cold, and he left his jacket inside, but he'd be damned if he would walk back in there. Instead, he crossed his arms and watched his angry breath take shape in the air before him. The night was filled with sounds. Music, a baby crying, a car horn. With the houses so close together, he couldn't tell where it all was coming from.

The door behind him creaked open. *Lucia*, he though, and closed his eyes. *You're angry and have every right to be.*

—Pop, here, take this. You'll catch cold.

His daughter Nikki draped his jacket over his shoulders.

—Your mother, she's angry.

—Yeah, but she don't like Uncle Bozo much, neither.

He turned back around.

—It's a beautiful night, *cara mia.*

—Pop, she said, leaning close. Pop, I'm gonna have a son and name him after you.

—Nicholetta, *mia dolce figlia.* You and Tommy, you been married these years and no child. And if God blesses you with a son, he'll be Vincent, after Tommy's pop.

He smiled sadly and patted her hand.

—Now you're gonna have two sons?

—Pop, I'm gonna name a son after you. I promise.

•

Tennessee rolls by in a succession of tobacco fields and small towns.

I spend one morning on a road that disappears into fog-shrouded mountains like something from *The Lord of the Rings*.

I spend another morning entertaining some women at the Carthage Wal-Mart who won't believe I'm from California until I show them my driver's license.

I spend the rest of that day climbing the Cumberland Plateau, an elevated swath of land that runs diagonally through eastern Tennessee. The heat and humidity make it hard enough, but then I exercise horrible judgment at a diner called Maddie's Place in Cookeville, where I stoke my body's furnace with a BLT, tater tots, and a bowl of fried Oreos.

I spend the morning after that on the gentle grades atop the Plateau, and while I'm there, I pause in my ride for twenty or so minutes to sit on a wooden bench at a roadside bait shop. In the distance, a red barn and silo sit among rolling wooded hills. Watching long shadows glide across those hills, I eat a vanilla Moonpie as a spotted dog unfolds itself from beside a Coke machine to see if I'll share.

While I sit there and give him a few pieces, I pull out my map of Tennessee. I bought it only five days ago, but it looks like an ancient parchment from another time. Folded and refolded several different ways, the sharp creases have become slack, and furred craters have appeared at the places where those creases meet. The paper is soft and soggy from the rain, and some of the town's names have flaked away. I can still see the shortcut that Lawson drew with a thin black marker over a blank area on the map, but the orange hi-liter I used to chart my intended path is almost completely bleached away by the sun. As I trace this ghosted path with my finger, my eyes wander to other towns north and south of it, towns with names like Goose Horn, Yankeetown, Hanging Limb, Difficult, and Wartburg. Maybe someday I'll take the time to visit these and other places, but right now the road I'm on is about all I can handle. Waiting for me up ahead is X the Unknown, and I've got the feeling that things are going to get harder before they get any easier.

# VOICES FROM THE ROAD

# 26

# Cherohala

"Do you know what it means?"

The girl in front of me—Maria, according to her nametag—can't be much older than seventeen. Around her neck she's wearing what I thought was a little gold unicorn but is actually a little gold centaur, and he's galloping around her collar as she bags my candy bars, pretzels, raisins, and almonds at the Tellico Plains Sav-A-Lot. She shakes her head in answer to my question and calls over her shoulder to the girl at the next register.

"Hey Sandy," she says. "What's 'Cherohala' mean?"

Sandy's line is empty. She studies her fingernails and doesn't look up. "Probably some Indian word."

Maria turns back to me.

"Some Indian word I guess," she says and hands me my bag.

Outside the Sav-A-Lot, traffic is light even though it's mid-morning on a Saturday. I'm about a block north of the intersection of Highways 68 and 165, and after I'm done eating the Three Musketeers bar I just unwrapped, I'm going to bike that block and head east on 165, which is known more commonly around here as the Cherohala Skyway. When Lawson helped me plot my course through the rest of Tennessee, he said that the Cherohala—a "scenic byway" running through the Appalachian Mountains and into North Carolina—was spectacular.

"Highlight of your trip, Professor," he said. "No doubt about it."

Three hours later, I'm having serious doubts about it.

The scenery was nice at first. Lots of trees, big rocks. It probably continued to be nice, but it's been hard to pay attention because for the entire time I've been on this road, it has twisted and turned upward with no relief in sight. Every time I round a bend, every time I catch a glimpse of sky and expect the road to level off and then drop, the road rises into yet another false peak. Two hours ago I had it in my head that the summit was just a little way off, another quarter mile at the most. I don't know why I thought that; it just seems that hours of climbing should amount to something. But the road keeps going up and so do I.

A roar grows behind me and builds until I can feel it in my chest. I keep pedaling; I've been on this road long enough to know what it is.

Seven motorcycles thunder past on my left.

Then more come the other way. Then some more after that. Then a huge pack—maybe fifteen bikes, all chopping up the air with loud, angry coughs—races by from behind.

And so has it been, and so does it go. All day, climbing and motorcycles. I hate them both, but I focus my rage on the cycles and their noise, their thick tires, their shiny chrome.

Their engines.

And I hate their riders, too, with their ZZ Top beards, leather vests, and thick, hairy forearms.

Okay, I don't hate them all. The ones who throw me a peace sign or a thumbs-up or a few quick taps on the horn as they pass, they're all right. But the rest of them need to get the hell off my mountain and let me suffer in peace.

Sometime later I stop at a scenic overlook to get my bearings, but this particular spot isn't marked on my map, which shows little more than a crooked line on a green background. I go to the bathroom, and when I come out, there's a family gathered around Rusty. We go through the usual script—they ask me where I'm from, and then they ask me if I'm crazy.

The dad is a guy named Randy, who's wearing a t-shirt that says "Save the Skunk Ape." After I try my best to convince him that I'm not crazy, I ask him if he knows where the peak is. But Randy and his family have come from Tennessee just like me, and this overlook is as far east as they're heading.

"Sorry, bud," he says. "Can I take a picture of you?"

"Are you hungry?" his wife, Sharon, asks me, and before I can answer, she adds, "I'll fix you a sandwich."

She retreats to a minivan while Randy poses me in front of Rusty and tells me all about the Skunk Ape. A few minutes later, Sharon comes back with two peanut butter and jelly sandwiches in Baggies and a bottle of Gatorade. Tethered to her wrist and waddling hard to keep up is a chubby little pug.

"You want more, you just say so, sweetheart," she says and pats my arm while her dog licks my shoe.

•

Back in Prescott, Arizona, I stayed with a guy named Dave who took me to a hole-in-the-wall Mexican restaurant that didn't serve alcohol but let customers carry in their own. The owners provided some help in the form of corkscrews and church keys hung on little hooks throughout the place. I had just used one myself to pry the cap from an icy Sierra Nevada that Dave passed to me.

Dave had forgotten more about biking than I would ever know, and the more we talked, the more I was convinced I had no idea what I was doing. The Sierra Nevadas kept coming along with questions about my ride, and the conversation slowly zeroed in on the hazards of the road.

"Been chased by a dog yet?" he asked.

When I told him I hadn't, he leaned back, smiled, and raised his bottle as if he was making a toast. "Don't worry. Before this is over, it'll happen."

He was right.

But before it happened, I received all kinds of advice about what to do when it did. Later that night Dave showed me a hand pump that he bent on a Rotweiller's back some years before. The clubbing approach was popular; two days later, when I told a ranger at the Grand Canyon that I planned to cut through the northeast corner of Arizona, she said to be sure I had a stick "for the rez dogs."

At a gas station in Utah, a guy approached me as I wolfed down a package of Twinkies. He also biked and favored a water bottle for dogs, saying, "A good shot of water in the face'll turn 'em every time."

Colorado bikers had their own ideas. A young guy I met just east of the Rockies said that whenever he saw a barking dog ahead, he just pedaled right at him and "backed the sonofabitch down." It made a lot of sense at the time, but I later wondered how it would work in a flank attack. Another guy was brief and direct: "Pedal your ass off." A couple I stayed with warned that I should "never, ever try to outrun them" because it just makes them charge harder. The thing to do, they advised, was to let them know I wasn't scared. *But how?* I thought. *And what if I was scared?*

And out on the plains, I met a guy who had been on the road for almost a year. His load was stacked high, covered in gray tarps and trussed tight with bungee cords. A crumpled cereal box poked out of the top. Sun and rain had faded its multi-colored four-letter name into a single, sickly hue of pinkish gray, but it was still legible—*l-i-f-e*. Under a clear sky with train tracks to our left and alfalfa to our right, he reminded me that dogs were pack animals, so they always obey the top dog. Then he smiled and said with the kind of assurance best displayed by the worst politicians, "Just bark at them. They'll back down if you're loud enough."

It sounded reasonable at the time.

So I practiced my bark on empty stretches of road. As it grew more robust and intimidating, I convinced myself it would repel any and all canine challengers.

When I was almost out of Kansas, I got my chance. A big red Chow popped through a hole in his fence and made straight for my rear tire. Or my foot. It was hard to tell. I turned my head at him and unleashed a staccato burst of *ugh-ugh-ugh*s. It was the bark I'd been working on, the one I sharpened into what I thought was a perfect announcement that I was Top Dog, Leader of the Pack, the One Who Must Be Obeyed.

It wasn't. It just made him madder.

He looked up at me and began to snarl and slobber in earnest. As our eyes locked, an unmistakable message passed from his to mine. *I'm going for that ankle, you sonofabitch.*

Three things worked in my favor. It was early, so I had energy; the road was flat; and this Chow had no doubt been living a cushy life of couch naps and Snausages on demand. I resorted to instinct and pedaled like hell. He was soon a memory.

It took a constant onslaught of farm dogs through Missouri, three big-shouldered mutts in Illinois, and a wild-eyed, mangy golden retriever in Kentucky to learn a very simple lesson.

Never, ever bark at what's chasing you.

•

Still climbing, I hear a metallic wheeze growing behind me. It's not a motorcycle; it sounds big—too big to share the road. I pull over and try not to think about how I'm going to get over three hundred pounds of gear, bike, and person moving up a steep grade from a dead stop. I turn and look at the bend behind me, where a laboring RV materializes, followed by a parade of vehicles waiting to pass. There's a white pickup with a long flatbed trailer, a red SUV, and—bringing up the rear—a car with a trunk painted in primer and a back window that's all plastic sheeting and duct tape.

•

Elizabeth drove our minivan and I drove our Geo Prizm, so when I left, I took the Prizm. At that point, the air conditioning had already conked out, and it wasn't worth the expense to get it fixed for the two or three weeks we might actually need it in temperate San Diego. At the time, it was the car's only real problem.

But then little things began to fail.

First was the cupholder. Some crucial plastic housing cracked, some tiny spring shot away and vanished, and then instead of ejecting from the dash with a smooth click while two little wings gently unflapped to support the cups, the holder snapped out harshly. No little wings, no gentle unflapping. Just a black plastic tray with two holes that couldn't hold anything.

Then the fabric on the ceiling developed holes. Small at first—no bigger than a pencil eraser—but then growing to the point where I could poke my thumb inside.

Then the fabric came unmoored from the ceiling. It sagged worst on moist, foggy mornings. When I drove, it felt like a hand rested lightly on my head.

Then the knob on my window crank snapped off.

Then the tab on my rear view mirror—the one that deflects bright lights behind me—gave with a soft click.

Then the inside door lever cracked off in my hand.

On one of my weekends with the boys, we went to a nearby baseball field where I hit them grounders and flies, and they ran the balls down and fired them back at me. The car was parked out of sight, and when we returned to it, we found a crumpled rear fender and no note from whoever hit it. One look told me it would cost more to fix than the car was worth.

This breakage was different. It was on the outside. More followed. Peeling paint on the trunk, a cracked hubcap, a hairline crack in the windshield.

I imagined that friends and neighbors and strangers looked at my car and thought the same thing I do whenever I see red tape over a broken tail light or a different colored front quarter-panel or a back window that's all plastic sheeting and duct tape.

*There is someone who will let things go.*

•

Another hour later, I notice that I'm not working as hard. The road has leveled, and then it starts to head down. But just as I breathe out a well-deserved "*Finally*," the road bends around an outcrop of rocks and rises again.

The next of these little saddles, about ten minutes later, fools me too, but the three after that do not.

It's insane. My climb to the Continental Divide only took two hours, and the crest of that was just under 11,000 feet. Here, the last elevation sign I saw was 3,700 feet, and I'm on hour four with no end in sight. I vaguely recall reading about the roads being cut differently in the Appalachians than in the Rockies. Not as high but steeper. In its current state, my mind can't process how this might be, so I let it go. All that matters is the single, simple fact that I'm fast approaching the point where I either give up or find some extra gear.

It could go either way, but the smart money is on the first.

•

Down the street from my buddy Daniel's apartment, where I lived for a while with him, his birds, and—on every other weekend—my boys, there was a grocery store the three of us walked to on Sunday mornings for doughnuts and, sometimes, a DVD from the Redbox.

One Sunday, doughnuts in hand, we got in line behind a father and son who were trying to rent a movie, but it wasn't working out too well; the dad used crumpled bills that kept getting rejected.

"It's okay, Dad," his son said. "Let's forget it."

He fished out a credit card, but that didn't work either.

Nick and Tony started fidgeting. The man's son looked at Nick and nodded.

I noticed the kid for the first time and thought he looked familiar. His father smiled and extended his hand when he saw me.

"Hey, Coach," he said.

"Oh, hey…how are you?"

His son, whose name I couldn't place, had been on one of Nick's baseball teams that I coached a season or two back.

"You playing ball this year?" the father asked Nick.

"I think so," Nick answered, looking up at me.

"Dad, c'mon…" His son was ready to go.

"Okay, let's try again," his dad said, turning back to the machine.

"Just forget it."

His dad looked at me and shrugged. "I don't know why it's not working…"

"Let's go, Dad."

"I thought we'd get a movie," he told me. "It's hard to know what to do sometimes. I don't live with him and his mom…" his voice trailed off.

*Jesus*, I thought.

He finally gave up. "Good seeing you again, Coach," he said, shaking my hand. He turned to Nick and Tony. "Have fun in ball this year, fellas."

We decided to pass on the movie, opting for a hike around a nearby lake instead. The whole time I thought about the look on the dad's face.

We were both members of the same group. The Helpless Sunday Dads. We weren't among those respectable fathers who came home from the church potluck and huddled around the big screen TV to watch the game and then play catch outside with their kids during halftime. Now we were living in apartments or with friends or both, trying to figure out how to fill the few remaining hours of the week's saddest day before we returned our children back to their real homes, where they clearly belonged.

●

Another, smaller rest stop. Two picnic tables, a tiny bathroom, and another directionless exchange, this time with a sweaty guy in a t-shirt who kneels by his motorcycle's engine with a wrench.

"You know where we are?"

"Tennessee."

"Right, but I mean, like, where the peak is?"

"Up a ways."

I try one more time. "You know what 'Cherohala' means?"

He just looks at me.

I thank him—for what I'm not sure—and start climbing again.

I used to tell myself that I preferred uphills to downhills. Downhills are dangerous, I reasoned; that was made clear by Interstate 8 on my second day out. As for uphills, not many bad things could happen other than tipping over. And I was all philosophical about it. *Uphills are like life. We need them to find out what we can do.*

*Fuck you, asshole*, is what I say to myself now. *Save it for a greeting card.*

Of course, the worst part about climbing right now isn't the fact that my legs are nearly dead. It's that my mind isn't.

●

I didn't tell anybody about the affair. The secret was too big, too dangerous, and at my worst moments I wondered if that's what it was all about, something to amuse and occupy Mistah Secrets. I wasn't a kid anymore, and maybe he decided that I needed to find a new way to get lost.

•

I cross the border between Tennessee and North Carolina. For some reason I thought the peak would coincide with this border, but I realize this makes no sense.

The road keeps rising, and I keep pedaling.

I decide that "Cherohala" means "twisting road that has no end."

On my sixteenth birthday, my friends gave me a copy of *Synchronicity* by the Police. It was 1983, so we're talking vinyl here, and with vinyl come skips. There was one on the second side, right in the middle of "Wrapped around Your Finger." I eventually exchanged the album, but before I did, I played it over and over, and as the song closed in on the skip, my body would tense in false hope that *this* time it would be all right and play through, but no, the needle would pop and land back on the same groove, the same part of the song, unable to move forward. *I know what you're up to* crik *I know what you're up to* crik *I know what you're up to…*

I'm stuck now, just like that needle. I want to keep going, but I can't move forward. At a mile marker on the right, I pull over, dismount, and prop Rusty against it.

I'm panting and my heart is beating angry and loud and I know at this moment, as sure as I've known anything, that the road goes nowhere, doesn't ever end, will climb and climb and climb until I give up.

The silence around me shatters as shouts crack in the mountain air like gunfire.

"Fuck you! Fuck! You! FUCK! YOU!"

I half expect to see an angry motorcyclist charging, tire iron in hand, because I gave him and his girlfriend a dirty look.

But no. The road is empty and I'm alone. Alone and shouting.

This has been coming for some time, since those first shaky

moments way back in San Diego, and I let go as if I'm letting go the brakes on a long, straight downhill. I shout at this road and the climbing and the who-the-fuck-knows where it's all heading. I shout at the dogs, at the rain, at the wind, at the heat. I shout at saddle sores, at bruised ribs, at acute patellar tendonitis. I shout at church, at confession, at secrets, at all the THINGS WE DON'T TALK ABOUT. I shout at those little rooms where we sit under fluorescent lights and pretend to read *Golf Digest* or *Sunset* while we wait for the news our mother is losing her past or our bodies have turned against us. And I shout at the two addresses on my kids' school forms, and I shout at Sunday nights, and I shout at Christmas cards that have an empty spot where I used to be. My chest heaves and my hands are on my knees. Something catches in my throat. I try to spit it out, but it turns into a hacking cough.

It's late in the day. I've been climbing for over six hours, and I still haven't reached the top. Of course it's up ahead somewhere, maybe one mile or ten miles or a hundred miles. It doesn't matter. It's out of reach.

I straighten up to a roar in the distance. I can't tell if it's coming from ahead or behind.

Ahead. Getting louder. Then they appear like stampeding horses. Ten…no, twelve…no, sixteen…Jesus, *twenty* motorcycles barreling downhill. A couple in the back start to slow down. One rider points his finger at me and then raises his head and flashes a thumbs-up. I immediately translate—*You okay?*

I nod and wave.

And then I climb on Rusty to look for someplace to stop because I'm done. Over and out.

I pull into the smallest rest area yet. A single picnic table and that's it. I lean Rusty against it and pull off my soaking jersey. The air is cool, and with my shirt still off, I unstrap my rear bag from the rack, pull out my tent and sleeping pad, and toss them both onto the table. The pad rolls to the end, falls off the edge, and rolls a little bit more on the soft grass. It's a narrow gash of lawn that almost immediately descends into forest, and it's the only place to pitch my tent. I rummage through my handlebar bag and pull out what food I have left. Half a peanut butter-and-jelly sandwich from Randy's wife, a little box with a few raisins stuck to the bottom, and a bag of pretzel crumbs and salt.

The day grows overcast as it heads into dusk. A blanket of trees covers the rolling mountains, and pockets of mist start to form in the low spots. In a few hours this forest will come alive, its inhabitants looking for food.

I read once that bears could smell food up to eleven miles away.

It's six-thirty. With rows of mountains behind me, the sun is already invisible, and its remaining light is being swallowed by long shadows that spill from the forest. In another forty-five minutes or so, those shadows will roll over me.

•

The morning I left Lawson's house, he told me a story.

A few years ago, he had a routine blood test that led to several other not-so-routine tests, which led to a diagnosis of chronic lymphocytic leukemia, or—as it's the custom of the medical profession to make the strange more manageable with abbreviations—CLL. It's a type of cancer that may not show symptoms for a while, and until it does, there's no need for treatment. Unfortunately, Lawson had recently begun showing symptoms and made the decision to begin chemotherapy at summer's end.

"It's not a cure," he said. "But after the chemo I should have six to ten years of clear sailing."

He went on to tell me about that moment when he knew something was wrong, about Beth and his two young children and wanting to stick around long enough to shepherd them into adulthood, about walking around the city where he spent his whole life and then realizing this city, like everything else, would continue to exist long after he'd been X'd out. Then it would be someone else's turn to sort through the scrapheap of history and someday, hopefully, find him there.

Back at Wolf Creek Pass, as I climbed the Rockies, I started to remember something and then quickly tamped it back down. A buried secret that Lawson's story dragged back up.

Near dinnertime during my second week of chemo, I felt a pain in my chest. A hot stab—sharper than heartburn—that nagged me throughout the early evening. Watching TV that night, I kept shifting around, trying to get comfortable, but every time I breathed, I felt the knife twist. I took a shower, hoping that would make it better.

It didn't. As bedtime approached, the pain grew. I pictured a bony hand wrapped around my heart and squeezing. I couldn't take a full breath; every time I tried to inhale, that hand clenched. It didn't matter whether I sat, stood, or lay down. My breathing became more and more shallow.

While Elizabeth made some calls and was eventually told to take me to the ER, I sat in a recliner and clutched the armrest. Focusing on one breath at a time—*this one...this one...this one*—I tried to ignore that hand around my heart. Just before we left, I staggered to the bathroom, put two pale hands on the counter, and stared into the mirror above the sink.

Hunched over, barely able to walk. Sunken eyes. Gray skin. Slack mouth. When I was a kid, I had to force myself to believe that the reflection was me, but now I knew all too well that it was. There was no escape.

On the way to the hospital, a curtain of pain crowded out most thoughts, but a few made it through. One of these was *I'm going to die tonight*.

And then another. Slumped in the passenger seat of our minivan with my head pressed against the cold glass window, I thought, *Good*.

I betrayed my wife, and my now my body betrayed me. It was fitting and just, and I was a rock in water, sinking into the dark. Soon I'd land on the bottom and everything would stop.

The bony hand turned out to be pericarditis. The sac of fluid around my heart had become inflamed and was slowly expanding, constricting its beat. It was a potentially lethal condition and a rare side effect of one of my chemo drugs. After consulting with the oncologist on call, the ER doctor prescribed some kind of steroid. The pain in my chest was reduced over the next couple of hours, but a faint knifing lingered for days.

What lingered longer—through that night, through the rest of my chemotherapy, through my recovery—was that aching desire to surrender, to fade away. Whenever I tried to imagine my future, it was a puzzle I couldn't solve, X the Unknown to the extreme. So I let Mistah Secrets take the wheel and pretended that we could drive like this for a while, pretended that the two of us weren't headed straight for a reckoning somewhere down the road. What I didn't know and couldn't guess was that reckoning would come a few years later on a Saturday night in early October as a confession.

•

At the picnic table I stare into the dark forest. I'm far from home. The farthest I've ever been, it seems.

My map is useless. I have no idea how it relates to me or where I'm supposed to be. My phone continues its deadpan message NO SERVICE, just as it has since Maria and her centaur rang me up at the Tellico Plains Sav-A-Lot.

I called Shannon early this morning, and I know that she's been waiting to hear from me all day. Maybe she'll finally make good on her threat to call the authorities, and a ranger or state trooper will rouse me out of my tent later tonight. Better one of them ready to write me a citation than a bear looking for a few raisins and the candy bar I ate hours ago.

But no, in the dark that's heading my way, no trooper will spot me. No bear, either.

And with this last thought comes another. This is exactly what I wanted as a kid—to bike away to a place where I couldn't be found.

•

A few months after my last chemo treatment, I got on my bike.

For the first couple of weeks, I took it easy, sticking to our tract and pedaling up and down the rows of identical houses that passed by in cartoon regularity. When those trips stopped tiring me out, I widened my circle and biked to a 7-11 about a half mile away. When I felt even stronger, I plotted a three-mile loop in my car and biked it two times a week. Then three.

One Saturday I was headed out to ride this very loop when the phone rang. It was Michelle, the social worker who ran my support group. She called to deliver the news that all of us who sat in a circle on the third Wednesday of every month knew was coming. Sara was dead.

I squeezed the cordless phone, which felt thin and fragile in my hand. Michelle went through the details, and I could hear in her voice that the task of reciting them to each of us was wearing on her. What made it worse was that I wasn't really listening; instead, I remembered my last conversation with Sara, when she said, "It is what it is."

After Michelle and I hung up, I replayed Sara's words in my head. There was resignation, but something else, too. Peace, maybe—the peace that comes when you look at the road you've been on, and even though it's nearing its end, you feel it was the right one. Would I have that when my time came?

The boys were at a friend's house across the street and Elizabeth was in the living room sorting mail. I could have very easily walked in there to tell her about Sara, to try and talk about what I was feeling.

But I went to the garage instead. I sat down on the concrete between our cars and felt myself slipping away until I saw a stranger, cross-legged and still, with a biking helmet by his knees. It was all more than I knew what to do with.

So I got on my bike. I didn't ride my usual loop. The truth is, I'm not sure where I went; I pedaled and kept on pedaling. When I finally made it back three hours later, tired and sweaty, I checked the cyclometer on my handlebars and saw that I had logged almost forty miles. It was the longest that I had ever biked in one stretch.

Not much, but a beginning.

•

At this table I'm outside myself again, watching a stranger stare into the trees as if there's some answer there. *Too dark*, I think, just before I become vaguely aware that this stranger is starting to move. He puts what little food is left back into the handlebar bag, and then he packs the tent and sleeping pad back into the rear bag and lashes it to Rusty's rack with bungee cords, and then he gathers up the wet clothes drying on the picnic table and stuffs them into whichever pannier has the most space. And as he moves, my mind starts to catch up. But I'm not so sure of this, not so sure of what my body thinks it has figured out. This is, after all, the same body that kept a terrible, horrible secret from me for most of my life and can't really be trusted. But then again, it's the only body I've got, so what choice do I have? My mind works itself out of first gear and has almost rejoined my body, which puts on helmet and gloves and then throws one leg over Rusty and turns toward the road, and we're nearly together now, mind and body, as I start to guess and then believe and then *know* what I've maybe known ever since I started out two months ago—or before that, when I wondered about the kind of father I could be under these new conditions; or before that, when I confessed my worst secret ever on a Saturday night in October; or before that, when Sara died; or before that, when I couldn't make it up the stairs without resting; or before that, when I wanted to die on my way to the ER; or before that, when I started keeping secrets, large and small; or maybe even before all of *that*, when I said goodbye to my training wheels and climbed aboard my AMF Roadmaster Renegade and pedaled into the world— which is that I don't want to run away, or be lost, or fade away into the shadow of this or any other forest, at least not without some kind of a fight. So I'm going to finish this fucking climb.

And waiting for me, less than a mile up the road, is the summit.

I pause for just a second before I hurtle down and race the dark to whatever town lies at the bottom. I stop just once, to talk to a couple of EMTs in an ambulance parked on the shoulder. One leans against the hood while the other sits in the front seat, looking at a clipboard. They were called in as support for an accident back up on the mountain.

"Anybody hurt?" I ask the guy by the hood.

"Coupla motorcycles hit each other," he says. "Both riders dead."

The guy in the ambulance nods. "Happens more than you'd think."

I wonder if I saw either of the riders up there. I wonder if either of them flashed me a peace sign or a thumbs up. What I don't wonder— because I know the answer—is if either of them woke up this morning and thought today might be their last day alive.

I'm about to leave when I remember something.

The guy by the hood shrugs in response to my question. "It's an Indian word, I'm pretty sure." He turns to his partner. "Hey, what's 'Cherohala' mean?"

The other guy looks up.

"Don't mean anything," he says. "It's these two forests here— Cherokee and Nantahala. Someone just put the names together and made up a new one."

"Huh," the first guy says. "Thought it was an Indian word."

"Nope," the second guy says and goes back to his clipboard. Then he looks up again. "Unless it was an Indian put them together."

# 27

# Road to Nowhere

I'm surrounded by blackness. Up ahead—though it's hard to tell how far—is a small half-circle of light about the size of a quarter held at arm's length. It doesn't do much; I can't see my feet or my hands or even my companion, who's somewhere to my right. Soon after we stepped inside this tunnel together, she vanished. I think I hear her steps, but it could just be the dull echo of my own feet. Water drips from above, but that sound is muted too, as if swallowed up by the dark. God only knows what happens with all that moisture in this place where the sun can't reach. It's easy to imagine fingers of mold and fungus reaching toward my body. I spread my arms to feel around me, and I grab a shoulder.

"You okay?" she asks.

"I can't see you," I say.

"We're almost there."

As we move forward, the quarter becomes a half dollar, then a silver dollar with its bottom edge shaved off. There's something on the ground to the left that looks like slumped-over body.

I clutch at her arm, but all I do is swipe at black air. "What is that? Is that a person?"

"I don't know," she laughs. "Hello!" she calls. The figure doesn't move.

We get closer and see it's a pile of rocks.

With the tunnel opening wider now, she comes into focus next to me. So does the heat and humidity, absent in the dark behind us. We step into sunlight, mottled by its passage through branches and vines, and about twenty feet ahead, long red-and-white striped boards stretch horizontally across dense vegetation. Somewhere beyond that is a lot of water, but I can't see it.

"Here it is," my guide says. "End of the road."

I have to admit it's not what I expected.

After the Cherohala Skyway thrashed me, I took refuge in Robbinsville, the tiny town at the bottom of the mountains, and reestablished contact with my dad, who said, "Make sure you stay on roads where there's food"; with my kids, who asked, "What happened to you?"; and with Shannon, who yelled, "Where the fuck have you been? I thought you were dead!"

I was all right, but I didn't sound that way, at least not to a guy named Jack in nearby Bryson City, who I called as a potential host. I told him about the climbing and the motorcycles, and my story may have strayed off in a couple of unintended directions because at some point I mentioned a little gold centaur and peanut-butter-and-jelly sandwiches and *Synchronicity*.

There was a pause. "Why don't you spend a couple of days with us. Rest up."

The "us" were Jack and his wife Raquel. They were both about my age and a study in contrasts. Where Jack had a calm, even-toned demeanor, Raquel moved in a flurry of physical gestures and talked nonstop in a thick New York accent. I immediately fell in love with her.

There was also a teenager named James, who I assumed was their son but found out later was their temporary foster child. The latest of many, as it turned out.

For the last several years, Jack and Raquel have worked as foster parents, and this work transformed their home into a carefully controlled environment. The rooms upstairs were completely off limits to the foster kids staying there, and the rooms downstairs had alarms that sounded a short, piercing *tweep* every time a door opened or closed in case anyone was wandering around at night or—more seriously—running away. Raquel told me all of this as if a teen climbing out of a window to escape was as ordinary as one asking to borrow the car. I opened my mouth to say something, but nothing came out. She laughed and put her hand on my arm.

"Don't worry…nothing like that's gonna happen while you're here."

"Have you had problems?"

"Oh yeah. One girl was a real piece of work. Constantly in my face. I'd ask her to help set the table and she'd be, 'Fuck you'; Jack would ask her to help him in the garage, she'd be, 'Fuck you.'"

"I couldn't handle that," I said.

"I'm with you. A kid gives me attitude, I wanna give it right back."

The foster kids came from rough situations. James, for instance, had no mother; she died in childbirth. His father, a junkie at the time, left James with his grandmother, who was an alcoholic and could barely take care of herself. Days would go by when James wouldn't eat. A concerned neighbor finally called Child Protective Services.

"He's moving to New York to be with his father again. He's clean now," Raquel said, then shrugged. "Who knows? Maybe it'll work out."

Later, over coffee, Raquel told me her own story. Even while sitting, she couldn't quite contain her energy. She waved and jabbed her mug in the air to emphasize what she said, and I kept waiting for coffee to spill out.

When she was seven years old, her parents were killed in a car crash. Her nineteen-year-old sister, who was in the police academy at the time, took her in and never let her forget it.

"She had a lot going on," Raquel said between sips. "She sure wasn't ready or willing to be a mom, too. But she was my only option."

Their brother was in Vietnam, where he got hooked on heroin. When Raquel was ten, he would stay with them for a few weeks, disappear for a few more, and then reappear. He would steal to support his habit. One morning at breakfast, her brother sat at the table without the bandana that he usually wore around his neck. When Raquel's sister walked in, she took one look at his neck and went crazy, beating him with both hands.

"She saw needle marks." She set her cup down. "I didn't know that at the time. I didn't know what the hell was going on. I just ran out of the room."

Raquel doesn't talk to her sister anymore and isn't sure what happened to her brother. To survive, she had to focus on herself, so she worked and put herself through school.

Jack's path was no less troubled. He ran away from home when he was seventeen and never looked back. He had a series of low-paying jobs, including one as a long-haul trucker, where he lived on the road for months at a time, his only companion a Bassett hound named Indio. Like Raquel, Jack put himself through school—earning a degree in social work—and has been helping other people ever since; in addition to the foster parent duties, he works full-time at a nearby group home.

"We saved ourselves and then each other," Raquel said, then laughed. "Now we're trying to save everybody else. Nobody would've predicted *that*." She rose to refill my cup when Jack and James came in from the garage. They were working on a goodbye gift to James's counselor, a young guy who played guitar. James showed me the gift—a hand-tooled leather guitar strap—and explained all the designs he stamped onto it.

"So my darling, what do you have planned for our guest tomorrow?" Jack asked.

"Show him the sights. Maybe drive up to Water Rock Knob."

"You should take him down the Road to Nowhere," Jack said.

"Sounds ominous," I said, and looked back and forth between their faces.

They just smiled.

On North Shore Road, just before it enters the Smoky Mountain National Forest, there's a loamy, leaf-strewn hillside that holds up a crooked little hand-lettered sign nailed onto two stakes with the words

Welcome to
The Road to Nowhere
A Broken Promise!
1943 – ?

In the early 1940s, events unfolded that would have a profound and lasting impact on a group of residents of local Swain County. The main people affected were the ones who lived on and near Highway 288, a road that no longer appears on any maps because it's a road that no longer exists.

During World War II, many industries were retooling and expanding in order to meet increased demands. One important company in this effort was Alcoa, whose aluminum plant in Knoxville, Tennessee, was crucial to the manufacture of American war planes. The energy they needed to process aluminum had outgrown their own means to produce it, so a deal was struck among Alcoa, the Tennessee Valley Authority, and Congress. What it amounted to was that Congress would fund the construction of a dam by the TVA, and the hydroelectric power generated by that dam would be made available to Alcoa.

But there was a *quid pro quo*. The dam was set to lie across the Little Tennessee River, and a substantial portion of the soon-to-be-flooded property was owned by Alcoa. In exchange for the energy that the dam would generate, the TVA would get control of that land. The rest of the area in question was privately owned, so the government purchased it from the 1,300 families that lived there.

The families were not given a choice. Their houses were sold, they were relocated, and the dam was built. In all, 44,000 acres of land was flooded to create Fontana Lake, which eradicated not just the homes but also Highway 288, the only access that the displaced families had to their ancestors' graves. Swain County insisted the government—in exchange for obtaining the land at a greatly reduced rate—build a new road along the north shore of Fontana Lake to replace the old one. In the meantime, the National Park Service would provide free ferry service across the lake twice a year for family members who wished to visit the now-isolated cemetery.

The building of the road progressed in piecemeal fashion, at the rate of a few miles every decade. Funds would be allocated and construction would commence, but then funds would dry up and construction would halt. There was a kind of cycle to it, one that spun out for years and years. This situation birthed lawsuits, mainly from county residents who had a stake in the building of the new road.

In the 1970s, the situation grew more complicated when someone discovered that rocks exposed by construction had released acids harmful to nearby land, water, and wildlife. A new set of lawsuits and litigants emerged, all with the intent to stop the project for good.

The last section of the road completed before that final, grinding halt was a 1,200 foot tunnel, the one Raquel and I now stand outside. And just beyond this tunnel, North Shore Road—more commonly referred to as "The Road to Nowhere"—simply ends.

We walk up to the barricade. I can't see Fontana Lake or even much beyond the thicket of forest in front of me, but I know that it's out there somewhere and that down below its surface is another world, drowned long ago. Places where people once lived and laughed and imagined their futures are now homes for fish and whatever plants grow in black water.

Also out there are the dead, at rest in their marooned graves.

"Strange story," Raquel says. "Even weirder ending."

When we're gone, what do we leave behind? Memories, of course, but memories change and fade, and so do the people in them. Documents? If we're very, very lucky, we might leave a few banker's boxfuls of papers, letters, and other items that actually have something to say about who we were and what we did. A physical marker in the form of ashes or a headstone? Sure, but what's the point of those?

Whatever remains of us will need caretakers.

My own ancestors' graves are scattered. My parents have plots waiting for them a few miles from their house in suburban Chicago, just off of the streets where I used to get lost on my bike. In a file somewhere I've got a map of the cemetery in New York where my mother's parents are buried. If I were there, I could find it. Somewhere else in that same city are the graves of my father's parents. I don't know exactly where, but I have cousins who could point me in the right direction. My godfather—my Uncle Barry—is buried at Arlington National Cemetery in Virginia. He was an air force pilot who spent the end of World War II in a German prison camp, something he never talked about. I've been to Arlington to pay my respects at his austere white headstone, which shares space with the graves of Robert and John Kennedy and the Unknown Soldier. In all its solemn splendor and pageantry and accessibility, Arlington is pretty much the opposite of the hidden graves out past the end of the Road to Nowhere.

Someday I'll come to the end of my own road. I imagine Nick and Tony will be my caretakers then, and maybe I'll end up in a well-tended plot they can visit every so often or maybe in an urn they'll take turns keeping. Or maybe they'll scatter my dust—along with those memories and stories that connect us—into the wind or water or someplace else so that whatever I leave behind keeps moving along.

# VOICES FROM THE ROAD

# 28

# No Simple Highway

When I left Bryson City, Jack told me that I would eventually hit the Piedmont—pancake flat roads that would take me to the coast—but three days later I'm still biking hills according to my legs and will be for a while longer according to my map. For now, though, I'm taking a break in Lincolnton, where I'm at a picnic table outside of a place called MOOSE'S with a woman named Lisa who just bought me a huge tumbler of sweet tea. At some point in our conversation, she asks where I'm going from here, and I tell her.

"Be careful on Highway 73," she says. "There's lots of traffic, and at least one biker gets hit there a month."

*Yeah, yeah,* I think.

As if reading my thoughts, she puts her hand on mine.

"Really, now," she says. "You be careful."

Two hours after I leave Lisa, I pull into a Wal-Mart to grab some lunch. The greeter there is a retired guy named Floyd, who looks at me through oversized, thick-lensed glasses. I ask if he'll watch Rusty while I eat, and he's happy to.

When I'm ready to leave, he asks where I'm heading and I tell him.

"Traffic's not too bad now," he says. "But once 73 crosses the interstate, watch out."

As with Lisa, I'm quick to dismiss Floyd's warnings. No way this guy bikes, and he hasn't seen what I have. Right?

A few miles west of Concord, the traffic picks up and Highway 73 narrows. As I approach the turn-in to a subdivision, I see a woman in front of a blue Suburban. She's waving her arms at me, so I stop.

"This is a very dangerous road," she says. "You shouldn't be on it."

Her name is Gabrielle, she's in her mid-thirties or so, and her blonde hair is cut short and sharp. She's wearing a thin black robe over a swimsuit, so I'm guessing that she's on her way either to or from a pool. Her son and dog both stare at me from inside the air conditioned Suburban, parked but still running. As I wave to the two of them, she tells me that a friend of hers, a cyclist, was hit on 73 just two weeks ago. She was thinking of this friend when she passed me on the road, so she stopped to flag me down.

We move into the shade and I grab my map. She shows me another route that goes about seven miles out of the way, bends around the southern edge of Concord, and then reconnects with Highway 73 on the city's eastern side, where the traffic is much lighter.

"More hills, but way safer."

She makes me promise to go that way, and I tell her I will. As I pull away, she says, for the fourth time, "Be careful."

"I'll be okay," I say, then add, "I'm kinda hard to kill." She looks unconvinced.

A little while later I come to Old Poplar Tent Church Road, the detour Gabrielle told me about. Up ahead on 73, the traffic doesn't look too bad. Off to the right, where I promised to turn, I can already see the hills. At the corner of this intersection there's a McDonald's, so I decide to get something to drink while I consider which way to go.

Before I can move, the gravel crunches on the shoulder behind me. I turn and see a familiar blue Suburban grind to a stop a few feet away. Gabrielle hops out, her hands bunched in front of her. In them he holds Clif Bars, energy chews, and a frozen fruit pop.

"I thought you could use these," she says, and passes the food from her hands to mine. "This is where you need to turn."

I remember Chuck in Colorado and how he gave me a lift when I needed one; I remember my first meeting with Roy and how he gave me his number in case anyone "gave me a hard time"; and I remember Jan and Bill and how they followed me for a few miles back in Missouri. All along the way, people have been looking out for me.

To hell with the hills or seven extra miles. At this point, Gabrielle's detour can be seven hundred miles out of the way, and I would still take it. I have to admit that I'm starting to believe in signs—at least the ones painted by the kindness of strangers.


My cousin Tom and his wife Ann live in Greenville, North Carolina, which is a few hours' ride from the Atlantic Ocean. I contacted him way back during the Planning Stage to see if he was willing to participate in my adventure, and of course he was. A biker himself, Tom was eager to help out, so I suggested he bike with me the last two days.

The plan—as we've pieced it together through calls, emails, and texts—is that he and Ann will meet me Saturday morning in Lillington, which is about a hundred miles west of Greenville. Ann will drive back to their house while Tom and I bike. Then, on Sunday morning, the two of us will again bike, and Ann will again drive, ninety more miles to Swan Quarter, where we'll catch a ferry that will take us to Ocracoke, a tiny beach community in the Outer Banks on the Atlantic Ocean.

The only problem with this plan is that I need to get to Lillington tomorrow, and Lillington is one hundred and twenty miles from this booth at Zaxby's, a fast food chicken place in Concord, where I'm sucking the remnants of a birthday cake-flavored shake through a straw that's way too thin for the job.

One hundred and twenty miles. A little more, actually. It's a crazy number that by far exceeds any single day on this trip, any single day in my entire biking career. I can't imagine going that far on flat grades with a tailwind while carrying a lot less weight in seventy degree weather, none of which I can expect tomorrow. North Carolina is, apparently, entering a heat wave. It's been toasty, but tomorrow temperatures are expected to be in the low triple digits and even higher with the heat index. As far as the grades go, I still haven't hit the Piedmont; instead, a good part of my route will run through the Uwharrie Forest, and in my experience out here, "forest" means hills.

When I call Tom that night, I try to keep a lid on my rising panic.

"So we'll be there by eight a.m. on Saturday," Tom tells me.

"Yeah," I say.

Tom must hear something in my voice, so he tries to take my mind off the ride tomorrow.

"So how long has it been?" he asks.

•

In 1976 I was nine years old. That Bicentennial summer, all of the fire hydrants in our townhouse development were repainted to look like little colonial figures. A minuteman here, a white-haired founding father there. All very patriotic. That was also the summer when we broke our pattern and drove not to New York but to Miami. Our chariot was a 1969 Oldsmobile Delta 88 with black-vinyl interior and no air conditioning that became a mini-torture chamber in the thick, wet southern heat.

We headed to my Aunt Angie's house, where my mom's mom, Granny, also lived. My mom and her three sisters had agreed that Granny couldn't live alone in Flatbush anymore, and Aunt Angie volunteered to take care of her. Two of my cousins were there, also. Linda—who thirty-one years later would read a Christmas card and think I was dead—and her brother Tom. I didn't even know I had these Florida cousins, but there they were. Soon after we arrived, they took Vince and me to the grocery store, and the two of them hopped in their car without putting on any shoes. With my own dark-socked feet tied tightly into brand-new vacation sneakers, I looked at Vince, but he shook his head in the way I knew meant *Just shut up.*

When I saw Tom move shoeless through the aisles of the store, I decided that he was one of the coolest people I had ever met, and this feeling was confirmed later when he effortlessly caught the little green lizards that were running all around their yard. The field behind our house back home was filled with toads and every once in a while a garter snake, but lizards were something exotic. They were quick, too, and I couldn't even get close before they vanished into the bushes. But Tom could pluck them off the wall or grass with ease, grabbing their bright bodies instead of their breakaway tails. He put them in my hands, and I tried to hold on to their wriggling bodies without crushing them.

●

The day is made of hills and heat.

I leave before the sun rises and tell myself that I'll stop as little as possible, but by the time I pull in front of J's Cash Mart in Cameron at about 4:30 in the afternoon, I've stopped to refill my water bottles over a dozen times, and now I have to again. Almost thirty miles remain between me and Lillington, and at the rate I've been moving and at the rate my energy has been dissipating, thirty miles should take another two and a half hours. I should have the light with me for the rest of the way. Barring any problems, of course.

As this last thought surfaces, I make a conscious effort not to look at my tires. I replaced my old ones in Paducah, so they're still new, but I don't want to jinx them. But then again, I've thought about them, haven't I? Won't that jinx them? And just how in the hell do jinxes work, anyway?

I shake my head before my mind starts spinning into those circles of non-logic I've been getting caught up in more and more. The combination of miles, heat, and low energy reserves is taking its toll. I feel that mind-body split again, only this time my mind is in charge. It's amazing what it can trick the body into doing. Time and again the last several weeks, I've collapsed at the end of the day and been grateful my energy held out just long enough for me to get where I was going. But I've been misreading the situation. It wasn't some supreme fortune of timing that exhaustion and arrival coincided so perfectly; it was my brain telling my muscles that if they could pedal up just one more hill, wait just twenty more minutes before cramping, then everything would be okay. Now, nearly two months after I started, my body is catching on that my mind's been shoveling it a steady, steaming load of horseshit.

Bottles filled, I get ready to hit the road again when a green SUV pulls up in front of me and a young couple gets out. Both are rail thin, wearing cutoffs and sunglasses, and holding cigarettes. The man moves to the back of his vehicle and begins to wrestle something out while the woman leans against the hood and looks at me.

"That's some bike," she says, stretching the last word into almost two syllables.

"Thanks," I say.

"Where you from?"

"California."

"California."

"Uh-huh."

"You rode here on that bike?"

I nod, and she looks at me over her sunglasses.

"No shit?"

"No shit."

"Chad!" she turns her head and shouts. "Getcher ass over here."

Chad clomps over with a giant red and white cooler in his arms. "Wassup?"

"This guy rode that there bike here from California."

"No shit!" He sets the cooler down and wipes his hands on his t-shirt, right over the picture of a fish and the words "Cooper's Pond."

He comes toward me, arm extended. "Mister, lemme shake your hand."

The woman's name is Rachel, and she asks me all kinds of questions while Chad hauls the cooler inside. When he returns, it's filled with beer and steaks that he invites me to share with them back at their place, just up the road.

"Hell yes," Rachel says. "We'll put you up."

I'm not sure I have another two and a half hours in me, and I can't think of anything that sounds better right now than beer and a steak.

"I wish I could," I tell them. "But I've got to get to Lillington."

"Shit," Chad says. "Have some steak and I'll give you a ride later."

I can just see how a nice, juicy steak will settle into my bloodstream along with a beer, and then another, and then possibly one more until the only thing I'll want to do is sink into Chad and Rachel's couch, sink so deep that a "ride later" will mean not later tonight but tomorrow morning. And not really *early* in the morning, either...

"I'll tell you what you can give me," I say, snapping out of it. "How about some directions out of here?"

Chad's more than happy to oblige, and even though I know where I'm going, I enjoy watching Chad get his entire body into his instructions. He doesn't just tell me the road bends; he shows me with a big twist of his torso, his arm curving around like he's delivering a knockout punch. And when he describes a hill I'll need to go over, his whole body arches like he's casting a line out to the middle of a lake.

Rachel hands me a card.

"Our numbers're on there, you change your mind," she tells me. The card says "yoga instructor," and as she holds it out to me, it's enveloped in a small cloud of smoke from the cigarette in her hand. It makes perfect sense that in North Carolina, even the yoga instructors smoke. At nearly every gas station and convenience store I've stopped, there's been a Styrofoam cup on the counter where you can buy cigarettes individually. I'm starting to wonder if, when you're born here, they give you a complimentary pack on your way out of the hospital.

We stand there waiting for someone to speak. Then Chad reaches into his pocket.

"Well, shit," he says, handing me something. "Least let us buy your dinner tonight."

"No, really," I say. "I can't take anything."

"Like hell you can't," Rachel says. She grabs the crumpled ten from Chad and stuffs it in my handlebar bag. "You getcherself a burger."

Before I can protest again, the two of them move in and gather me up in their arms.

We say goodbye and I take off. And then, over those last thirty miles to Lillington, two things happen that I credit, irrationally, to Chad and Rachel's kindness: the heat dissipates, and the road—finally, mercifully—levels out, this time for good.

In Lillington I stop at a Microtel that they really should call the "Micromanage-tel." When I check in, walk to my room, and settle in, the trip is punctuated by little signs announcing policies that seem designed to harass the guests.

On the front desk: "We will not rent rooms to people who live within a 30-mile radius of Lillington."

At the breakfast bar: "Do not use milk from the cartons in your coffee. We provide creamers for this."

At the ice machine: "Do not fill ice chests or bags."

In the bathroom: "If you require shampoo, you must request it at the front desk."

Enough already. I just want to eat and sleep, hopefully in that order.

But after I've eaten a burger at the Waffle House next door, I can't sleep. Earlier, on my way through town, I saw people gathering at a restaurant for dinner. I couldn't see the name of the place; it was mostly covered by a big yellow banner that proclaimed "All U Can Eat Fish Fry-day," and the scent of beer-battered catfish or trout or whatever they pull fresh from the Cape Fear River was nearly enough to make me steer right off the road and into a booth with the locals. Had it been the end of any day other than one with triple-digit miles and triple-digit heat, I would have done it.

Instead, I pressed on and had to settle for what I could imagine about the Lillingtonians—their conversations, their easy hellos to fellow neighbors who also make a ritual of Fish Fry-day, their rides or walks back home where they might spend the last hours of the day with a cup of coffee or a beer in front of the local news.

Most of this trip has been on two-lane roads, the kinds that are hidden on all but the most detailed maps. As opposed to high-speed interstates, these roads meander through hundreds upon hundreds of small towns—places where people like Lisa, Floyd, Gabrielle, Chad, and Rachel might take a few minutes to connect with some nut on a bike. And when I haven't been too exhausted or frustrated or self-absorbed, I've tried to return the favor, my reward being glimpses of everyday people at home in their everyday lives.

In Mount Pleasant, where I passed through this morning, the "Movie in the Park" scheduled for tonight was *Up*. The sky is now dark, so parents are no doubt trying to corral their kids to come sit on the blanket and watch the movie. For the next hour and a half or so, those parents will be a nonstop whirl of crisis management as they hand out snacks, change diapers, and break up wrestling matches between kids.

Yesterday, I pedaled past a high school in Cherryville and spotted a bunch of girls—probably from the softball or volleyball team—doing exercise runs up, down, and across the football bleachers. I steered my bike to the side of the road and watched their clockwork pattern for a few minutes. Then I looked across the street and saw a guy with a big straw hat move slowly over a church lawn on a rider mower. In the parking lot off to the right, there were two ladies chatting, and while they did, one of them kept moving a big bag of groceries from one arm to the other.

In Monterey, Tennessee, there's a Phillips 66 at Exit 301. When

I stopped in to get a map of North Carolina a few days ago, I asked some of teens leaning against the counter what they did for fun. One kid in a faded cap with "STP" stitched on front said, "This is it."

In Deerfield, Kansas, people from there and neighboring Holcomb are probably just finishing their own outdoor movie at the park. When I passed through in mid-June, the upcoming film was *Sergeant York*; no telling what tonight's fare is.

Further west, in Durango, Colorado, young professionals are well into their weekend at the Steamworks Brewing Company, knocking back pints of Lizard Head Red.

And way back in Tuba City, Arizona—where I was, it seems, a lifetime ago—local teens are gathered at the Sonic on Highway 160, filling the outdoor tables beneath the wide desert sky. I remember listening to their chatter while I sat alone off to the side.

Even though I haven't lived there for over twenty years and even though I couldn't wait to leave, I'll always consider Downers Grove, Illinois, my hometown. A lot has changed in that time. The townhouse where I grew up used to be surrounded by fields, but they've long been replaced with more housing developments and suburban strip malls anchored by the likes of Wal-Mart, Home Depot, and Best Buy. My elementary school is gone, converted into offices for the park district. The Just Games on Ogden Avenue where my friends and I would waste time and quarters playing Galaga and Tempest and Space Invaders is history, as is the Venture on 75th Street and the Dynamic Video off of Fairview Avenue. Then there's Omega, a restaurant where my friends and I spent most Friday nights after playing Dungeons and Dragons or seeing *Ghostbusters* for the fifth or sixth time. We would guzzle coffee, flirt ineffectively with our waitress, then go back to our homes, watch *SCTV*, and recite all the best bits on Saturday night, when we did the whole thing all over again. Omega was always our last stop of the night. One late Saturday night at college, Jerry and I got the idea to drive up there. It was already close to midnight, and Omega lay two and a half hours north of Champaign, but we made the trip, drank our coffee, ate our meals—Jerry's standard was the patty melt and mine was the "Downers Grove Burger"—and then drove back to school. I remember being too wired to sleep even though it was almost dawn, so instead of going to bed, I climbed the stairs to the third floor of our fraternity house, where there was an access panel to the roof, and I sat up there to watch the sun rise over campus. That building is long gone now, razed to make room for apartments.

So much of my life was spent in places that don't exist anymore.

But some things remain. Two important places in my youth— the Tivoli Theater and Anderson's Bookshop—are still thriving in Downers Grove. The Tivoli might endure for a while yet, if its past is prologue; it's a single-screen theater that's remained that way since it was built in 1928, and it's rumored to have been the second theater in the country to show sound movies.

Someday my boys will be old enough to explore the corners of their hometown, find their own hangouts, establish their own rituals, and shape their own histories free from the boundaries set by their mom and me. Someday beyond that—not as far down the road as I might like to think—they'll be looking back on their time here, marveling at what's changed and what's remained. Now, though, they're young enough that we travel this terrain together. In our reordered life, we have our "Pizza Fridays," our ballfields and tennis courts, our different hiking trails—the one where we saw a rattlesnake eating a rabbit, the climb where we bushwhacked a new path to the top, the spot where we spent an entire afternoon creating a river from a giant rain puddle.

Later that night, I check my progress on an online map that I set up before I left. With an iPhone app whose workings lie far beyond my understanding, I've been dropping "waypoints"—little markers of pictures and brief comments—for two months now. Shannon and Nick and Tony have been watching these waypoints appear and panicking when they didn't. On the map, the markers look like upside-down raindrops, red with a black dot in the center, each one a place where somebody calls home. Compressed onto my phone's tiny screen, the image I'm staring at looks like a giant red caterpillar stretched across the entire country.

I zoom in on various waypoints and try to remember what was going through my head at those moments. One of them—at the southern edge of Monument Valley—is crystal clear. I pulled over and took a picture of a tiny cluster of houses wedged in between a giant sandstone monolith and the ever-flowing highway. I wonder now as I did then about the people who live in that difficult space; do they feel torn by those oppositional forces—permanence and wanderlust—or have they found some kind of balance?

A few days earlier, in Asheville, I got a call from a biker friend of mine named Truman. I met him on that very stretch of road through Monument Valley, about a half hour after I took the picture. We ran into each other again in Colorado, exchanged phone numbers, and have been sporadically updating each other about our adventures. When I first met him, he had been on the road for nine months. A true vagabond, he rode without any clear destination, stopping whenever he was tired and could find some reasonable shelter. He knocked on church doors, huddled behind stores, and one night even slept in a large, handicapped-accessible Porta-Potty. At the Grand Canyon, he headed into the woods when there were no cars in sight, quickly changed into a camouflage t-shirt, and set up camp. In Berkeley he lived in a young couple's basement for a week, and in Texas he stayed in a stranger's heated garage for two, earning his keep by painting, raking leaves, and going for walks with the man's twenty-year-old autistic son.

I couldn't get a handle on Truman's non-biking experiences; of those, he was stingy with details except to say that he was fifty-three and had lived alone his whole life.

When he called, he was back in Chicago.

"At your apartment?" I asked.

"No, with some friends in Evanston."

"What are you up to?"

"Oh, nothing important," he said.

"What now?" I asked.

"I dunno," he said. "I can't stay still."

I thought about his words after I hung up, and I'm thinking about them now as I sit here alone in this motel room.

*I can't stay still.*

That's a good mindset for riding a bike. That moment you learn to stay up on just a few millimeters of rubber feels like magic, but it's not. You just need to move.

But you don't need to pedal like a maniac; you can stay up when you slow down, too. In fact, you can stay up even when you're stopped, provided you get your feet on the ground in time. The trick is knowing when to pedal, when to coast, when to stop, and when to start again.

I zoom in on my very first marker. Ocean Beach. What was I thinking at the moment just before I took off? The whole country spread out before me—all those miles; all those aches and pains; all that heat, wind, and rain; all that desert; all those mountains; all those people waiting to be met, and all those memories—and I had yet to bike a single inch. It took unbelievable innocence—or stupidity—to make that initial push. If I had any real sense of how hard it was going to be, I'm not sure I would have been able to move. It's so easy not to move. But this road and everything on it is something I couldn't even imagine a few years ago, when I was pointed in a direction I didn't want to go. I guess we need to be that innocent—or that stupid—to move ourselves and find the road we need. And to slow down when we do.

# 29

# Road to Somewhere

Finales are tough.

Maybe the best way is to get right into it.

As I crest the sandy hill with Rusty and catch my first real glimpse of the Atlantic Ocean—

Nope. Can't start there. I'm not ready yet.

I'll start on Saturday morning in Lillington, when Tom and Ann showed up.

We loaded my front and rear panniers and my rear bag into their station wagon, ate grapes out of Baggies, and slathered ourselves in sunscreen for the ride to Greenville, another ninety-eight miles to the east.

Biking with Tom was a perfect capstone to this adventure. Free of all my baggage and so close to the end, I felt like I was flying on Rusty. Tom and I fell into an easy rhythm as we talked biking and family and politics. I also lapsed into a comfortable silence as we pedaled. Of course, I was conserving my energy so that I could finish the ride and was happy to listen to Tom outline options for Sunday in terms of ferries. My Aunt Angie told me she named Tom after my dad. Even though the two of them don't share DNA, they do share a love of detail and planning. I remember once—

Wait. I guess I've been here before. Personal reminiscences, family anecdotes.

Maybe the best way to capture the end is by collecting details:

Wringing out disgusting brown liquid from my sweat-soaked riding gloves at each stop along the way to Greenville.

Eating nearly half of the lasagna that Ann baked that night.

The red glow of the sun just over the horizon on Sunday as Tom and I pedaled out of the dark and into the final day.

A gray egret lifting itself majestically from a marsh in the distance.

Saving one more turtle, a prehistoric-looking snapper that Tom had to nudge off the road and into the weeds with his shoe.

Wheeling to a stop at the ferry station in Swan Quarter, calling my dad to tell him that it was almost over, and hearing him exhale, "Thank God."

The diesel fumes and rumbling turbines of the ferry cutting through the Pamlico Sound.

Here on the ferry, I stand by myself at the railing. Tom and Ann have wandered away, probably to let me meditate on my journey's end. A dark gray body of land lies as if asleep on the water ahead, and I can see what might be a lighthouse near one end. Beyond that lighthouse is the coast. End of the road. I try to zero in on a clear emotion, but I can't do it. The harder I try to conjure something, the faster my mind works, refusing to land on any one image.

The lighthouse grows bigger, but instead of thinking about the end, I think about the journey itself.

I think about all of the people who took me in, or talked to me, or gave me something—strangers wanting to connect with another stranger. A guy who pulled alongside me on Highway 160 in Arizona to see if I needed any water, another one who handed me a bottle of Gatorade at a gas station in North Carolina, a couple in Colorado who pulled over to see if I needed a place to stay that night. Family of friends in Wickenburg and Wichita.

I think about Chuck Carpin, who came along and saved my ass

in Colorado.

I think about Dr. Candace in Alamosa. And about Gabrielle with her big blue Suburban of mercy.

I think about the nightly shoot-'em-up in Dodge City and all those copies of *The Spirit of the Plains* stacked nice and neat.

I think about Miranda following her dream to the ocean, Brian and Glen in search of vineyards, and Truman who can't stay still.

I think about Springview Farm, about Suzy, Bill, and especially Mama Owl Jan and all of her stories of the things that can kill you.

I even think about ol' Rod in Blythe.

I think about all of those unleashed dogs that tried and failed to catch me.

I think about those places that will still be around when we're gone—the Grand Canyon, Monument Valley, the Rockies, the Great Plains, the rivers, the Appalachians, even the Goddamn Ozarks.

I think about Herman and his rainbow, about *Santa Claus, the Great Imposter.*

I think about Dennis Hopper, easy riding his way into the beyond.

I think about soaring through the Kansas sky with Roy in his dying friend's plane.

I think about Miss Fortune. *Luck's not bad or good,* I imagine her telling me. *Luck just* is.

I think about the workers of USW Local 7-669 and their families looking for a fair shake from Honeywell.

I think about Superman and Big John.

I think about all those lives touched by disasters. The people flushed from their homes by the San Diego fires, the people in the Gulf, and the people of Greensburg, Kansas, who vowed to REBUILD.

I think about the homeless men in Durango along *El Rio de las Animas Perdidas.*

I think about my family in Chicago. My brother, who's taken a vicarious thrill in my ride, sending me little notes across the ether almost every day. My dad and the strange orbit we're in—sometimes close, sometimes far away. My mom, who's fading away.

I think about X the Unknown, and the Road to Nowhere, and the Cherohala Skyway.

I think about John and his Harley and his road atlas, and I wonder if he ever patched things up with his old lady. I can almost hear him now. *Fuck guys on bikes. What are you gonna do?*

I think about the end of Mistah Secrets.

I think about Sara, who lost her fight but found some peace. And about Lawson, who said that cancer gave him "focus." About how I wouldn't be here if not for my cancer. I wouldn't be out of my marriage if not for my cancer. I wouldn't have found had what I needed to find if not for my cancer.

I think about the people I love, waiting for me back at my own home—friends from work, students, and of course, Shannon, Nick, and Tony.

And I think about those two boys of mine and how I can't wait to see them again. But most of all I think about how the three of us occupy spots on a vast web that defies understanding and how that web divides backwards into generations that have intersected in the most improbable ways to bring us together in this here and now. I think of my three grandparents who once crossed the ocean in front of me to set foot on the shore of their new lives. My grandfather Vincenzo—Grandpa—who came to America from Reggio Calabria when he was twenty-one. My grandmother Lucia Milillo—Granny—who came to America from Bari when she was nineteen because her father wouldn't buy her a sewing machine, or so the story goes. And my grandfather Rocco—a man I never met but whose name I carry—who came to America when he was eighteen. Like his future wife, he came from Bari, but the two didn't know each other in Italy; it took a mutual family friend in Brooklyn to bring them together. None of these ancestors, when they reached this shore, knew what lay ahead for them. They couldn't possibly have envisioned that their grandson would one day bicycle back in this direction to touch the same waters that carried them here.

As we pull closer to Ocracoke, my throat tightens. For a second I envision breaking down into a blubbering mess, forcing Tom and Ann into the awkward and uncomfortable role of having to hold me together. But it passes.

We get off the ferry. Ann is in the car and we decide that she should and scout out a place for us to get to the beach while Tom and I follow on bike.

We pedal through the touristy downtown part of Ocracoke on Route 12. The buildings soon fall away and the road is stark, caressed by wind-blown threads of sand. Even though I stretched on the ferry, my legs cramp up. It gives me an excuse to hang back and savor the moment.

We round a bend and I see Ann up ahead. She's found a road that leads to the beach. Tom and I pull in behind her, and while he stops to talk, I keep pedaling.

As I crest the sandy hill with Rusty, I catch my first real glimpse of the Atlantic Ocean. Ann pulls ahead of me in the car and drives onto the sand, heading for the shore. I dismount and start walking Rusty to the water.

This is it. The moment I've been trying to imagine ever since I first got this insane idea—THE TRIUMPHANT ARRIVAL. I take a deep breath.

And then Ann wedges the car in the beach about fifty yards from the ocean. She revs the motor, and the front tires sink further into the sugary sand. Tom gets behind the wheel to see if he has better luck. Ann walks in front of the car toward me. Her arms are folded in front of her, and when she looks at me I can almost see the thought bubble above her head and the words in it. *Oh dear Lord, I've ruined everything.*

But she hasn't ruined anything. I smile at her and help to try unearth the car. We let some air out of the front tires and push against the blazing hot hood as Tom tries to reverse, but all that happens is that we inhale the thick metallic scent of burning clutch.

A guy in a tow truck rolls up and offers to pull the car out. Ann and I wait while Tom parks it back by the entrance road, and while we wait I try to knock some of the sand from my shoes and bike with little success. My legs and arms—sticky from sunscreen and sweat—are caked with so much grit I look like a Shake 'n' Bake chicken.

Tom rejoins us at the crest of the hill. I turn and catch my second glimpse of the Atlantic Ocean.

And mother of God the wind is strong. Kansas has nothing on the gale forces slapping me in the face right now. Between the wind and the sand, it's slow going. I lift Rusty up because it's easier than trying to roll him. Plus, he's carried me these last two months, so now it's my turn to carry him.

A family of four falls into step beside us, and two of the kids hold boogie boards by their leashes while the gusts make them flutter horizontally above the sand. One of the kids loses his grip, and the board whizzes by my face.

"Careful, honey" his mother says. "You'll hurt someone."

*Hurt someone? He'll* kill *someone.*

They continue to walk upwind beside us, and I keep one eye on the Atlantic and the other on their deadly boards. We're right in their path. Only an eleven year old's grip stands between me and a new set of teeth.

And then we're at the water's edge. Tom and Ann take pictures of me as I position myself in the foamy waves. The kids can't hold those boards to save their lives, so Tom takes a solid blow to the arm and a glancing shot to the head. I'm not sure why these kids are right next to us. The entire beach in both directions is empty. Don't they know how hard I worked to get here?

I want so much for this moment of arrival to match the size it's grown to in my mind. I'm waiting for a gargantuan wave of meaning and importance, the final triumph that at once captures and transcends clichés of victory—crossing the finish line, grabbing the brass ring, ascending the pedestal, planting the flag.

But it isn't there. Or if it is, it's an arbitrary end point that seems to be so much less than the trip itself. So what happens is this—I dip Rusty's front tire into the Atlantic Ocean and the three of us walk back to the car.

I call Shannon, and she starts to cry. It's a little joke among the boys and me how easily she's moved to tears.

"Any epiphanies?" she manages.

"One or two. I'll tell you about them later."

"Just get your furry butt back here."

I call Nick and Tony. They both get on the line and say they've been watching my progress that morning and were waiting for the call.

Nick tells me they ran into his old math teacher at Target yesterday. I'm not sure why he brings this up until he says, "Y'know, she bikes too."

"Did you tell her what I was doing?"

"Well, no…"

"Right," I say, imitating my son imitating me: "Dad, you're so lame—"

"No, Dad," Nick says. "You're like the opposite of lame. It's just that…"

He goes on, I imagine, to explain why it's uncool to talk with your teachers outside of school, but I don't hear much of anything he says after "the opposite of lame." I can't think of a higher compliment, and I'm afraid that if I try to talk, I won't be able to.

Back on the ferry, it's pretty clear that we're all worn out. Tom and Ann head below deck, but I stay above to watch Ocracoke recede in the distance.

My body knows the ride is over and just wants to rest, but my mind—still propelled by the momentum of the road—races forward to later tonight, at the seafood restaurant Ann has already picked out; to tomorrow, when we'll bring Rusty to the Bicycle Post so that Tom's mechanic friend, Ken, can break him down and ship him back to California; to the day after that, when I'll catch a flight in Raleigh; and to several hours after that, when I'll descend into the San Diego airport, feel the plane come to a halt outside of the gate, grab my bag from the overhead compartment, and move through the cabin, then through the airport, then to a life that looks different to me now than it did when I left a little over two months ago. I think about this road I'm on, this road I've found. It's my own personal Cherohala—winding and difficult, sure, but also a one-of-a-kind scenic byway that bridges two places, that combines parts of other things into something new and different. A life reimagined. A home reimagined. A home with Shannon and my boys, new stories, new Christmas cards, and new mirrors that—when I look into them—reflect a "me" that feels right and true and solid.

I lean against the railing a few feet down from an older couple. She's smoking a cigarette and he's got a cigar, and I imagine they're breaking a posted rule somewhere until I remember these waters are, technically, North Carolina, and in North Carolina everyone smokes.

Just then I hear a screech. Then another. I look around to see who or what it is.

The man points with his cigar to the sky where, maybe twenty feet above the ferry, is a gull. His wings are still as he hovers in midair. I'm not sure whether he's fighting the current or letting it carry him. He lets loose another screech.

"Quit yer complaining," the guy says.

I look at that bird up in the wild wind. He's not complaining, and he's not crying. He's laughing, enjoying the ride, because he knows where he is and he knows his way home.

# Acknowledgments

I thought this would be a lot easier.

I don't mean the bike ride. I knew that would be tough and it was. No, I mean writing this book. Way, way back, I thought, *How hard could this be?* I blogged regularly when I was on the road, and I kept a journal, too, so the book was pretty much already written. All I had to do was string together the posts, add a few things from the journal, do a little editing, and *ta-DA*...a book!

Well, it didn't work out that way at all, and I've been writing and teaching writing long enough to have known better. In fact, I shouldn't have been surprised to discover that in every way except for physical strain, the riding was a lot easier than the writing. It certainly took a lot less time. I'm reminded of something I wrote very late in the book, something about being incredibly innocent or stupid or (most likely) both as I stood on Rusty at the beginning of the ride with no real idea of what I was getting into.

Turns out, that's a pretty accurate way to describe writing a book, too. Not a single word written, and all those pages to go...

And like the bike journey, I wouldn't have gotten through the writing journey without a lot of help from a lot of people. So a number of thanks are in order.

First, the ride. Deep thanks to everyone who helped me along the way—the people who stopped to see if I was all right or needed anything, the people who housed and fed me, the people who read my blog and left a comment or two, and the many people who just saw a guy with a ton of crap on his bike and decided to talk to him for a few minutes. All of you made a lonely endeavor a lot less so. I especially want to thank the people who were a big part of my trip but—due to the mercenary demands of storytelling—didn't make it fully into the narrative proper: Brian and Angie McNeece, Eileen and Richard Travis and family, Jody and Dave Travis and family, Dave and Pamela Craig, Paul Winer, Daniel Young, Tom and Stanna Galbraith, Jake Heath, Karen and Jeff Wilson, Ron from Boulder (I never did get his last name), John and Sharlene Sampson, Bill Haddan and family, Alan White, Lance, Michelle, and Christian Freezeland, David and Erin Anthony, Eddie West, Christine North, and Chris Nielsen.

Special thanks to Jan and Bill Montgomery, who were the perfect guides through the "heart" of this journey, and to Tom and Ann McConnell, who were the perfect guides through the "tail" of it.

Thanks to all my family and friends who helped me recharge during my Chicago "intermission": my brother Vince, his wife Jean, and their family, my mom and dad, Pat Gonder and Teresa Aguinaldo, Jerry Karlin and Karen Klebba, Paul Sternenberg, Marc Kaplanes and Julie Hubbard. And a special thank you to Greg Hart for the dance and plane ticket (two separate things).

Finally, the ride would have been possible but a lot harder without the work of whoever created the iPhone apps for "Track My Tour" and "Warmshowers." Many thanks.

Along those lines (and as regards the book), I owe a big debt to whoever created and maintains Google Earth and Wikipedia; both were instrumental when my memory or perspective failed, or when I needed to find out something about Dodge City, or the Irwin Cobb Bridge, or the Tennessee Valley Authority. I'm also indebted to Elliot Willensky's *When Brooklyn Was the World* (Harmony Books, 1986) for helping to add a little color to my dad's memories.

Big thanks and an even bigger hug to my favorite geologist and dear friend Suzy Gonder, who patiently answered all my questions about rocks and geological time, and for the chocolate that sustained me while I drove that behemoth of a Silverado up to Chicago.

Thanks also to Lawson Mabry, who closely read and reread the sections about his family and its history and has offered nothing but hospitality and encouragement to me since I met him. Thanks also to Brian McNeece and Erin Anthony for their generous and rigorous readings of an early draft of the book. Big thanks to members of my Palomar family for the same: Barb Neault Kelber, Deborah Paes de Barros, Jack Quintero, and Carlton Smith. My colleagues are, quite simply, the best, and I'm also grateful for the friendship and encouragement of Leanne Maunu, Andrea Bell, Teresa Laughlin, and Jenny Fererro (to whom I might still owe a Clif Bar). And thanks, too, to my other readers: Pat Gonder, John Lucas (who also helped with the comics), and Colin Rafferty.

In terms of reading, I owe quite a bit to two assistant agents at two different agencies—Jennifer Herrera and Lena Yarbrough—who gave me invaluable notes that resulted in a much, much better final version.

Special thanks to Robert James Russell and the editors of *Midwestern Gothic* for publishing sections of this book. Many thanks to Hannah Krieger and the editors of the *Georgetown Review* for the same.

A big thank you to the good folks who run the San Diego Book Awards for honoring my work at a time when I needed some encouragement.

Huge thanks to Kevin Atticks, Alexandra Chouinard, Nicole DeVincentis (and her infinite patience with me), and all of the other hard workers at Apprentice House Press for their support, insight, and direction—all of which helped turn my dream into the reality you now hold in your hands.

Big hug to my Aunt Angie McConnell, who helped fill in some of the blanks about my grandfather, Rocco Tursi.

Thanks, too, to my dad, Thomas Versaci, who patiently retold many stories, answered a ton of questions, enumerated details, and didn't really care when I added some of my own. One of the gifts of this entire journey has been to sort through his memories with him.

As always, I'm deeply thankful for my students, many of whom were interested in my trip and some of whom had the energy and patience to read parts of this book. Working with all of them inspires me daily (Sarah Bates, Nolan Turner, the jokers in our English Majors

Club—I'm looking at you).

And finally, I am grateful beyond words for Shannon Lienhart, Nick, and Tony, without whom this book wouldn't exist.

# About the Author

Rocco Versaci grew up in the Chicago suburb of Downers Grove and is the product of an Italian-American family, too much TV, and countless books. He currently lives in San Diego, where he is an English professor at Palomar College. In addition to teaching composition, creative writing and literature (including comics), he is the co-advisor for the school's award-winning literary journal, *Bravura*. He is the author of *This Book Contains Graphic Language* (Bloomsbury, 2007), and his writing has appeared in *The English Journal*, *The International Journal of Comic Art*, *Midwestern Gothic*, and the *Georgetown Review*. *That Hidden Road* won a 2015 San Diego Book Award for outstanding memoir. He has two sons, two bikes, and only a few regrets.

Apprentice House is the country's only campus-based, student-staffed book publishing company. Directed by professors and industry professionals, it is a nonprofit activity of the Communication Department at Loyola University Maryland.

Using state-of-the-art technology and an experiential learning model of education, Apprentice House publishes books in untraditional ways. This dual responsibility as publishers and educators creates an unprecedented collaborative environment among faculty and students, while teaching tomorrow's editors, designers, and marketers.

Outside of class, progress on book projects is carried forth by the AH Book Publishing Club, a co-curricular campus organization supported by Loyola University Maryland's Office of Student Activities.

Eclectic and provocative, Apprentice House titles intend to entertain as well as spark dialogue on a variety of topics. Financial contributions to sustain the press's work are welcomed. Contributions are tax deductible to the fullest extent allowed by the IRS.

To learn more about Apprentice House books or to obtain submission guidelines, please visit www.apprenticehouse.com.

Apprentice House
Communication Department
Loyola University Maryland
4501 N. Charles Street
Baltimore, MD 21210
Ph: 410-617-5265 • Fax: 410-617-2198
info@apprenticehouse.com•www.apprenticehouse.com

CPSIA information can be obtained
at www.ICGtesting.com
Printed in the USA
FSOW02n0829311016
26795FS